Text copyright © 2011 by Zov Karamardian
Photography copyright © 2011 by Pornchai Mittongtare
Cover and book design by Donna Giovannitti

All rights reserved. No part of this book may be reproduced, stored in a retrieval system or transmitted in any form or by any means electronic, mechanical, photocopying, recording or otherwise, without prior permission in writing from the publisher.

Library of Congress Cataloging-Publication Data

ISBN- 978-0-9759558-2-6
First Edition 2011

Zov's Publishing, LLC
17440 E. 17th Street, Tustin, CA 92780 U.S.A.
Phone: 800 980-ZOVS (9687)
www.zovs.com

Zov's Bistro and Zov's Neighborhood Cafés
Tustin, Newport, Irvine

Printing by Continental Colorcraft
1166 W. Garvey Avenue
Monterey Park, CA 91754
323-283-3000

Printed and bound in the United States

Rustic classics with a Mediterranean twist

Recipes from the internationally acclaimed restaurant *Zov's*

By Zov Karamardian ✦ Photographs by Pornchai Mittongtare

ALSO BY ZOV KARAMARDIAN
Zov: Recipes and Memories from the Heart

◆ I dedicate this book with passion and love to my husband Gary, my daughter Taleene, my son Armen and my daughter-in-law Mikelle, and my grandchildren, Morgan, Nicholas and Gia. I also want to dedicate this book to the memory of my mother, who instilled in me a deep appreciation for food, family, culture and the arts, and who told me I could do anything I put my mind to. I love you all very much.

CONTENTS

acknowledgments **8**

author's note **12**

pantry and produce **16**

appetizers **24**

breakfast **80**

soups **122**

salads **144**

seafood **166**

meats **190**

poultry **222**

side dishes **244**

sauces, etc. **290**

sweets **314**

index **364**

ACKNOWLEDGMENTS

Eleanor Roosevelt once said, "If life were predictable it would cease to be life, and be without flavor." I simply could not imagine life without flavor. This cookbook, which is bursting at the seams with flavor, simply could not have been created without my talented and loving friends and colleagues whom I would like to thank for their continued help, support, wisdom and talent. | I have been truly blessed in every possible way in life to be able to achieve my dream, but that dream would never have been made possible without the support of my family. I would like to thank, for absolutely everything, the love of my life and my other half, my husband, Gary. My daughter, Taleene, my son, Armen, and his wife and my daughter-in-law, Mikelle, who all bring me strength and courage. Also, my grandchildren, Morgan, Nicholas and Gia, all of whom I love so much and who all shine a light in my life that nothing can extinguish. Everyone in my family brings me such joy and happiness and helps me to realize how important life is. »

To those of you who worked tirelessly through drafts, edits, deadlines, headaches, and even those moments of inspiration, without you this book would have not been possible.

My sincere thanks to Donna Giovannitti for your outstanding book design. Wow, Donna, your creative, innovative and cutting-edge design is incredible and it could not have turned out better. Thank you from the bottom of my heart. Your hard work and dedication truly impressed me.

Pornchai Mittongtare, how can I ever thank you for your outstanding vision and direction of the project. Your photography and eye for detail brought my recipes to life. The images are beautiful, immaculate, and most importantly, mouthwatering. Even though I have made these recipes many times, these pictures inspire me to cook them all over again. Pornchai, in my opinion, you are one of the very best food photographers in the country, not only for your amazing eye, but your ability to capture the most tantalizing essence of every dish. Behind every master of the arts there are his assistants and a big thank you to Kawa Wong and Sarah Olson for assisting Pornchai in the studio, even providing subtle hand modeling when needed. Thank you for making this project fun.

Special thanks to my remarkable editor, Grace Jidoun, who guided me so brilliantly and patiently, who edited and re-edited the manuscript and recipes with an incredibly keen eye. Grace, I don't know what I would have done without you. Your ability to see through each recipe and give me feedback is unbelievable. Thank you very much. You are amazing. You are truly a gifted editor!

My deep appreciation to Rochelle Palermo, my recipe editor. Rochelle, you have an unsurpassed ability to test, edit and lend your invaluable advice to ensure the perfection of each recipe. Rochelle, you tested every recipe in this cookbook with passion and enthusiasm, guiding me on how to simplify my recipe preparation for the readers. Thank you.

To Basil Friedman, thank you for spending countless hours preparing the food for the photo shoots. The food looked delicious and appetizing. Your culinary styling tricks to make the food be the star amazed me! Your job was the most challenging and yet most fascinating. You were always at the top of your game, even when the food did not behave. Thank you for being so detail-oriented and meticulous. You are truly an artist.

I would also like to thank Basil's assistant, John Galang. Thank you John for your punctuality and for cooking whatever Basil asked you to cook.

I would like to thank Robin Turk for doing the prop styling and providing and finding the finest and most unusual props to stage each dish. Robin, I know that you have gone miles and miles to find that perfect dish, glass bowl or pitcher to use in each shoot. I appreciate all of your input on this project.

Thank you, Brad Wright, for taking this project on. What a terrific job you did in copy editing. I am forever grateful.

Alexandra Nickerson, thank you for graciously rescuing me at the last minute to compile the index. In my opinion, no cookbook would be complete without a great index. Alexandra, you are truly a gifted professional.

Thank you, Joe and Sharon Hernandez of Melissa's World Variety Produce, not only for providing us with the freshest and the best produce available, but also for your sincere friendship. A special thanks to the team at Melissa's for always giving us top-notch service and finding us the finest and rarest produce. Many thanks to James Waseloff for always making sure that each item you provided for the cookbook and the three restaurants is of the best quality.

Last but not least, I would like to thank our entire Zov's Bistro and Neighborhood Café family and staff members, whose passion for hospitality and excellence is as keen as ever and remains the true secret of our success. Without you Zov's does not exist. Thank you. You are all the best! |

AUTHOR'S NOTE

I once found myself, in the early dawn, walking down an old cobblestone path lined by tall stone buildings in the South of France. A subtle breeze of sea and salt seemed to wrap around my entire body, drawing me forward. The small corridor opened up onto a beautiful sight: brightly colored, striped awnings that sheltered baskets of French baguettes, barrels of beans and lentils, and flats piled high with fresh fruits, vegetables, fish and meats. People meandered from stall to stall, chatting joyfully and admiring the fresh quality and dazzling colors. | As I strolled up and down the aisles, I was astonished by the beauty and abundance displayed by the vendors. I was overwhelmed; the recipe possibilities were endless. With such ingredients, what meal would not taste amazing? I wished then that back home in America it was easier to find fresh ingredients and incorporate them into everyday meals. »

sour grapes

Some years later, away from the sea air, I sat in my office contemplating what direction to take my new cookbook. Should it be a continuation of my previous cookbook, *Zov: Recipes and Memories From the Heart*, featuring those Armenian and Mediterranean recipes from my homeland, the Middle East, that are so rich in flavor and full of life? Or should I dip into my catering roots and teach readers how to throw the perfect party? Every time I sat down to think, the phone would ring, someone at the restaurant would need my assistance, or one of my children, although adults, would need their mother's help. Finally, in the middle of all the chaos, surrounded by the bustling of chefs and servers, and stacks of paper threatening to implode at any minute, it came to me. My next book would be perfect for someone who has a busy family and a budget, but wants to use farm-fresh ingredients in their cooking. It would be for someone who wants easy every-night meals without sacrificing flavor.

For those of you who are thinking of writing a cookbook, let me tell you, writing a book in the middle of an already hectic day is no easy task. So why am I doing this then, you might be thinking. Well, the answer is simple. I want to inspire people to cook, but beyond that, I want to teach people about all the interesting spices that are now so easy to find. And I want to show how simple it is to incorporate these flavors into delicious do-ahead meals. I wanted to write a cookbook that was diverse, unique, and above all, practical.

The recipes in this book are easy and cost-effective, and most can be prepared ahead, which means more time enjoying guests. The base ingredients are items that most of you probably already have, but this book may introduce you to some new flavors. My refrigerator at home is full of fresh citrus, tomatoes, peppers, garlic, mint, green onions and ginger. My pantry is never without preserved lemons, red pepper paste, harissa, and of course, my "delectable dozen": allspice, cayenne pepper, cinnamon, cumin, garlic, ginger, nutmeg, oregano, paprika, rosemary, thyme and turmeric. These flavors, which somehow always find their way into my cooking, add that extra sparkle. Here, I am sharing my pantry list (as well as a few chopping techniques) so that you can easily navigate my recipes. Like you, I rely mostly on supermarket staples, but I never miss a chance to search through the spice aisle, never knowing what I might find.

As Americans continue to discover different tastes and ethnic cuisines, I hope that through the recipes in this book, you too will embrace new spices and seek out high-quality, flavorful ingredients. One your way home from work one night, bypass your local grocery store and venture into an ethnic market. I bet you'll be intrigued by what you find.

I have lived in this country for nearly all of my life, and I wanted to include plenty of tried-and-true recipes of familiar favorites too. American classics like meatloaf and mac 'n' cheese are now as much as part of my culinary heritage as the traditional Armenian foods that I grew up with. For me, American cuisine represents a culture of food that blends spices, techniques and ingredients from different parts of the globe to create something fresh and exciting, but also comforting. American cuisine is a melting pot of fast-paced eating, slow cooking, convenience and tradition.

As a chef and restaurant owner, I find inspiration everywhere: in the music that fills my heart with memories, the countries I visit, the people I meet, and the food I taste along the way. I have found that the beauty and "Spice of Life" lies in the ability to transcend borders and oceans to find comfort in any cuisine. My hope is that through this cookbook, you will too!

PANTRY AND PRODUCE

One of my favorite smells in the world can be found by simply walking into a pantry and pulling out a drawer that's filled with bottles of fresh spices like oregano, thyme and cinnamon.

The smell is bold and aromatic. It tingles your nose and makes your mouth water. You linger there for a moment, basking in the earthy aroma. Right there in front of you, the possibilities are endless. More than anything, beautiful spices and fresh herbs start the creative process and are the ultimate inspiration. | Knowing how to use and mix the proper spices can turn any boring meal into something amazingly delicious. Even if you're trying to cut calories, you don't have to sacrifice flavor if you know how to jazz things up with something extraordinary from the pantry. Throughout this cookbook I use particularly flavorful Indo-European spices that most of us are familiar with like cumin, cardamom, turmeric, paprika and ground ginger. These come from countries in North Africa, India and the Eastern Mediterranean. | But two of the most popular spices from this region are ones that American households don't know very well: Aleppo pepper and Zahtar. You will learn about them here, along with my other go-to ingredients, including grains and citrus, that give life and pizzazz to my food. | By becoming familiar with these key ingredients you will be able to incorporate flavors from around the world into your cooking. You will discover lemongrass, the secret herb that gives my Coconut Chicken Chowder its distinct flavor. You will find out where to buy nigella seeds for the popular cocktail appetizer Cheese Boreg, and learn all about the nutrititional benefits of pelted wheat, the base for my Armenian porridge Harisah, a comforting dish that always leaves everyone smiling from ear to ear. »

PANTRY AND PRODUCE

Aleppo pepper: Aleppo pepper comes from the city of Aleppo, located along the Silk Road in northern Syria. It is an earthy, slightly spicy crushed chile that has the consistency of fine sand and a deep red color. Its complex flavor slowly unfolds, adding a nice bite to soups, salads, and appetizers. It also makes a nice rub for chicken. Though Aleppo pepper is becoming more mainstream, it is still predominantly used in Middle Eastern cuisine. If it is not available, substitute 4 parts paprika to 1 part cayenne pepper. You can order Aleppo pepper online at Penzeys Spices (penzeys.com).

Barley: This hardy grain dates back to the Stone Age and has been used throughout the eons in dishes ranging from breads to soups to salads. Most of the barley grown in the Western world is used for animal feed or, when malted, to make beer or whiskey. Barley is very nutritious. It's probably best known for being an excellent source of fiber, but it's also rich in vitamins B and E, and folic acid. Barley helps to lower blood sugar and cholesterol, and slows down the absorption of carbohydrates. As an extra bonus, barley acts as an appetizer suppressant by making you feel full. Hulled (also called whole-grain) barley has only the outer husk removed and is the most nutritious form of the grain. Pearl barley has had the bran removed and has been steamed and polished. It comes in 3 grades of texture: coarse, medium and fine. When combined with water it expands to triple its volume. Barley flour or barley meal is ground from hulled barley and must be combined with gluten containing flour for use in yeast breads. All of these types of barley can be found at natural foods stores and Whole Foods markets.

Bulgur: For centuries, bulgur has been the staple grain of Eastern Europe and the Middle East. In the Old Testament it was called "Arisah." Bulgur is a whole grain made from wheat that has been washed and stemmed, then hulled and either parched or dry-cooled. It is then cracked and sifted into 4 grades of texture, from 1 (a fine grind) to 4 (the coarsest grind). It is widely used in tabbouleh and pilafs. You can find it at Whole Foods markets, some supermarkets and online at Kalustyan's (kalustyans.com) or Amazon.com.

Cocoa Powder: There are 2 types of cocoa powder: natural, unsweetened cocoa powder and Dutch process. Natural unsweetened cocoa powder has a bitter taste, but adds deep chocolate flavor to baked goods. Dutch-processed, which is darker in color, has been treated with small amounts of alkaline solution, which neutralizes the acidity in the cocoa. The result is a smoother, silkier flavor. It's a bit more expensive, but not unreasonably so. I love the Callebaut and Valrhona brands. You can substitute natural cocoa for Dutch process, but not vice versa. If you do substitute, keep in mind that there will be slight flavor and/or color differences in the end products. You can find both products at many supermarkets and specialty food stores. »

Coriander: Widely used in Indian and Mediterranean cooking, coriander seeds come from the same plant that produces cilantro. You either love it or you hate it. Coriander is a wonderful complement to soups, cauliflower and eggplant dishes. It also teases out the sweetness in cooked carrots. It's sold as whole seeds or in powder form. For optimal flavor, I like to lightly toast the seeds and then grind them just before using. Coriander can be found at Whole Foods markets, some supermarkets and at ethnic markets.

Extra-virgin olive oil: Many of my recipes call for extra-virgin olive oil. It's considered the finest and fruitiest of the olive oils. It's derived from the first cold pressing of the olives and has the most delicate flavor and antioxidant benefits. Anyone from the Mediterranean region will sing the praises of a good dose of olive oil on salads, pasta, fish and almost anything else.

Flat-leaf parsley: Italian parsley has dark green, flat leaves that are the most flavorful of all the parsleys, making it the preferred plant of gourmets. This herb is used widely in Mediterranean cuisine. It's an excellent source of vitamins A and C, as well as some minerals. Try growing your own. It's harvestable through much of winter, even in colder climates, and is very easy to grow, especially in window boxes and pots either inside or out. Grow parsley near roses to improve the flowers' scent and health.

Hydroponic watercress: Most of us are familiar with the peppery flavor of watercress. This member of the mustard family grows naturally around streams. Commercially grown hydroponic watercress grows in similar soil-free conditions, where the roots are regularly flooded with water. These hydroponic plants are exposed to ample oxygen, and as a result, grow much faster than plants grown in soil. They also absorb nutrients better. Hydroponic gardening may soon be our future, as it offers many benefits to our environment including fewer diseases and much less (if any) pesticide use. Look for hydroponic watercress at Whole Foods Markets and some supermarkets.

Lemongrass: Lemongrass is a wonderful herb to cook with. Popular in Asian cuisine, especially Thai food, it has a strong lemony aroma, and gives soups, sauces and even drinks a light, refreshing taste with a hint of ginger. I love infusing tea with lemongrass, but I mostly use the chopped stalk or stem in soups, salads, stir-fries and pickles. Use the tender inner root of the stalk. When buying lemongrass, pick fresh-looking stalks that are not dry or brittle. An extra bonus of lemongrass (also known as citronella root) is that it's a natural bug repellent; the oil drives away mosquitos. You can find lemongrass at nurseries, Asian markets and some supermarkets. You can also plant them in your garden, but plant sparingly; they do grow like weeds.

Lemons: You might be surprised to see common lemons on this list, but every part of this citrus fruit, from the peel to the flesh, is an integral part of my cooking. Fresh lemon juice is like a bright canvas of flavor on which I layer other spices. I squeeze the juice into soups and sauces, over salads, and use it to season savory foods. Adding a pinch of zest instead of salt is a healthful trick to enliven dishes. Salt makes flavor pop; lemon makes flavor bounce! And of course, you can't beat a cool glass of water with lemon wedge in it. There is nothing better.

Mahlab: There are many different spellings for this popular Middle Eastern flavoring — mahleb, mahaleb, mahlab — but they all refer to this unusual, fragrant spice. The seeds are extracted from the pits of a small black cherry tree that grows wild in the Mediterranean. The dried kernels are oval and buff-colored, with finely wrinkled skin. Once ground, the powder is yellowish (similar to mace). I love its subtle aroma. It's particularly delicious in cheeses and buttered cookies. If used sparingly, it will offset bitter flavors. For optimum freshness, freeze mahlab whole and then grind as needed. You can find mahlab online at Penzeys Spices (penzeys.com)

Nigella seeds: Since antiquity, Asian herbalists have used nigella seeds (also called kalonji) for their healing qualities. The long, jet-black seeds flavor many Indian dishes, particularly from the northern regions, as well as Middle Eastern cuisine. They typically flavor breads and flatbreads, including the famous Indian bread naan, as well as cheeses, vegetables, legumes and salads. The seeds are quite aromatic and slightly bitter, but when cooked take on a peppery, smoky flavor. Though they may smell a bit like onions, they are not related. You can buy nigella seeds online at Amazon.com.

Pelted wheat: This wild grain grows throughout the Middle East, Armenia and Iran. The domesticated form is grown mostly in Georgia, and American cooks are beginning to discover its many benefits. These pearled and polished wheat kernels are high in fiber and a good source of protein. It's used widely in the Armenian community, especially for the popular chicken (or beef) porridge called Harisah (page 234). It's also delicious in pilafs and salads. You can find pelted wheat at Middle Eastern markets.

Pomegranate molasses: Pomegranate molasses is a thick, syrupy reduction of pomegranate juice. It lends a delicious sweet-tart flavor to any dish. Concentrated pomegranate juice can be substituted, but be sure to add a bit of sugar to balance out its slightly bitter flavor. Both pomegranate molasses and concentrated pomegranate juice can be found at Middle Eastern markets, most specialty foods stores and in the ethnic section of some supermarkets. Pomegranate molasses is also sold at Whole Foods markets and online at Amazon.com. »

Preserved lemons: Preserved lemons are essential to Moroccan, Middle Eastern and Mediterranean cuisines. Having a jar in my pantry is a must. Its distinctive taste provides that extra layer of flavor, and balances out so many dishes. Though they take a few weeks to make, it's very easy to do. Essentially, lemons are preserved in a brine of kosher salt and their own juices until they're soft and silky. See my recipe on page 296.

Red pepper paste: This mixture of sweet and spicy red peppers is an integral part of Eastern Mediterranean cooking, used to enliven soups, sauces, stews, dressings and much more. Typically, the peppers are sun-dried, then slow-cooked in an oven. The finished paste is then topped off with olive oil and stored in the refrigerator. I use a food processor and a slow-cooker to cut down on the work (see my recipe on page 305), but you can also buy jars of pre-made paste at Middle Eastern markets under the brand Sera in hot or mild versions, or online at Parthenon Foods (parthenonfoods.com).

Seasoned salt: This is one of my secret spice weapons. Seasoned salt is typically made up of salt, sugar, and equal amounts of dry spices such as black pepper, garlic powder, cumin, chile powder, dry mustard, paprika, turmeric and thyme. Of all the different brands on the market, I prefer Lawry's. It's a wonderful combination that enhances the flavor of many of my dishes.

Sriracha: Originally from the city of Sriracha in the eastern part of Thailand, this is one of the hottest sauces I have ever tasted. it's mostly used as a condiment or spicy dipping sauce. The bright-red paste is made from ground sun-ripened chiles along with garlic, sugar, salt and distilled vinegar. It's quite addictive; almost like eating a spicy, fresh chile pepper. Needless to say, a little goes a long way. Now made in the United States, Sriracha is available in squeeze bottles in the Asian foods section of many supermarkets.

Turmeric: Turmeric imparts a wonderful woodsy fragrance and a deep orange color to cooked foods. It is a very strong spice, so a little goes a long way. It's particularly delicious with lentils, rice, soups, stews and vegetables. Its yellow pigment dyes anything it comes into contact with so be sure to use pots and pans that are stain-resistant. Turmeric can be found at Whole Foods markets and many supermarkets.

Zahtar: Also spelled za'atar, this popular Middle Eastern spice blend has a nutty, toasty flavor, and a nice lemony accent thanks to sumac, its main ingredient. Sumac is an Eastern Mediterranean powder that's esteemed for its distinctive sour taste. Zahtar's other ingredients are marjoram, oregano, toasted sesame seeds, wild thyme and salt. It's great for sprinkling on meats and vegetables. You can find zahtar at Middle Eastern markets and online at Kalustyan's (kalustyans.com).

APPETIZERS

beef pirozhki with mushrooms **28**

che kofta **32**

crispy onion rings **34**

cheese boreg **36**

parmesan bruschetta **40**

crispy vegetable croquettes (falafels) **42**

gravlax **46**

grilled eggplant, olive and tomato bruschetta **50**

koufta **52**

old world sliders **58**

olive tapenade **60**

spicy pomegranate-glazed chicken wings **62**

perfect guacamole **64**

spicy sesame seed flatbreads with pepper paste **66**

pureed bean dip with yogurt and dill **72**

zucchini fritters with gravlax **74**

tomato-basil risotto fritters **76**

APPETIZERS

When I think about planning a meal for a dinner or an event, I think of the whole production as a play. There is the entrée, which is the star; the side in a supporting role; and dessert, the grand finale. But as in any play, there is always an opening scene or attention grabber, something that makes you want to continue watching. It has to be exciting and eye-catching. To me, the role of the appetizer is just that: the stage setter. Appetizers are deliciously tasty tidbits, snacks or dips that whet your appetite for more. Appetizers are seemingly effortless and impressive all at once, and sometimes steal the show. | In our house and in the Armenian culture, we refer to appetizers as mezze, and no dinner party is complete without them. Mezze is a variety of dishes that are served on small plates (with or without drinks) at the beginning of a large spread. The Middle Eastern culture is famous for serving appetizers at gatherings and sometimes appetizers are the entire meal. The beauty of the recipes in this chapter is that many can be made ahead and frozen until you're ready to entertain. | In my home there will always be Boreg, with its thin and crispy layers of buttery pastry and its cheese filling that oozes out after baking. For my grandchildren, I also love making Perfect Guacamole, which is a staple in our home. And I remember when my mother used to come down from Northern California to visit me in Orange County. My family always requested that she make the same dish. Her kibby (Koufta) is the most delicious appetizer you will ever have. The flavors are so balanced and perfect that you will beg for more. | In this chapter you will learn about many fun, easy appetizers. You don't need to shuffle through cookbooks looking for recipes anymore. Everything you need is right here in these pages. Go ahead and experiment. Before you know it, you will be the star of the show. |

APPETIZERS: beef pirozhki with mushrooms

Pirozhki are a comfort-food staple in Eastern Europe and Russia, but many versions of this flavorful meat turnover are served throughout the world. In South and Central America they're called empanadas. In the Middle East they're known as boreg (for Cheese Boreg, see page 36). And we're all familiar with Asian won tons. Nowadays you will find these delicious meat pies mostly baked as more people cut back on fried foods. I'll be honest, I love mine fried, but then this is not a typical recipe. If you don't have time to make the dough, look for pirozhki or empanada wrappers for frying (La Salteña brand) at Middle Eastern and Latin markets. The commercial brands are so perfected they come close to the quality of homemade.

MAKES ABOUT 45

Make the filling: Fill a large saucepan with enough water to come 2 inches up the sides of the pot. Cover the pot and bring the water to a boil. Add the potatoes and cook until tender, about 15 minutes. Drain the water and return the potatoes to the saucepan. Using a fork, coarsely mash the potatoes, then set aside to cool completely.

Meanwhile, heat the oil in a large skillet over high heat. Add the beef and cook until the juices evaporate and the meat is dark brown, stirring often and breaking up the meat into large clumps with the back of a spoon, about 8 minutes. Add the onions, mushrooms and garlic, and cook until the onions soften, about 10 minutes. Reduce the heat to medium and continue cooking until the onions are caramelized and the mixture is dark brown, stirring frequently, about 18 minutes. Stir in the mashed potatoes. Remove the skillet from heat. Add the parsley, Monterey Jack, Parmesan, eggs, thyme, kosher salt, Aleppo pepper, lemon pepper, seasoned salt and cayenne pepper, if using. Cool completely.

Do-ahead tip: The filling can be refrigerated for up to 2 days or frozen for up to 3 months. Transfer to a container, cover and store.

Meanwhile, prepare the dough: Mix the warm water and yeast in a medium bowl. Let stand until the yeast is dissolved, about 5 minutes. »

Filling

- 2 medium russet potatoes (1½ pounds total), peeled, cut into ¾-inch pieces
- 2 tablespoons canola oil
- 1 pound lean (15% fat) ground beef
- 3 onions, chopped (about 4 cups)
- 8 ounces fresh white mushrooms, chopped
- 2 tablespoons minced garlic
- 1 cup chopped fresh flat-leaf parsley
- 1 cup grated Monterey Jack, Gouda or cheddar cheese
- ½ cup grated Parmesan
- 3 large hard-boiled eggs, peeled and chopped
- 1 tablespoon chopped fresh thyme
- 1½ teaspoons kosher salt
- 1 teaspoon Aleppo pepper (see *Pantry and Produce*)
- 1 teaspoon lemon pepper
- 1 teaspoon seasoned salt (see *Pantry and Produce*)
- ¼ teaspoon cayenne pepper (optional)

Dough

- ¼ cup warm water (105°F to 115°F)
- 1 ¼-ounce package active dry yeast
- 1 cup lukewarm whole milk
- 3 large eggs, at room temperature
- ½ cup canola oil, plus more for deep-frying
- 4½ cups all-purpose flour
- 1 tablespoon granulated sugar
- 1 teaspoon kosher salt
- Nonstick cooking spray

Whisk the warm milk, eggs and ½ cup of oil in a large bowl to blend. Mix in the yeast mixture and set aside. Whisk 4½ cups of the flour, sugar and salt in another large bowl to blend. Make a well in the center of the flour mixture and pour the egg mixture into the center. Using a wooden spoon, mix the flour until the dough comes together. Transfer the dough to a lightly floured surface and knead until the dough is smooth and elastic, about 5 minutes. The dough will be soft and tacky; when you touch the dough it will feel sticky but will easily release to the touch.

Spray 2 baking sheets with nonstick spray. Form the dough into ping-pong sized balls, using about ¾ ounce of dough for each. Line the balls on the prepared baking sheet, spacing apart, and cover loosely with a moistened cloth. Set aside in a warm draft-free area until the dough balls double in size, about 1½ hours.

Make the pirozhki: Working with 1 ball of dough at a time, roll each on a lightly floured work surface to a 3-inch round. Place 1 heaping tablespoon of the filling over the bottom half of the dough round and fold the top half of the dough over to form a half-moon shape. Press the edges of the dough very firmly to seal. Using a fork, crimp the edges firmly. As you form the pirozhki, keep them covered with a moistened cloth so they do not dry out.

Pour enough oil in a heavy, large pot or deep fryer to reach a depth of ¾ inch. Attach a deep-fry thermometer and the heat oil to 375°F. Working in batches, fry the pirozhki until the dough is cooked through and dark golden brown, about 3 minutes per side. Serve warm.

Do-ahead tip: It's best to eat the pirozhki right away, but they can be made in advance. After frying, cool them completely and refrigerate in an airtight container for up to 2 days or freeze for up to 2 months. To rewarm, wrap the pirozhki in aluminum foil and bake in a 350°F oven until heated through, about 15 minutes for refrigerated pirozhki and 35 minutes for frozen.

Zov's kitchen note: The dough is easy to handle. Just make sure that you don't puncture the dough with the fork when you are crimping it, otherwise the filling will ooze out. Sometimes the pirozhki will brown nicely on top but will still be raw inside, so it's especially important to follow the specified time and temperature when frying.

A touch of Aleppo pepper and fiery cayenne give this filling a distinct flavor. >

APPETIZERS: che kofta

I would call this dish the steak tartare of the Mediterranean, with the exception that bulgur is added to the mix. It's typically reserved for parties and special occasions. The Tomato-Cucumber Relish (page 309) is a must; it adds delicious flavor and is the perfect cooling complement.

SERVES 12

Make the che kofta: Place a large, flat serving platter and a large bowl in the refrigerator to chill. Mix the bulgur in a large bowl with 1 cup of cold water to moisten. Set aside until the bulgur softens and all the water is absorbed, about 30 minutes. Mix in the pepper paste, basil, paprika, cumin, salt, Aleppo pepper, cayenne pepper and black pepper.

Do-ahead tip: The bulgur mixture can be made up to 4 hours ahead. Cover with plastic wrap and refrigerate.

Meanwhile, pulse the onion in a food processor until it is pureed and watery. Transfer the onion puree to a large bowl and toss with the cold beef cubes to coat. Working in 2 batches, pulse the beef cubes and the pureed onion mixture in the food processor until the meat becomes almost like a smooth paste and the onions are no longer visible. Transfer the mixture to the chilled bowl and set the bowl over ice to keep the meat mixture cold.

Fill a small bowl with ice water (this is to keep your hands cold as you knead the che kofta). Working in 2 batches, knead the meat mixture into the bulgur with both hands, dipping your hands in the ice water often to ensure they stay very cold, until the che kofta is very well blended.

Serve the che kofta: Pat the che kofta evenly over the chilled flat platter, forming about a 1/4-inch-thick layer.

Using a fork, make diamond-shaped designs on top of the che kofta. Top with the pine nuts and drizzle with the oil. Sprinkle with parsley and green onions. Serve the che kofta immediately with the tomato-cucumber relish and a platter of radishes and mint alongside.

Zov's kitchen note: The meat should be extremely lean and kept in ice at all times. High-quality lamb, top sirloin or London broil would be great substitutes. For a variation, shape into patties.

- 1 cup fine-grade bulgur (#1) (see *Pantry and Produce*)
- 1 cup cold water
- 3 tablespoons Red Pepper Paste (page 305)
- 1 tablespoon dried basil
- 1 tablespoon paprika
- 2 teaspoons ground cumin
- 2 teaspoons kosher salt
- 1 teaspoon Aleppo pepper (see *Pantry and Produce*)
- 1/2 teaspoon cayenne pepper
- 1/2 teaspoon freshly ground black pepper
- 1 small red onion, coarsely chopped (about 1 cup)
- 1 3/4 pounds lean top round beef, all fat and gristle removed, meat cut into about 1/2-inch pieces, chilled (about 1 1/4 pounds trimmed)

Garnishes

- 1/2 cup pine nuts, toasted
- Extra-virgin olive oil or chile oil
- 1/4 cup chopped fresh flat-leaf parsley
- 2 green onions, thinly sliced diagonally (about 1/2 cup)
- Tomato-Cucumber Relish (page 309)
- 2 bunches radishes, trimmed
- 2 bunches fresh mint

APPETIZERS: crispy onion rings

These onion rings have an addictive spicy-crunchy quality that makes them a true crowd pleaser. Try them as an accompaniment to Old World Sliders (page 58), or all on their own with Chile-Lime Chipotle Sauce (page 303) or Blue Cheese Dressing (page 294). I also love them as a garnish for my homemade meatloaf (page 220), as they add beautiful height and texture. The onions need to soak in the buttermilk for at least an hour, so plan accordingly.

SERVES 4 TO 6

Pour the buttermilk into a medium bowl. Separate the onion rings and toss them in the buttermilk to coat. Cover the bowl with plastic wrap and store the onions in the refrigerator for at least 1 hour and up to 1 day.

Pour enough oil into a heavy, large pot or deep fryer to reach a depth of 3 inches. Heat the oil to 350°F (over medium heat if using a pot). Mix the rice flour, all-purpose flour and cayenne pepper in a large bowl to blend. Working in batches, remove the onion slices from the buttermilk and toss them in the flour mixture to coat completely. Shake the excess flour off of the onions and fry the onions until they are golden brown and crisp, 2 to 3 minutes. Be sure to fry the onions in small batches and to allow the oil to return to 350°F before adding each batch. Using a slotted spoon, transfer the crispy onions to paper towels to drain the excess oil. The onion rings will be crisp and delicate, so handle them carefully to ensure the rings stay intact. Immediately season the hot onion rings with seasoned salt. Serve with the chile-lime chipotle sauce.

Zov's kitchen note: Rice flour in the batter gives the onion rings an extra crispy crust. Use this method with any fried foods where you want a real crunch. Fry the onion rings in batches so as not to overcrowd the pan. Overcrowding lowers the temperature and makes the onion rings greasy.

1½ cups buttermilk
2 large yellow onions (1½ pounds total), very thinly sliced into rings (⅛-inch thick)
Canola oil for deep frying
1 cup rice flour
½ cup all-purpose flour
¼ teaspoon cayenne pepper
Seasoned salt (see *Pantry and Produce*)
Chile-Lime Chipotle Sauce (page 303)

APPETIZERS: cheese boreg

Boreg is a delicious Armenian appetizer of puff pastry (or phyllo) traditionally stuffed with a savory meat mixture. A party food staple, this version is filled with three types of cheese, and it just does not get any better than this. The combination of melted cheese and flaky pastry is hard to resist. I think this will be your new appetizer standby. Unbaked boregs freeze beautifully for easy do-ahead. The dough needs to chill overnight, so plan accordingly.

MAKES 32 BOREGS

Prepare the dough: Whisk the water, eggs, egg yolk, oil, vinegar and salt in a large mixer bowl to blend. Using a wooden spoon or a heavy-duty stand mixer with the paddle attachment, slowly mix 4¼ cups of flour into the egg mixture until the dough comes together.

Transfer the dough to a lightly floured work surface and knead the dough until it is smooth and elastic, about 5 minutes. Wrap the dough in plastic wrap and refrigerate for 30 minutes. Chilling the dough will help relax it and make it more firm, thus easier to roll out.

Dust a heavy, large baking sheet with flour. Turn the dough out onto a lightly floured work surface. Roll out the dough to a 24x17-inch rectangle that is about ¼-inch thick. Position the dough so that one long side is closest to you. Brush away any excess flour. Spread the softened butter over the dough, leaving a 1-inch border around the edge so that the butter will not ooze out. Fold one-third of the dough over the center third, then fold the remaining third over the folded two-thirds, as is done for folding a letter. Set the dough on the prepared baking sheet, then cover tightly with plastic wrap and refrigerate for 2 hours.

Remove from refrigerator. Once again, set the dough on the work surface so that the long edges of the dough are parallel to the edge of the work surface and so that the side with the seam is closest to you. Roll out the dough to a 24x17-inch rectangle. Fold the one-third of the dough over the center third, then fold the remaining third over the folded two-thirds, as done previously. Return the dough to the baking sheet, then cover and refrigerate for 1 hour. Repeat this rolling and folding 2 more times, refrigerating the dough for 1 hour after each turn. Now, refrigerate the dough overnight. Be sure the dough is covered well with plastic wrap each time it is refrigerated. »

Dough

- 1 cup lukewarm water (110° to 115°F)
- 2 large eggs
- 1 large egg yolk
- 3 tablespoons olive oil
- 2 tablespoons white distilled vinegar
- 1 teaspoon kosher salt
- 4¼ cups (about 1½ pounds) all-purpose flour, plus more for dusting
- 12 ounces (3 sticks) unsalted butter, softened at room temperature

Boregs

- 3 cups grated Monterey Jack cheese
- 2 cups crumbled feta cheese
- 1 cup grated Fontina cheese
- 1 cup chopped fresh flat-leaf parsley
- 3 large eggs, lightly beaten to blend
- 1½ tablespoons nigella seeds (see *Pantry and Produce*)
- 1 large egg, beaten to blend for egg wash

Do-ahead tip: Instead of refrigerating overnight, the dough can be frozen for up to 3 months. Cover with plastic wrap and store.

Assemble and bake the boregs: Mix the Monterey Jack, feta, Fontina, parsley, 3 beaten eggs and nigella seeds in a large bowl to blend.

Line 2 heavy, large baking sheets with parchment paper. Cut the dough crosswise in half. Roll out 1 of the dough halves on a floured work surface to a 15-inch square (keep the remaining dough half refrigerated). Using a sharp knife, cut out 16 dough squares.

Place 1 generous tablespoon of the filling in the center of each dough square, then fold each square to form a triangle. Pinch the edges of the dough to seal, then use a fork to crimp the edges to prevent the filling from oozing out too much. Place the boregs on the prepared baking sheet. Cover and refrigerate the boregs until cold, about 1 hour. Repeat with the remaining dough half and filling. This dough is very tender, with many layers of butter, so keeping it cold makes it easier to handle and allows the dough to puff well when baked.

Do-ahead tip: Freeze the boregs for up to 2 months in an airtight container or freezer bag. You do not need to thaw before baking.

Preheat the oven to 400°F. Brush the boregs with the egg wash. Bake until the boregs are golden brown, puffed and cooked through, about 25 minutes. Some of the cheese filling may ooze out a little, which makes them look even more delicious.

Zov's kitchen note: Acid in the dough (in this case, vinegar) helps relax the gluten, which will make the dough easier to roll out. Boreg dough is typically cut into square shapes, stuffed with an assortment of savory fillings and then folded in half to create a triangle. Boregs are usually baked, but you will sometimes see them fried.

The ingredients for the cheese filling are simple, but the results are sublime. >

APPETIZERS: parmesan bruschetta

Bruschetta is a popular Italian hors d'oeuvre that is a snap to make. It can be served as a first course paired with any type of spreadable cheese and thinly sliced prosciutto. Or try toasting the bread slices first, brushing them with olive oil and then lightly grilling them. Bruschetta is a nice accompaniment to dips, soups and stews.

MAKES 12 SLICES

¼ cup extra-virgin olive oil
½ tablespoon finely chopped fresh basil
1 garlic clove, minced
½ loaf (about) French baguette
2 tablespoons freshly grated Parmesan cheese

Preheat a ridged grill pan or barbecue (medium heat). Combine the olive oil, basil and garlic in a small bowl to blend.

Cut the bread on a sharp diagonal into twelve ½-inch-thick slices. Brush both sides of the bread with the olive oil mixture, then sprinkle 1 side of the bread with the Parmesan. Grill until char marks form and the bread is crisp on the outside but soft on the inside, about 3 minutes per side. Alternatively, toast the bread in the toaster oven just until golden.

Do-ahead tip: Store in an airtight container for up to 1 day. Rewarm on a baking sheet in a 350°F oven for about 2 minutes.

APPETIZERS: crispy vegetable croquettes (falafels)

This crunchy and tasty street snack is one of the most popular vegetarian appetizers in the Middle East. Nearly every corner has a vendor selling falafels stuffed into pita bread with fresh tomatoes, cucumbers and Tahini Sauce (page 304). They are also traditionally served on a plate, drizzled with Tzatziki Sauce (page 303) and accompanied by an array of fresh vegetables like sliced tomatoes and lettuce. The fava and garbanzo beans need to soak overnight, so plan ahead.

MAKES 6 DOZEN

Drain the fava beans and garbanzo beans. Place just the garbanzo beans in a saucepan and cover with 2 inches of water. Bring the water to a boil, then boil for 10 minutes. Drain immediately, then scatter the garbanzo beans over a baking sheet to cool. Meanwhile, peel the fava beans and set them aside. To peel a fava, peel back the skin from one end, then pinch the bean between two fingers to pop it out of the skin. Do not boil the fava beans.

Pulse the fava beans in a food processor until they are coarsely chopped. Add the garbanzo beans and pulse until the beans are finely chopped and gritty and resemble large grains of sand (they should not be ground into a paste), scraping the bowl as needed. Transfer the beans to a large bowl.

Combine the onion, ginger, garlic, cilantro and parsley in the food processor and pulse until the mixture is gritty and brilliant green but not pureed. Scrape down the sides of the bowl and add a few tablespoons of water, if necessary, to release some of the mixture that might be stuck to the sides of the bowl. Transfer the mixture to the fava and garbanzo mixture. Stir in the coriander, cumin, salt, Aleppo pepper, granulated garlic, granulated onion, black pepper and cayenne pepper. Add the potato flakes and panko. Using your hands, mix until well blended. Cover and refrigerate for at least 1 hour and up to 2 days.

Do-ahead tip: At this point, the mixture can be divided into several portions, stored in airtight containers, and frozen for about 3 months. Thaw before continuing. Don't forget to add the appropriate amount of baking powder to the mixture after it has thawed. »

2 cups dried shucked fava beans, soaked overnight
1 cup dried garbanzo beans, soaked overnight
1 large onion, coarsely chopped (about 2 cups)
1 piece (2 inches) peeled fresh ginger, finely chopped
¼ cup minced garlic
1 bunch fresh cilantro (about 1½ cups)
1 bunch fresh flat-leaf parsley (about 1½ cups)
1 tablespoon ground coriander (see *Pantry and Produce*)
1 tablespoon ground cumin
1 tablespoon kosher salt
2 teaspoons Aleppo pepper (see *Pantry and Produce*)
2 teaspoons granulated garlic
2 teaspoons granulated onion
1½ teaspoons freshly ground black pepper
¼ teaspoon cayenne pepper
1 cup instant potato flakes
½ cup panko (Japanese breadcrumbs)
1½ quarts canola oil
1 tablespoon baking powder
Tahini Sauce (page 304)

Garnishes

Sliced or diced ripe tomatoes,
Cilantro leaves
Mint sprigs
Chopped cucumber
Romaine lettuce leaves for garnish

Heat about 2 inches of oil in a large saucepan or a deep fryer over medium heat until it reaches 350°F on a deep-fry thermometer. Just before frying, mix the baking powder into the falafel mixture. Scoop rounded tablespoonfuls of the falafel mixture into disc-shaped rounds. Working in batches of about 6 falafels per batch, fry the falafels until they are brown and crisp on the outside, about 2 minutes. Using a slotted spoon, transfer the falafels to a plate lined with paper towels to drain. Make sure the heat does not get too hot, otherwise the falafels will brown too much before the center is cooked. Serve hot with tahini sauce, tomatoes, cilantro, mint, chopped cucumber and lettuce.

Zov's kitchen note: Baking powder makes the falafels light and fluffy. Be sure to add the baking powder just before frying the falafels so as not to diminish its rising power.

Dried fava beans can be found at Middle Eastern markets. Though dried fava beans are shucked from their pods, the skin surrounding the bean must be peeled away. Peeling takes a bit of time, so enlist help from friends and family — their reward will be the most amazing falafels they've ever eaten.

Dried garbanzo and fava beans are more tender when cooked than their canned counterparts. >

APPETIZERS gravlax

Gravlax is a Scandinavian delicacy of fresh salmon cured in a mixture of spices, dill, salt, sugar and vodka. It's one of the most popular breakfast items at our restaurants, and we use it in many delicious ways: folded into soft scrambled eggs, in place of Canadian bacon in eggs Benedict and as a luscious first-course appetizer. Traditionally sliced paper-thin and served cold, gravlax captures a terrific combination of texture, temperature and flavor. So soft and sweet, it literally melts in your mouth. At home, try it on thinly sliced dark rye bread with a simple drizzle of Mustard Aïoli (page 299), a squeeze of lemon and a dollop of crème fraîche. It also makes an excellent passed hors d'oeuvre at a cocktail party. However you serve it, this is one recipe that will impress family and friends. The salmon needs to cure for at least three days, so plan ahead.

SERVES 16

½ cup kosher salt
½ cup granulated sugar
2 tablespoons lemon zest (from about 4 lemons)
2 2-pound high-quality boneless salmon fillets (preferably center-cut), skin on
1½ bunches fresh dill, stems removed
½ cup aquavit or vodka
2 teaspoons olive oil

Accompaniments
Pumpernickel bread, toasted
Unsalted butter
Mustard Aïoli (page 299)
Red onion, thinly sliced
Capers, drained

Mix the salt, sugar and lemon zest in a small bowl to blend. Lay a long sheet of plastic wrap over a 13x9x2-inch baking dish, extending well beyond the edges of the dish. Place 1 salmon fillet skin down on the plastic wrap in the dish. Pack ½ cup of the salt-sugar mixture all over the salmon fillet in the dish. Lay the dill over the salmon fillet. Then pour the aquavit over the salmon fillet. Pack ½ cup of the salt-sugar mixture over the second salmon fillet. Lay the second fillet flesh side down atop the fillet in the dish, as if you were making a sandwich. Rub any remaining salt-sugar mixture all over the stacked fish. Wrap the salmon fillets with the plastic wrap. Set a second baking dish on top of the fillets and weigh down the baking dish with 2 large cans. Refrigerate until the flesh of the salmon is translucent around the edges, basting the salmon with the accumulated juices every day, at least 3 days and up to 1 week.

Remove the fillets from the baking dish and scrape off the dill and any brine. You can also wipe off the brine with paper towels. Removing any excess brine ensures the salmon will not be too salty. Rub the fillets all over with olive oil.

Do-ahead tip: At this point, the gravlax can be made 1 week ahead. Wrap each salmon fillet tightly with clean plastic wrap, then place them in a clean glass container and wrap with another sheet of plastic wrap and refrigerate. The gravlax can also be stored in freezer bags and kept frozen for up to 1 month; thaw in the refrigerator before serving. »

To serve, lay the salmon, skin side down, on a cutting board. Using a knife with a long, thin blade, thinly slice the salmon diagonally at a 45-degree angle from the top of the fillet toward the skin.

Butter the toasted pumpernickel bread, then top with the gravlax slices. Spoon a small dollop of mustard aïoli on top of the gravlax, and then garnish with red onion and capers. Transfer to a platter and serve. Alternatively, arrange sliced gravlax decoratively on a platter, and sprinkle with the capers and red onion. Serve mustard aïoli and buttered pumpernickel toast alongside for guests to assemble themselves.

Zov's kitchen note: Always use the freshest, best-quality salmon you can find. There are so many delicious ways to serve gravlax. It pairs well with rye, multi-grain bread or bagels. Instead of homemade aïoli, you can serve the gravalx with lemon wedges and a dip of whole grain mustard mixed with mayonnaise on the side. You can also use half of the salmon in a sandwich (save the other half for another use). Try it on dark bread with soft scrambled eggs, a thick slice of juicy heirloom tomato, thinly sliced red onions and crème fraîche. For an elegant appetizer, serve the gravalx with toast points and sesame lavash crackers.

For melt-in-your-mouth texture, thinly slice the salmon at an angle, against the grain. >

APPETIZERS grilled eggplant, olive and tomato bruschetta

This is one of those great stand-by appetizers for a summer barbecue that you can pull together quickly when company drops in. You probably have most of the ingredients on hand, and the flavors can be tailored to suit your taste. Try it with roasted red or yellow peppers, add sun-dried tomatoes for extra flavor, or grill the bread, instead of baking it, for another layer of smokiness. The eggplant-tomato topping is also delicious spooned over grilled meats.

SERVES 8 (MAKES 16)

Prepare the barbecue (medium-high heat). Brush the eggplant slices with 2 tablespoons of olive oil and grill until tender and charred on both sides with grill marks, about 12 minutes total. Set aside until cooled slightly. Coarsely chop the grilled eggplant and set aside.

Meanwhile, preheat the oven to 400°F. Spoon 2 tablespoons of the olive oil onto a baking sheet and dip both sides of the bread slices in the oil to coat lightly. Arrange the bread slices in a single layer on the baking sheet and bake until golden brown and crisp, about 12 minutes.

Do-ahead tip: The toasts can be made 2 days ahead; store in an airtight container at room temperature. The eggplant can be grilled and chopped 1 day ahead; refrigerate in an airtight container. Allow the eggplant to come to room temperature before using.

Toss the eggplant pieces, tomatoes, olives, basil, cilantro, capers, shallots, lemon juice, ¾ teaspoon of salt, pepper and remaining 2 tablespoons of olive oil in a medium bowl. Season the mixture to taste with more salt. You will have about 3½ cups of the eggplant mixture. Divide the mixture evenly among the toasts and sprinkle with Parmesan. Garnish with parsley sprigs and serve.

Zov's kitchen note: Most of the ingredients can be prepared ahead, just make sure not to mix them together until you're ready to serve. The herbs and tomatoes should be freshly chopped, as oxidation alters the taste. Use any leftover mixture on grilled fish or chicken.

- 1 medium eggplant, cut into ½-inch-thick slices
- 6 tablespoons extra-virgin olive oil, divided
- 16 ½-inch-thick diagonally cut baguette slices
- 2 plum tomatoes, seeded and diced
- ½ cup kalamata olives, pitted and diced
- ¼ cup chopped fresh basil
- 2 tablespoons chopped fresh cilantro
- 2 tablespoons drained capers
- 2 tablespoons finely chopped shallots
- 2 teaspoons fresh lemon juice
- ¾ teaspoon kosher salt
- ¼ teaspoon freshly ground black pepper
- 3 tablespoons freshly grated Parmesan cheese
- Flat-leaf parsley sprigs, for garnish

APPETIZERS koufta

Koufta is one of the Middle East's most popular appetizers, often served as one of many mezza items on a buffet table. Growing up, no holiday was ever celebrated without my mother's koufta, one of the best I have ever tasted and now a tradition in my home. The beef filling is a bit time-consuming, but the end result makes it all worthwhile. To serve, garnish with lemon wedges, mint sprigs and cherry tomatoes.

MAKES 50 KOUFTA

Make the filling: Heat 3 tablespoons of oil in a large skillet over high heat. Add the beef and cook until the liquid evaporates and the meat is dark brown and caramelized, stirring often and breaking up the meat into large clumps with the back of the spoon, about 20 minutes. Add the onions and the butter. Reduce the heat to medium-high. Cook the meat mixture until it is a dark chocolate brown color and the onions are completely caramelized and incorporated into the meat, stirring frequently, about 35 minutes.

Stir the basil, granulated garlic, cumin, 1½ teaspoons of kosher salt, lemon pepper, seasoned salt, cayenne pepper and black pepper into the meat mixture. Remove the pan from the heat. Mix the parsley and pine nuts, if using, into the meat mixture. Cool. Season the mixture to taste with more kosher salt. You will have about 12 cups of filling.

Do-ahead tip: Transfer the filling to a freezer bag and freeze for up to 2 months. Thaw in the refrigerator before using.

Make the shell: Remove any fat or gristle from the beef, then cut the beef into ¾-inch cubes. Working in 3 batches, place the beef cubes in a food processor and process until the beef forms into a ball and becomes very smooth. Transfer the meat to a bowl and cover and refrigerate. (Do not clean out the food processor bowl.)

Mix the bulgur with 1½ cups of cold water in a large bowl, then set aside until the bulgur softens, about 10 minutes. Add the chopped onion to the food processor and pulse until it is very finely chopped. Stir the chopped onion, pepper paste, basil, cumin, kosher salt, seasoned salt, lemon pepper, paprika and black pepper into the bulgur. Working in batches, add the bulgur mixture to the food processor and pulse until well blended and the onion is pureed. Transfer the bulgur mixture to a large baking sheet. Add the beef paste and, using your hands, knead until the bulgur mixture and beef paste are completely blended.

(continued on page 56)

Filling

- 3 tablespoons vegetable oil
- 3 pounds lean ground beef
- 3 pounds onions (about 4 large onions), sliced
- 8 ounces (2 sticks) unsalted butter, cut into pieces
- 1 tablespoon dried basil
- 1 tablespoon granulated garlic
- 2 teaspoons ground cumin
- 1½ teaspoons kosher salt
- 1 teaspoon lemon pepper
- 1 teaspoon seasoned salt (see *Pantry and Produce*)
- ½ teaspoon cayenne pepper
- ½ teaspoon freshly ground black pepper
- 1 cup chopped fresh flat-leaf parsley
- 1 cup pine nuts (optional)

Shell

- 2 pounds beef eye of round
- 2 cups (12 ounces) fine-grade bulgur (#1) (see *Pantry and Produce*)
- 1½ cups cold water
- 1 small onion, coarsely chopped (about 1 cup)
- ½ cup Red Pepper Paste (page 305)
- 1 tablespoon dried basil
- 1 tablespoon ground cumin
- 2 teaspoons kosher salt
- 1½ teaspoons seasoned salt (see *Pantry and Produce*)
- 1¼ teaspoons lemon pepper
- 1 teaspoon paprika
- ½ teaspoon freshly ground black pepper
- Canola oil, for deep frying

koufta
STEP BY STEP

1. When making the shell, knead until the bulgur mixture and beef paste are completely blended.

2. Using about 1½ tablespoons of the shell mixture for each koufta, roll the mixture into 1½-inch balls using wet hands.

3. Poke a small hole into the center of each ball.

4. Spoon about 1 tablespoon of the filling into the center.

5. Reform the ball, making sure the filling is completely enclosed. Pinch off any excess patty. Roll the meatball between the palms of your hands to form a firm and smooth oval ball with tapered ends.

(continued from page 52)

Form the koufta: Using about 1½ tablespoons of the shell mixture for each koufta, roll the mixture into a 1½-inch ball using wet hands. Poke a small hole into the center of each ball and insert about 1 tablespoon of the filling, then reform into a ball. Pinch off any excess patty. Roll the meatball between the palms of your hands to form a firm and smooth oval ball with tapered ends. Arrange the koufta on a baking sheet. Cover and refrigerate the formed koufta as you continue to make more.

Do-ahead tip: At this point, the koufta can be covered and refrigerated for up to 2 days or frozen for up to 2 months. Place covered baking sheets in the freezer until the koufta are frozen and solid. Then transfer the koufta to an airtight container and store in the freezer. Defrost before continuing.

Heat 2 inches of oil in a heavy, large frying pan over medium heat until a deep-fry thermometer registers 350°F. Working in batches, fry the koufta until they are brown and heated through, about 5 minutes. Transfer the koufta to a baking sheet lined with paper towels to drain.

Zov's kitchen note: Caramelizing the onions and meat for the filling is a key step – make sure to sauté the mixture until it becomes a beautiful brown color. The filling can also be used for Pirozhki (page 28). The meat for the casings should be extremely lean; top sirloin or London broil can be used in place of the eye of round.

The koufta filling can be made up to 2 months ahead and frozen. >

APPETIZERS **old world sliders**

These miniature burgers are fantastic for cocktail parties. It's impossible to eat just one. Here, I updated the classic slider by adding cumin, mint and cayenne to make the flavor pop. Tomato-Mint Salsa and a tangy feta spread are vibrant garnishes. For a variation, top each slider with caramelized onions. The patties need to chill for at least an hour before grilling, so plan accordingly.

MAKES 12

Combine the panko and soda water in a large bowl and soak until all of the liquid is absorbed, about 5 minutes. Add the beef, parsley, mint, shallots, garlic, cumin, salt, black pepper and cayenne pepper. Gently knead until the herbs and spices are well combined.

Using about ⅓ cup for each patty, shape the meat mixture into twelve 2-ounce mini patties that are 2½-inches in diameter and ¾-inch thick. Place the patties on a baking sheet lined with plastic wrap. Cover and refrigerate for at least 1 hour and up to 1 day to allow the flavors to marry.

Preheat the barbecue or a grill pan (medium-high heat). Cook the patties until browned with grill marks, about 2 minutes per side for medium. Transfer the patties to a platter and tent with foil to keep warm.

Spoon 1 tablespoon of the yogurt and feta cheese spread over each bun bottom. Top with the patties, and then the tomato-mint salsa. Spoon 1 tablespoon of the yogurt spread over each bun top, then set them atop the burgers. Insert a toothpick into the center of each slider. Serve the remaining yogurt spread and salsa alongside.

Yogurt and Feta Cheese Spread: Using a fork, mash all ingredients in a medium bowl until mixture is nearly smooth. Refrigerate until ready to use. *Makes 1¾ cups*

Tomato-Mint Salsa: Stir all the ingredients in a medium bowl. Set aside at room temperature until ready to use or up to 2 hours. *Makes 1½ cups*

Zov's kitchen note: Both the Yogurt and Feta Cheese Spread and the Tomato-Mint Salsa make excellent appetizers all on their own. Serve them in separate bowls surrounded by toasted pita wedges.

¾ cup panko (Japanese breadcrumbs)
½ cup soda water
1 pound lean ground beef
½ cup finely chopped fresh flat-leaf parsley
½ cup finely chopped fresh mint
½ cup minced shallots
2 garlic cloves, minced
1 tablespoon ground cumin
1½ teaspoons kosher salt
½ teaspoon freshly ground black pepper
½ teaspoon cayenne pepper
12 mini burger buns (about 2-inches in diameter; preferably brioche)

Yogurt and feta cheese spread

1½ cups plain whole-milk Greek-style yogurt
¾ cup crumbled feta cheese (about 5 ounces)
3 tablespoons finely chopped fresh oregano
¾ teaspoon kosher salt
¾ teaspoon freshly ground black pepper

Tomato–mint salsa

1 cup finely chopped seeded fresh tomatoes
1 cup finely chopped seeded hothouse cucumber
½ cup finely chopped red onion
1 tablespoon finely chopped fresh mint
1 tablespoon fresh lemon juice
1 teaspoon kosher salt
½ teaspoon freshly ground black pepper
½ teaspoon garlic powder

APPETIZERS: olive tapenade

Black olives, capers, anchovies and olive oil come together in this versatile spread that hails from the Provence region of France. How do you improve on a classic? Mix in my Preserved Lemons (page 296) for wonderful, bright-tasting complexity. If you don't have time to make preserved lemons, just increase the lemon peel and juice slightly. Avoid store-bought preserved lemons, as they often have a preservative-laden flavor.

This simple tapenade is the foundation for many stunning dishes. Spread creamy burrata cheese on slices of toasted baguette and serve the tapenade alongside. Use it as a tangy dip for assorted raw vegetables like carrots, celery, mushrooms or cucumbers. Or spread a thin layer on sandwich bread and top with a thick slice of heirloom tomato, fresh mozzarella cheese and a drizzle of olive oil. Tapenade also makes a delicious topping for grilled fish or chicken.

MAKES 2 CUPS

Grate the flesh side of the tomato halves into the food processor bowl; discard the tomato skins. Add the sun-dried tomatoes and pulse once to combine. Let stand 15 minutes to allow the sun-dried tomatoes to soften slightly in the tomato juices. Add the olives, 2 tablespoons of the capers, and the next 11 ingredients. Pulse until a very chunky puree forms. With the machine running, pour the oil through the feed tube, blending just until a coarse puree forms. Transfer the tapenade to a bowl. Garnish the tapenade with the remaining 1 tablespoon of capers.

Do-ahead tip: Refrigerate in an airtight container for up to 1 week.

Zov's kitchen note: Any cured black olive can stand in for kalamata. The consistency of the tapenade should be slightly chunky, but not too thick. Burrata cheese is a luscious triple-cream mozzarella from Italy. If you can't find burrata, use fresh mozzarella. Instead of baguette slices, use lavash crackers, toasted pita or plain French bread.

- 2 ripe tomatoes (about 8 ounces), halved and seeded
- 1½ ounces sun-dried tomatoes (not packed in oil; about 1 cup)
- 1 cup pitted kalamata olives
- 3 tablespoons drained capers, rinsed, divided
- 2 anchovy fillets
- ¼ cup fresh flat-leaf parsley
- 1 tablespoon chopped shallots
- 1 tablespoon chopped Preserved Lemons (page 296; optional)
- 2 teaspoons coarsely chopped fresh rosemary
- 2 teaspoons coarsely chopped fresh thyme
- 1½ teaspoons fresh lemon juice
- 1½ teaspoons finely grated lemon zest
- 2 garlic cloves
- ⅛ teaspoon dried crushed hot red pepper
- ⅛ teaspoon freshly ground black pepper
- ½ cup extra-virgin olive oil

APPETIZERS: spicy pomegranate-glazed chicken wings

There are hundreds of recipes for Buffalo wings, ranging from hot to sweet to savory and every variation in between. My version gives a nod to the original by using Frank's hot sauce, but I turn up the flavor with Sriracha and pomegranate molasses. Instead of deep-frying the traditional way, I think wings are just as delicious baked, and it's much easier to do. My secret: a heavily-greased baking sheet creates a similar crispiness to frying. Another trick is to brine the wings beforehand to lock in moisture. Customer demand for these wings reaches a fever pitch during football season. Now, when a big game is on TV, sports fans can make their own wings at home. Serve with Tzatziki Sauce (page 303) or ranch dressing. The wings need to be refrigerated for an hour before baking, so plan ahead.

SERVES 8

Prepare the chicken: Using a sharp knife, cut the tips off each wing then cut through the joints to divide the wings in half. Combine 4 cups of water and 3 tablespoons salt in a large bowl, stirring to dissolve. Add the chicken and set aside for 30 minutes. Drain and pat the wings dry.

Generously coat 2 large, rimmed baking sheets with vegetable shortening, forming a thin white coating. Mix the flour, seasoned salt, black pepper and remaining 2 tablespoons of kosher salt in a large bowl. Add the chicken wings and toss to coat with the flour mixture until they are evenly and thickly coated. Arrange the chicken wings on the prepared baking sheets, dividing equally and spacing evenly apart. Cover and refrigerate 1 hour.

Preheat the oven to 400°F. Bake the chicken wings until golden on the bottom, about 30 minutes. Turn the wings over and continue baking until the wings are crispy and brown all over, about 30 minutes longer.

Meanwhile, prepare the sauce: Stir the hot sauces, pomegranate molasses, vinegar, granulated garlic, butter and paprika in a small saucepan over low heat until the butter is melted and the mixture is blended.

Transfer the roasted chicken wings to a large serving bowl. Add the sauce and toss to coat. Serve immediately with ranch dressing alongside.

Zov's kitchen note: Chances are you're making chicken wings for a crowd, so it's best to buy them in bulk packs. Chicken wings are sold pre-cut or whole. Whole wings are cheaper, but you'll have to do the cutting yourself, which is easy once you get a feel for it. Start by holding the wing at the base upright. Spread the wings out and with a sharp knife gently slice between the bones. Softly move the knife around to find the easiest way through.

Chicken

- 4 pounds whole chicken wings
- 4 cups cold water
- 5 tablespoons kosher salt, divided
- 4 tablespoons solid vegetable shortening
- 1¼ cups all-purpose flour
- 2 tablespoons seasoned salt (see *Pantry and Produce*)
- 1 tablespoon freshly ground black pepper

Sauce

- 1 5-ounce bottle hot chile sauce (preferably Frank's hot sauce)
- 3 tablespoons hot chili sauce (such as Sriracha) (see *Pantry and Produce*)
- ¼ cup pomegranate molasses (see *Pantry and Produce*)
- 3 tablespoons white distilled vinegar
- 2 tablespoons granulated garlic
- 2 tablespoons unsalted butter
- 1 tablespoon paprika
- Ranch dressing, for dipping

[handwritten note: Don't forget must cover/leave wings for 1 hr before baking]

APPETIZERS: perfect guacamole

Who doesn't like guacamole? The famous Mexican dip shows off the subtle nutty flavor of avocados, complements a variety of vegetables (not just tortilla chips), and is packed with nutrients. The trick to perfect guacamole, though, depends on having good-quality Hass avocados, which are creamier than other varieties. The skin is sturdier too, which makes them easier to peel. Go beyond the classic tomato-based salsas and try mixing Hass with diced red onions or mangoes. Serve with pita chips and artfully arranged crudités.

MAKES 2 CUPS

Using a fork, mash the avocados in a large bowl, making sure they stay a bit chunky. Stir in the tomatoes, cilantro, shallots and jalapeño. Stir in the lemon juice, lime juice, salt, black pepper and crushed red pepper, if using.

Do-ahead tip: The guacamole can be made 5 hours ahead. Press a sheet of plastic wrap directly on the surface of the guacamole, then wrap tightly with another sheet of plastic. Refrigerate until ready to serve.

Zov's kitchen note: If you make the guacamole ahead, be sure to seal the bowl tightly to prevent any air from getting in. Exposure to air causes avocados to turn brown. Also, wash your hands thoroughly after touching any hot chile. The oils can cause irritation to the skin, but most importantly, avoid touching your eyes or the area near your eyes for several hours.

- 4 ripe Hass avocados, pitted and peeled
- 1 ripe tomato, seeded and finely chopped
- ⅓ cup chopped fresh cilantro
- ¼ cup minced shallots
- 1 jalapeño chile, seeded and minced
- 1 tablespoon fresh lemon juice
- 1 tablespoon fresh lime juice
- 1 teaspoon kosher salt
- ½ teaspoon freshly ground black pepper
- ⅛ teaspoon dried crushed hot red pepper (optional)

APPETIZERS ## spicy sesame seed flatbreads with pepper paste

These mini flatbreads are so delicious it's impossible to eat just one. A generous amount of olive oil gives this typical Mediterranean appetizer extra texture and flavor.

MAKES 30 FLATBREADS

Prepare the dough: Mix the yeast, sugar and ½ cup of the warm water in a medium bowl. Let stand until the yeast is dissolved and the mixture is frothy and foamy, about 5 minutes.

Mix 7 cups of the flour and salt in the bowl of a stand mixer fitted with the dough hook until a well forms. Add the yeast mixture and the remaining 3 cups of warm water to the well. Mix on low speed until a dough forms. Transfer the dough to a floured board and knead until the dough is elastic, about 5 minutes. Place the dough in an oiled bowl. Cover and rest until the dough doubles in size, about 45 minutes. Punch down the dough, then cover and let rest another 30 minutes.

Meanwhile, prepare the topping: Heat 1 cup of olive oil in a heavy, large saucepan over medium-high heat. Add the onions and sauté until almost tan in color, about 18 minutes. Remove the pan from the heat and stir in the ricotta cheese, pepper paste, tomato paste, zahtar, sesame seeds, oregano, thyme, black pepper, cumin and salt. Mix in ½ cup of olive oil. You should have 7 cups of topping.

Prepare the flatbreads: Preheat the oven to 500°F. Lightly oil a large baking sheet. Using about 2 ounces of dough for each flatbread, shape the dough into thirty 2-inch balls and line them on the oiled baking sheet.

Do-ahead tip: Store the uncooked topping and dough balls separately in freezer bags and freeze for up to 1 year. Thaw before proceeding.

Preheat another large baking sheet in the oven until it is very hot, about 5 minutes. Using oven mitts, transfer the hot baking sheet to a heat-resistant surface or set it on the stove top (the baking sheet will be very hot so be sure to use oven mitts and set it on a surface that won't scorch). Place a third baking sheet in the oven to preheat while assembling the flatbread on the first preheated baking sheet.

(continued on page 70)

Dough

- 2 ¼-ounce packages rapid-rise yeast
- 1 teaspoon granulated sugar
- 3 ½ cups warm water (105°F to 115°F), divided
- 7 cups all-purpose flour
- 2 teaspoons kosher salt

Topping

- 1 ¾ cups extra-virgin olive oil, divided
- 2 large onions, finely chopped (about 3 ½ cups)
- 16 ounces ricotta cheese
- 1 ½ cups Red Pepper Paste (page 305)
- 1 cup tomato paste
- ½ cup zahtar (see *Pantry and Produce*)
- ½ cup sesame seeds
- 2 tablespoons dried oregano
- 2 tablespoons coarsely chopped fresh thyme
- 1 teaspoon freshly ground black pepper
- 1 teaspoon ground cumin
- 1 teaspoon kosher salt

spicy sesame seed flatbreads with pepper paste
STEP BY STEP

1. Shape the dough into 2-inch balls.

2. Dip a paper towel into ¼ cup of olive oil and lightly coat a sheet of parchment paper.

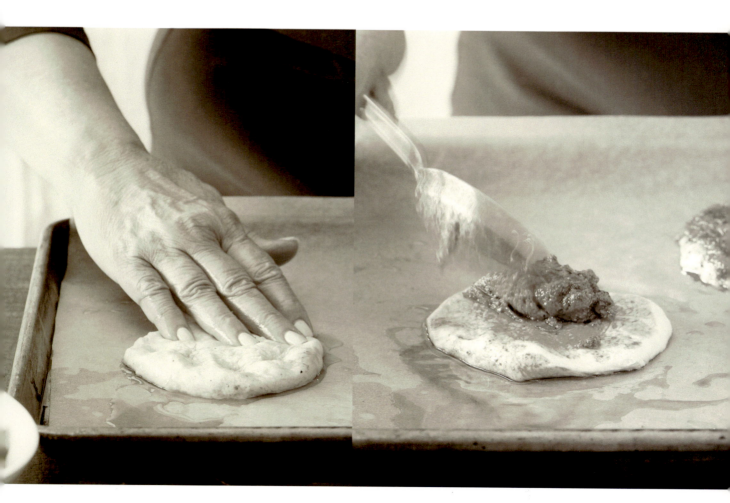

3. Using oiled fingers, press each dough ball into 3½-inch discs. Flattening the dough on a hot baking sheet helps prevent it from shrinking back.

4. Spoon about 2 tablespoons of the topping onto the flatbread. Using your hands, flatten the dough to a 4½-inch-diameter disc as you spread the topping all over the flatbread.

(continued from page 66)

Dip a paper towel into the remaining ¼ cup of olive oil and lightly coat a sheet of parchment paper with oil. Lay the parchment paper on the hot baking sheet. Arrange 6 of the dough balls on the parchment paper, spacing evenly apart. Using oiled fingers, press the dough into 3½-inch discs. Using your hands and about 2 tablespoons of the topping for each flatbread, spread the topping all over the surface of the flatbreads, flattening the dough to 4½-inch-diameter discs as you spread. Flattening the dough on a hot baking sheet makes it easier to stretch the dough and helps prevent it from shrinking back. When assembling the flatbreads, occasionally mix the topping to ensure the oil is well blended throughout.

Bake until the dough is browned on the bottom, about 12 minutes. Make sure you don't overbake the flatbreads, otherwise the bread will be very dry. While the first baking sheet of flatbread is in the oven, remove the second baking sheet and assemble more flatbreads. Working with 2 trays in this manner makes it much faster to assemble the flatbreads.

Do-ahead tip: Freeze leftover baked flatbreads in an airtight freezer bag for up to 3 months. To rewarm, arrange flatbreads on a baking sheet, cover with foil and bake at 350°F until heated through.

Zov's kitchen note: If you don't have time to make your own red pepper 0aste, you can find it at Middle Eastern markets. Look for paste that is thick, not saucy. Mild versions are also available (see Pantry and Produce for more information). For extra tangy flatbreads, mix in to the topping ¼ cup each of crumbled blue cheese and grated Gouda.

Red pepper paste, sesame seeds and zahtar >

APPETIZERS: pureed bean dip with yogurt and dill

The recipe for this bean dip comes from one of my employees, Cat Mosley, who loves to experiment with food. One day, she brought a sample of her creation to work and I fell in love with it immediately. So flavorful and simple — the main ingredients are garbanzo beans and yogurt — this recipe offers a healthier take on traditional hummus by forgoing high-fat tahini. It's a smart alternative to sour cream dips, which can be high in calories and saturated fat. Serve with an assortment of celery sticks, cauliflower, radishes, cucumber, red and green bell peppers, carrot sticks, mushrooms, cherry tomatoes, asparagus and warm toasted pita wedges. Beware, it is quite spicy and has a nice kick.

MAKES 3 ½ CUPS

Finely chop the garlic in a food processor. Add the garbanzo beans and blend until a coarse puree forms, stopping the machine occasionally to scrape down the sides of the bowl. Add the pickled jalapeño chiles, lemon juice, yogurt, dill, cumin, paprika, salt, cayenne pepper and black pepper. With the machine running, slowly drizzle the oil through the feed tube, blending until the mixture is smooth and creamy and stopping the machine to scrape down the sides of the bowl occasionally. Transfer to a decorative bowl and serve.

Do-ahead tip: The dip can be made 2 days ahead. Cover and refrigerate.

Zov's kitchen note: For a milder version, omit the cayenne pepper and pickled jalapeños. To turn up the heat, add more jalapeños or increase the cayenne pepper. You can use regular paprika, if you like, but I love the bolder flavor of Hungarian paprika.

- 4 garlic cloves
- 2 15-ounce cans garbanzo beans, drained
- ⅓ cup pickled sliced hot jalapeño chiles (drained from jar)
- ¼ cup fresh lemon juice
- ¼ cup plain whole-milk Greek-style yogurt
- 3 tablespoons chopped fresh dill
- 2 teaspoons ground cumin
- 2 teaspoons paprika (preferably Hungarian paprika)
- 1 teaspoon kosher salt
- ½ teaspoon cayenne pepper
- ½ teaspoon freshly ground black pepper
- ⅔ cup extra-virgin olive oil

APPETIZERS: zucchini fritters with gravlax

So simple and fun to make, these fritters work as tasty appetizers, a satisfying snack or even a meatless main course. For a gorgeous addition to a buffet table, arrange them on a platter with Greek-style yogurt on the side; garnish with mint, radishes, fresh parsley leaves, lemon slices or teardrop tomatoes. I also love the fritters stuffed into pita bread with fresh tomato slices, avocados and crumbled feta cheese.

MAKES 12

Wrap the grated zucchini in a paper towel and wring it to remove the excess liquid. Whisk the eggs in a large bowl to blend. Add the zucchini, parsley, green onions, mint, chives, dill, garlic, lemon zest, salt and pepper and stir until all the ingredients are combined. Stir in 1 cup of the panko. Let stand for 1 minute. If the mixture is too wet, add more panko 1 tablespoon at a time.

Using about ¼ cup of the zucchini mixture for each, form 12 patties that are about 3 inches in diameter.

Heat 3 tablespoons of oil in a heavy, large skillet over medium-low heat. Lay 4 patties in the hot pan, making sure the fritters are spaced a few inches apart. Cook until the patties are firm and begin to turn golden brown on the bottom, about 5 minutes, being careful not to burn them. Using a spatula, turn the fritters over and cook until brown on the bottom, about 5 minutes. Transfer the fritters to a baking sheet lined with paper towels to drain. Repeat with the remaining fritters, adding more oil as needed.

Place the fritters on a flat platter, top each with the gravlax then with a dollop of yogurt. Garnish with dill sprigs and serve.

Zov's kitchen note: Serve the fritters hot or at room temperature. When frying the fritters, don't crowd the pan; they need room to expand. Make sure to drain the zucchini thoroughly. If the mixture is wet, it will create foam in the oil and the fritters won't brown evenly. You can substitute cocktail shrimp or lump crabmeat for the gravlax, and sour cream for the yogurt.

- 3 medium zucchini (about 1 pound total), coarsely grated (about 3 cups)
- 4 large eggs, beaten lightly to blend
- ½ cup chopped fresh flat-leaf parsley
- ½ cup minced green onions
- ⅓ cup chopped fresh mint
- 3 tablespoons minced fresh chives
- 2 tablespoons chopped fresh dill
- 2 garlic cloves, minced
- 1 tablespoon lemon zest
- 1 teaspoon kosher salt
- 1 teaspoon freshly ground black pepper
- 1 cup (or more) panko (Japanese breadcrumbs)
- 6 tablespoons (about) olive oil
- 6 ounces thinly sliced Gravlax (page 46)
- 1 cup Greek-style yogurt
- Dill sprigs, for garnish

APPETIZERS: tomato-basil risotto fritters

This recipe was created by our former chef Kellie Rabanit. She always came up with clever ways of creating a recipe within a recipe. This fun cocktail appetizer is one example. Every bite has a satisfying crunch and oozes a surprise filling of delicious melted cheese. It looks beautiful, tastes amazing and elevates boring leftover rice to something spectacular. They're perfect for an elegant party. I like them best with Tomato-Basil Sauce (page 308), but you can also use Marinara Sauce (page 306) or your favorite store-bought dipping sauce. The risotto needs to chill for at least two hours, so plan ahead.

MAKES ABOUT 75 FRITTERS

Bring the broth and the tomato sauce to a simmer in a heavy medium saucepan, then cover and keep over very low heat.

Heat the butter with the oil in a heavy 4-quart saucepan over medium-high heat. Mixing the oil and butter helps prevent the butter from burning while still imparting a buttery flavor to the risotto. Add the onion and sauté until translucent, about 2 minutes. Using a wooden spoon, stir in the rice and garlic. Continue stirring to make sure the rice is coated and nicely toasted, about 4 minutes. Stirring creates friction on the grains of rice and releases a little of its starch.

Reduce the heat to medium. Stir ¾ cup of the hot tomato broth into the rice mixture. Continue stirring until the broth is absorbed. Continue adding the broth ¾ cup at a time and stirring and simmering gently until the rice is al dente and the mixture is creamy, about 20 minutes. Don't allow the rice to dry up completely before adding more broth, but also make sure there is no excess liquid in the saucepan.

Stir in the Parmesan, cheddar cheese, salt, black pepper and crushed red pepper. The risotto should be thick and not too loose or the fritters will not come together to form a ball after chilling. »

---

7 cups chicken broth
1 8-ounce can tomato sauce
2 tablespoons unsalted butter
¼ cup olive oil
½ cup finely chopped onion
2 cups arborio rice
2 tablespoons minced garlic
1½ cups grated Parmesan cheese (about 6 ounces)
½ cup grated cheddar cheese (about 2 ounces)
1 teaspoon kosher salt
½ teaspoon freshly ground black pepper
¼ teaspoon dried crushed hot red pepper
8 ounces cooked, peeled and deveined shrimp (optional)
½ cup fresh basil, finely chopped
3 cups panko (Japanese breadcrumbs), divided
12 ounces whole-milk mozzarella cheese, cut into ½-inch cubes
Canola oil for deep-frying
Tomato-Basil Sauce (page 308)

Pulse the shrimp, if using, in a food processor until minced but not pureed. Stir the shrimp, basil and 1 cup of the panko into the risotto. Spread the risotto in an even layer over a large, rimmed baking sheet. Cover and refrigerate until the risotto is firm to the touch, at least 2 hours or overnight.

Moistening your hands with water to prevent the risotto from sticking, flatten 1 heaping tablespoon of the risotto in the palm of your hand. Place 1 cube of the mozzarella in the center, then fold the edges of the risotto over the cheese, pressing firmly to encase the cheese and form a 2-inch ball. Repeat with the remaining risotto and mozzarella cubes. Dredge the risotto balls in the remaining 2 cups of panko and pat gently to coat. Cover and refrigerate for at least 30 minutes or overnight.

Add enough oil to a heavy large saucepan to fill it halfway. Heat the oil over medium heat to 350°F. Working in batches, fry the risotto balls in the oil until golden brown, about 3 minutes. Using a slotted spoon, transfer the fritters to a baking sheet lined with paper towels to drain the excess oil.

Do-ahead tip: The fried risotto balls can be kept warm in a 200°F oven for up to 1 hour. Alternatively, the uncooked risotto balls can be stored in an airtight container and frozen for up to 1 month; do not thaw them before frying.

Transfer the fritters to a platter and insert a small cocktail skewer into each fritter. Serve the tomato sauce alongside for dipping.

Zov's ktichen note: Fontina cheese is a good substitute for mozzarella.

Do-ahead tip: Refrigerate for up to 2 days or freeze for up to 1 month.

> The risotto shell is easy to prepare, but depends on having a few top-quality ingredients in your larder. >

BREAKFAST

apricot jam **84**

breakfast bake with soujouk and potatoes **88**

bananas foster french toast **90**

oatmeal brûlée **92**

breakfast potato cakes **94**

old-fashioned pancakes with blueberry syrup **98**

crunchy granola with almonds, oats and dried fruits **100**

eggs benedict with gravlax and creamy hollandaise sauce **102**

sour cherry jam **104**

torte milanese with spinach **106**

simple buttermilk biscuits **110**

quince jam **112**

spanish omelet with manchego and cheddar cheese **114**

super easy fig jam **116**

ultimate cinnamon buns **118**

BREAKFAST

Whether tiny or large or blue, brown or speckled, eggs are one of nature's most elegant creations. They are not only the beginning of life, but they're also a truly perfect food. The stunningly yellow yolk and pristine egg whites are both packed with nutrients. The outer shell, which protects its delicate insides, is perfectly packaged for today's on-the-go lifestyle. And the egg is emblematic of my favorite meal of the day: breakfast. | The wonderful thing about an egg is that it can be cooked so many different ways. I like them poached so that the warm, gooey yoke spills out over a crunchy piece of toast when you spear it with your fork; or made into a small, simple omelet that's light and fluffy, and packed with flavorful fillings. Whether you prefer them scrambled, soft-boiled, hard-boiled, sunny side up or over easy, eggs are a great way to start any day. | Paired with a buttermilk biscuit or a piece of toast covered with Apricot Jam, eggs become a simple, satisfying meal. But they are also essential to delectable breakfast foods like Bananas Foster French Toast covered with sweet, ripe bananas or Old-Fashioned Pancakes drizzled in a rich, thick blueberry syrup. | Throughout this chapter, you will learn how to make many different dishes that are, like the egg, versatile, from eat-on-the-run meals to sophisticated Sunday brunches. |

BREAKFAST apricot jam

This versatile jam can be used as a luscious filling for pastries and cookies or just for your morning toast. Making jam is much easier and safer than most people think. It simply involves cooking fresh fruit with lots of sugar and some lemon juice, then pouring the mixture into sterilized jars. This jam keeps well in the refrigerator for more than a year.

MAKES FOUR 16-OUNCE JARS

Place the apricot halves in a heavy, wide 5-quart pot, then add the sugar, water and lemon juice. Let the mixture stand for 1 hour at room temperature, stirring occasionally, to allow the apricots to release their juice and most of the sugar to dissolve into a syrup.

Cook over high heat, stirring often, until all of the sugar melts and the mixture boils, about 12 minutes. Set a bowl of ice water and a pastry brush on the counter near the pot and brush all along the inside walls of the pot to remove any sugar granules that are clinging to the side. Keep brushing the sides of the pot until the sugar is completely dissolved. Brushing the sides with ice water prevents the jam mixture from crystallizing; if one granule of sugar clinging to the side of the pot gets into the jam, the whole batch of jam will crystallize.

Reduce the heat to medium-low and simmer, stirring often to prevent the jam from sticking to the bottom of the pot, until the apricots break down completely, about 35 minutes (just a few lumpy pieces should remain and the jam should thicken slightly). As the apricots cook, the color will change to a darker shade of orange and small bubbles will form on top; don't worry about skimming off the bubbles, as they will dissolve. Don't allow the jam to thicken too much since it will thicken considerably when cooled. To test if the jam will be thick enough, drop a tablespoon onto a frozen plate and let cool. It should be firm but not hard. If it is too thin, continue cooking. If it is too firm, add some water to thin it to the desired consistency.

Ladle the hot jam into dry sterilized jars, leaving about ¼-inch of room at the top. Cover and refrigerate for up to 2 weeks.

Do-ahead tip: To store longer, follow the canning instructions on page 86.

Zov's kitchen note: The key to a successful jam is not to overcook it. Overcooked jam will harden overnight and end up as hard as rock candy. If the finished jam does end up too thick, place the entire jar into a pot »

3 pounds apricots, halved and pitted
6 cups granulated sugar (about 3 pounds)
¾ cup water
1 tablespoon fresh lemon juice

Special equipment:
four 16-ounce glass jars and canning tongs, both sterilized (for Sterilization and Canning Instructions, see page 86)

of water and let it come to a boil. After the jam heats up, it will turn to liquid. At this point, add a small amount of water to the jam to thin it out. Use the freezer-plate method described in the recipe until you get the right consistency.

Sterilizing Jars: Wash the jars and lids with hot, soapy water. Set a rack in the bottom of a large pot. Set the jars and the lids on the rack, then fill the pot and jars with water. Be sure the jars and lids are completely submerged. Bring the water to a boil. Boil for 15 minutes.

Dip the ends of the canning tongs into the boiling water for 3 minutes to sterilize them. Remove the pot of boiling water from the heat. Using the sterilized tongs, remove the jars and lids from the boiling water and tilt the jar to drain the excess liquid. Allow the heat to steam dry the jars and lids.

Canning Instructions: Wipe the sealing surface of the jars with a clean paper towel, dampened with hot water. Adjust the lids.

Set the jars of jam upright in a large pot of water. Be sure the jars are completely submerged. Bring the water to a boil and boil for 5 minutes. Remove from the heat and let stand in the water for an additional 5 minutes. Using the canning tongs and keeping the jars upright, carefully remove the jars from the water and set them on a cooling rack. Set aside until cool, about 12 hours. Store the jams in the refrigerator indefinitely.

BREAKFAST breakfast bake with soujouk and potatoes

Sausage and potatoes have found each other in a whole new way. This make-ahead casserole shows how good that combination can be, and is just one of the reasons why breakfast is my favorite meal of the day.

SERVES 8

Preheat the oven to 350°F. Butter a 2½-quart baking dish. Cook the soujouk in a nonstick sauté pan over medium heat until it is heated through and most of its oils have exuded, about 5 minutes. Using a slotted spoon, transfer the soujouk to a plate lined with paper towels to drain the excess oil.

Whisk the eggs, milk and ½ cup of the sour cream in a large bowl to blend. Stir in the cooked soujouk, cheddar cheese, Gouda, green onions, shallots, salt and pepper. Grate the potatoes into the egg mixture. Stir to blend. Pour the mixture into the prepared baking dish.

Bake uncovered until the mixture is golden brown on top and slightly puffed and the potatoes are very tender, about 1½ hours. Cut the mixture into squares and transfer to plates. Top each with a dollop of sour cream and garnish with parsley. Serve the tomato-cucumber relish alongside.

Zov's kitchen note: Soujouk (also spelled soujuk) is an Armenian spicy dried sausage that can be found at Middle Eastern markets. Diced ham, chicken sausage or bacon can be substituted for the soujouk. Yukon Gold potatoes can stand in for the russets, or you can substitute a thawed 32-ounce package of frozen hash browns to save time. Add sautéed mushrooms for a delicious variation.

Do-ahead tip: This hearty breakfast dish can be aseembled the day before and baked before serving. Cover tightly with plastic wrap and refrigerate overnight.

8 ounces soujouk, finely diced (see note)
8 large eggs
2 cups whole milk
1½ cups sour cream, divided
2 cups grated white cheddar cheese
1 cup grated Gouda cheese
5 green onions, chopped (about 1 cup)
1 tablespoon minced shallots
1½ teaspoons kosher salt
1 teaspoon freshly ground black pepper
2 pounds russet potatoes, peeled
Flat-leaf parsley, for garnish
Tomato-Cucumber Relish (page 309)

BREAKFAST: bananas foster french toast

A delicious twist on a classic dessert, bananas Foster is reinvented for breakfast. The sturdy texture of challah bread gives this dish a wonderful richness, while the homey flavor of caramelized bananas appeals to kids of all ages. I also like to drizzle banana sauce over pancakes, ice cream and pound cake.

SERVES 6

Make the banana sauce: Melt the butter in a large stainless-steel skillet over medium heat. Add the brown sugar and whisk until it melts, about 2 minutes. Add the water and whisk until well blended and smooth. Cover and set aside while you prepare the French toast.

Prepare the French toast: Whisk the whole eggs and egg yolks in a large bowl to blend. Gradually whisk in the milk, whipping cream and vanilla. Dip the bread slices into the egg mixture, turning to coat and soak until they are completely moistened with the custard.

Heat a heavy, large griddle pan over medium heat. Melt 1 tablespoon of butter on the griddle. Working in batches, transfer the soaked bread to the pan with a slotted spatula and cook until golden brown and cooked through, about 3 minutes per side. Add more butter as needed for each batch.

To serve, add the banana slices to the sauce and cook until the bananas are almost tender, tossing gently, about 3 minutes. Transfer the French toast to plates. Top each with the banana sauce and whipped cream, if desired.

Banana sauce
- 4 ounces (1 stick) unsalted butter
- ½ cup (packed) dark brown sugar
- 2 tablespoons water
- 4 bananas, peeled and cut diagonally into ½-inch-thick slices

French toast
- 3 large whole eggs
- 3 large egg yolks
- ½ cup whole milk
- ¼ cup whipping cream
- 1 teaspoon vanilla extract
- 6 slices (¾-inch thick) challah bread or brioche
- 3 tablespoons (about) unsalted butter
- Whipped cream (optional)

BREAKFAST oatmeal brûlée

Individual servings of nutritious rolled oats get a wake-up call with a caramelized sugar topping. What a luxurious way to incorporate whole grain into your diet. For even more sparkle, add toasted candied walnuts, figs or dried cranberries. This recipe requires a kitchen torch.

SERVES 4

Bring 5 cups of milk to a simmer in a heavy medium saucepan over high heat. Add the oats and salt and stir over medium heat until the oats soften, about 10 minutes. Stir in raisins and cinnamon. Reduce the heat to low and cook until the oats are very tender, the raisins are plump and the mixture is thick and creamy, stirring often, about 3 minutes. If the oatmeal becomes too thick, add more milk to thin it to the desired consistency.

Divide the oatmeal among 4 ceramic bowls and smooth the tops. Sprinkle the sugar over the entire surface of the oatmeal. Using a kitchen torch, wave the flame in a circular motion over the sugar until the sugar is melted and golden brown. Garnish with blueberries, raspberries, strawberries and mint sprigs and serve.

Zov's kitchen note: There are so many ways to customize your bowl of oatmeal. My favorite combinations are banana, walnut and raisin and chopped apples with maple syrup. You can find coarse sugar crystals at gourmet markets and cookware stores.

- 5 cups (or more) 2% milk
- 2 cups old-fashioned rolled oats
- ⅛ teaspoon kosher salt
- ½ cup golden raisins
- ½ teaspoon ground cinnamon
- 4 tablespoons coarse sugar crystals or turbinado sugar
- 1 cup fresh blueberries, raspberries and sliced strawberries, for garnish
- Mint sprigs, for garnish

BREAKFAST breakfast potato cakes

Who doesn't crave a simple, delicious potato now and then? It's the familiar comforts that we like best. A subtle hint of chives and sweet shallots accent these potato cakes, which are a perfect match with poached eggs. Try them as a replacement for English muffins in Eggs Benedict (page 102) or alongside scrambled eggs and omelets. At our restaurant, when the breakfast rush hits, we cannot make these fast enough.

MAKES 12

Place the raw potatoes in a heavy 2-quart saucepan and add enough cold water to cover them by 1 inch. Bring the water to a boil over medium-high heat. Reduce the heat to medium and simmer until the potatoes are soft, about 15 to 20 minutes. Strain the potatoes, then return them to the hot pot and set aside to steam dry for 3 minutes. Using a fork or a potato masher, mash the potatoes and set aside. You should have about 1½ cups of mashed potatoes.

Combine the 1½ cups of mashed potatoes with the thawed hash browns, 1 cup of the panko, Parmesan, melted butter, parsley, chives, shallots, kosher salt, seasoned salt and pepper in a large bowl. Using your hands, mix the potato mixture until it is well blended.

Sprinkle the remaining ¾ cup of panko in a pie dish. Line a baking sheet with parchment paper. Set a 3-inch-diameter biscuit cutter on the prepared baking sheet. Spoon a generous ½ cup of the potato mixture into the cutter. Using the heel of your hand, press the potato mixture firmly to form a 1-inch-thick disc. Remove the cutter and repeat with the remaining potato mixture, forming 12 patties total. Coat the top and bottom of the potato cakes lightly with panko (do not coat the sides). Place the potato cakes on the prepared baking sheet.

Do–ahead tip: At this point, the potato cakes can be covered and refrigerated for up to 2 days or stored in an airtight container and frozen for up to 3 months. Thaw the frozen cakes before continuing. »

- 3 medium russet potatoes (about 20 ounces total), peeled and quartered
- 1 30-ounce bag frozen shredded hash browns (such as Ore-Ida Country Style), thawed
- 1¾ cups panko (Japanese breadcrumbs), divided
- ½ cup freshly grated Parmesan cheese
- 5 ounces (1¼ sticks) melted unsalted butter
- ¼ cup chopped fresh flat-leaf parsley
- 3 tablespoons chopped fresh chives
- 1 tablespoon minced shallots
- 1 teaspoon kosher salt
- 1 teaspoon seasoned salt (see *Pantry and Produce*)
- ½ teaspoon freshly ground black pepper
- 12 tablespoons canola oil, divided

Preheat the oven to 350°F. Working in 3 batches, heat 2 tablespoons of oil on a nonstick griddle pan or in a heavy, large skillet over medium heat. Add 4 potato cakes and cook until the bottoms are golden brown and crisp, about 9 minutes. Turn the cakes over. Add 2 tablespoons of oil to the pan, reduce the heat to medium-low and continue cooking until the cakes are cooked through and crisp and golden on the bottom, about 9 minutes. If the cakes are not cooked through by the time they are golden brown on both sides, transfer the cakes to a baking sheet and bake until they are fully cooked.

Transfer the potatoe cakes to a plate lined with paper towels to absorb any excess oil. Serve immediately.

Zov's kitchen note: You can use fresh boiled grated potatoes instead of frozen hash browns, if desired, but I find that frozen hash browns provide more consistent results. These potato cakes are not just for breakfast; they make a delicious side for many of the entrées in this book.

Use a biscuit cutter to make perfectly shaped potato cakes >

BREAKFAST: old-fashioned pancakes with blueberry syrup

When it comes to breakfast, sometimes only the fluffiest, most decadent pancakes will do. This is a recipe that's fun to make, easy to eat and guaranteed to get raves from the whole family.

MAKES ABOUT TWENTY-FOUR 4-INCH PANCAKES

Make the blueberry syrup: Place 3 baskets of the blueberries and all of the orange juice, maple syrup, sugar, lemon juice, orange zest and salt in a heavy, medium saucepan over medium-low heat. Stir until the sugar dissolves, the mixture simmers, and the blueberries begin to split, about 8 minutes. Remove from the heat. Using an immersion blender, puree the blueberry mixture in the saucepan until it is thick and smooth. Stir the remaining 1 basket of blueberries into the warm syrup and set aside.

Do-ahead tip: The blueberry syrup can be stored in a jar and refrigerated for up to 3 days. Rewarm in a small saucepan over low heat or in the microwave before serving.

Make the pancakes: Whisk the flour, sugar, baking powder, baking soda and salt in a large bowl to blend; set aside. Whisk the buttermilk, melted butter, eggs, lemon zest and vanilla in another large bowl to blend.

Make a well in the center of the dry ingredients and pour in the liquid mixture. Fold until the batter is evenly moistened but with many lumps. The batter will be thick and lumpy. Do not stir the batter or overmix it. Allow the batter to rest for at least 5 minutes before making the pancakes.

Preheat a heavy, nonstick griddle pan over medium heat. Working in batches, drop the batter onto the griddle by ¼ cupfuls. Spread the batter with the back of a spoon, if necessary, to form a round shape. Cook until bubbles appear on top and the bottom is golden brown, about 2 minutes. Turn the pancakes over and cook until the bottom is lightly golden brown, about 1½ minutes. Transfer the pancakes to plates. Spoon the blueberry syrup over and serve immediately.

Zov's kitchen note: Do not flatten the pancakes with a spatula or turn them more than once or they will become tough and heavy. You can add ½ cup of fresh or frozen berries or fresh sliced bananas to the pancake batter for extra flavor and texture. You can also substitute whole milk, yogurt or sour cream for the buttermilk, although the pancakes may not be as tender.

Blueberry syrup

- 4 6-ounce baskets fresh blueberries, rinsed, divided
- ½ cup freshly squeezed orange juice
- ½ cup pure maple syrup
- ½ cup granulated sugar
- 1 tablespoon fresh lemon juice
- 1 tablespoon orange zest
- ⅛ teaspoon kosher salt

Pancakes

- 2 ½ cups unbleached all-purpose flour
- ¼ cup granulated sugar
- 1 tablespoon baking powder
- 1 teaspoon baking soda
- ½ teaspoon salt
- 3 cups buttermilk
- 4 ounces (1 stick) unsalted butter, melted
- 3 large eggs
- 1 tablespoon lemon zest or orange zest (optional)
- 1 teaspoon vanilla extract

BREAKFAST: crunchy granola with almonds, oats and dried fruits

A healthful mix of nuts, oats and dried fruits makes this crunchy granola an especially good way to start the morning. Keep the recipe handy and use with all sorts of fresh summer berries. I like to layer the granola with yogurt in a tall parfait glass. The granola makes a delicious topping for ice cream as well.

MAKES ABOUT 8 CUPS

Preheat the oven to 250°F. Spray a heavy, large baking sheet with nonstick cooking spray. Mix the oats, brown sugar, pecans, walnuts, almonds, cinnamon and orange peel in a large bowl.

Whisk the maple syrup and melted butter in a medium bowl to blend. Pour the maple-butter over the oat-nut mixture and toss until all the ingredients are well coated. Transfer to prepared baking sheet, forming an even layer.

Bake until the granola is golden brown, stirring every 25 minutes, for about 1 hour and 30 minutes. Stir the figs, blueberries and cranberries into the granola and continue baking for 15 minutes. Cool the granola and store in airtight glass jars.

Do-ahead tip: The granola will keep in an airtight jar at room temperature for up to 3 months.

Zov's kitchen note: You can also add 1/2 cup of shredded sweetened coconut and 1 cup of dark raisins to the granola. Give it as a hostess gift in a decorative clear bag tied with a pretty ribbon.

- Nonstick vegetable-oil cooking spray
- 4 cups old-fashioned rolled oats
- 1/2 cup (packed) dark brown sugar
- 1/2 cup pecan halves, coarsely chopped
- 1/2 cup walnut halves, coarsely chopped
- 1/2 cup sliced almonds
- 1 1/2 teaspoons ground cinnamon
- 1 teaspoon finely grated orange peel
- 1/2 cup pure maple syrup
- 4 tablespoons (1/2 stick) unsalted butter, melted
- 1/2 cup dried Black Mission figs, diced
- 1/2 cup dried blueberries
- 1/2 cup dried cranberries

BREAKFAST: eggs benedict with gravlax and creamy hollandaise sauce

Eggs Benedict has the perception of being difficult to prepare, but my version is easy *and* delicious. Try this brunch classic as an elegant main course for a special event. You can poach the eggs the day before. Just store them in the refrigerator completely submerged in water. When ready to assemble the dish, drop the poached eggs in hot water to warm them. My Breakfast Potato Cakes (page 94) make a fabulous replacement for the English muffins.

SERVES 6

- 1 tablespoon distilled white vinegar
- 1¼ teaspoons kosher salt, divided
- 12 extra-large eggs
- 12 ¼-inch-thick slices beefsteak tomatoes
- 2 tablespoons olive oil
- ½ teaspoon freshly ground black pepper
- 2 tablespoons thinly sliced fresh basil
- 6 English muffins, split and toasted
- 12 ounces thinly sliced Gravlax (page 46)
- Creamy Hollandaise Sauce (page 295), warm
- Fresh dill sprigs or basil sprigs, for garnish

Fill a large baking dish with cold water. Pour enough water into a large, deep skillet to reach a depth of 2 inches. Add the vinegar and ¾ teaspoon of salt to the water in the skillet and bring to a simmer. Reduce the heat to medium-low so that the water just barely simmers. Crack 1 egg into a small bowl or cup and then gently slide the egg into the simmering water. Repeat with 5 more eggs, spacing them apart in the simmering water. Cook until the whites are set but the yolks are still creamy, about 3 minutes. Using a slotted spoon, remove the poached eggs from the simmering water and carefully place them in the baking dish of cold water. Repeat with the remaining 6 eggs.

Do–ahead tip: The poached eggs can be refrigerated for up to 1 day. Keep them submerged in cold water in the baking dish. Cover and store.

Position the rack 3 to 4 inches from the broiler heat source, then preheat the broiler. Gently toss the tomato slices, olive oil, remaining ½ teaspoon of salt, and black pepper in a medium bowl to coat the tomatoes well. Place the tomato slices in a single layer on a rimmed baking sheet. Broil until the tomatoes soften slightly, about 2 minutes. Sprinkle the basil over the tomatoes.

Meanwhile, rewarm the eggs by placing them in the same skillet of simmering water just until hot, about 30 seconds. Using a slotted spoon, gently remove the eggs from the skillet and set them on a paper towel to absorb any excess water.

Top each toasted English muffin half with 1 ounce of gravlax, then top each with a tomato slice. Top with the poached eggs, and spoon the warm hollandaise sauce over the eggs. Garnish with fresh dill sprigs or basil sprigs and serve immediately.

Zov's kitchen note: Instead of gravlax, try it with Canadian bacon or regular bacon.

BREAKFAST sour cherry jam

How do you capture the flavor of summer? Make this delicious cherry jam. The season is so short that the minute I see cherries at the market I know I need to hurry to preserve their sweet, succulent flavor at the peak of ripeness. This recipe brings back many wonderful memories of cherry picking with my children. When they were young kids, I'd often pile them (along with their friends) into the car and drive to Cherry Valley in Riverside, where we would pluck the fruit right off the trees. Most of the cherries were gobbled up before we even got home, but whatever was left would be preserved in this simple syrup. This jam makes a great hostess gift during the holidays.

MAKES FOUR 8-OUNCE JARS

Place the cherries in a heavy, large pot and sprinkle the sugar and lemon juice over the cherries. Set aside for 1 hour, stirring occasionally, until most of the sugar dissolves in the accumulated cherry juices.

Set a bowl of ice water and a pastry brush on the counter near the pot. Stir the cherries over medium-high heat until the sugar is completely liquefied. While the cherries cook, dip the brush into the ice water to moisten thoroughly and brush the water all along the inside walls of the pot to remove any sugar granules that are clinging to the sides. Keep brushing the sides of the pot until the sugar is completely dissolved. Brushing the sides with ice water prevents the jam mixture from crystallizing. Bring the jam to a boil and cook until some foam rises to the top of the jam (this foam will eventually blend into the jam), about 10 minutes. Reduce the heat to medium-low and continue cooking the jam until the juices thicken to your desired consistency, about 30 minutes.

The jam will continue to thicken considerably when cooled, so do not allow it to thicken too much at this point. To test if the jam will be thick enough, drop a tablespoon of the hot jam onto a frozen plate and let cool. It should be firm but not hard. If it is too thin, continue cooking. If it is too firm, add some water to thin it to the desired consistency.

Ladle the hot jam into dry sterilized jars, leaving about ¼-inch of room at the top. Cover and refrigerate for up to 2 weeks.

Do-ahead tip: To store longer, follow the canning instructions on page 86.

Zov's kitchen note: This recipe works well with any type of cherry.

3 pounds fresh cherries, pitted
2 cups granulated sugar (about 1 pound)
1 tablespoon fresh lemon juice

Special equipment:

four 8-ounce glass jars and canning tongs, both sterilized (for Sterlization and Canning Instructions, see page 86)

BREAKFAST: torte milanese with spinach

When I first opened Zov's Bistro in 1987, I created this recipe as a light lunch. It is a delicious addition to a brunch buffet and an easy main course for a ladies luncheon or shower, as it can be made ahead and served at room temperature. Slicing the torte reveals beautiful layers of green, red and yellow inside. Serve with a light salad or fruit, and pop open a bottle of bubbly or crisp white wine.

SERVES 10

Preheat the oven to 375°F. Whisk 11 eggs in a large bowl with the cream, ½ teaspoon of the kosher salt, ½ teaspoon of the seasoned salt, and ¼ teaspoon of black pepper until well blended.

Melt the butter with 1 tablespoon of the oil in a heavy, large, nonstick sauté pan over medium heat. Add the egg mixture and cook until most of the eggs are no longer runny but some egg is still very creamy and runny. As the eggs cook, use a silicone spatula to scrape the cooked egg from the bottom and sides of the pan and fold it into the rest of the egg mixture. This will take about 3 minutes. Spoon the egg mixture over a large plate and set aside to cool completely. Wipe out the pan.

Heat 2 tablespoons of the oil in the same sauté pan over medium-high heat. Stir in 1 tablespoon of the shallots and the garlic, then stir in all the bell peppers. Add the remaining 1 teaspoon of the seasoned salt, ½ teaspoon of the kosher salt, and the lemon pepper. Sauté until the bell peppers are tender and all their liquid has evaporated, about 12 minutes. Transfer the bell peppers to another large plate and set aside to cool completely.

Heat the remaining 1 tablespoon of oil in the same sauté pan over high heat. Stir in the remaining 1 tablespoon of shallots and ½ teaspoon of kosher salt. Add the spinach to the pan one handful at a time, stirring to coat the spinach with the oil and shallots, until all the spinach has been added and is wilted, about 3 minutes. Transfer the spinach to a colander and set over a bowl to drain and cool. Once the spinach is cool, squeeze it to extract as much liquid as possible. »

- 12 large eggs, divided
- ¼ cup heavy cream
- 1½ teaspoons kosher salt, divided
- 1½ teaspoons seasoned salt, divided (see *Pantry and Produce*)
- ¼ teaspoon freshly ground black pepper
- 1½ tablespoons unsalted butter
- 4 tablespoons olive oil, divided
- 2 tablespoons minced shallots, divided
- 2 teaspoons minced garlic
- 2 red bell peppers cut into matchstick-size strips
- 2 yellow bell peppers cut into matchstick-size strips
- ½ teaspoon lemon pepper
- 2 9-ounce bags fresh spinach
- 2 17.3-ounce packages frozen puff pastry (4 sheets)
- Nonstick vegetable-oil cooking spray
- 1 pound grated Gruyère cheese
- 8 ounces thinly sliced good-quality ham
- 1 tablespoon whole milk

Using the bottom of a 9-inch springform pan as a template, cut out a round disc from 1 sheet of pastry; set it aside. Assemble the 9-inch springform pan, then spray the pan with nonstick spray. Roll out 2 sheets of puff pastry to form two 13x11-inch rectangles, then lay them on a work surface with the long sides slightly overlapping. Press the seam of the pastry sheets to seal. Press the pastry over the bottom and up the sides of the pan, allowing the excess to hang over the edge of the pan. Spoon the egg mixture into the prepared pan, forming an even layer. Sprinkle ¼ of the cheese over the eggs. Spoon the bell pepper mixture on top. Sprinkle ¼ of the cheese over the bell peppers. Arrange the spinach on top. Sprinkle ¼ of the cheese over the spinach. Cover with the ham, then sprinkle with the remaining cheese. Fold the overhanging dough over the top. Set the pastry disc on top and press gently to adhere.

Whisk the remaining 1 egg with 1 tablespoon of milk in a small bowl to blend. Cut ten ½-inch-wide strips from the remaining sheet of pastry. Lightly brush the egg over the pastry disc. Lay 5 pastry strips over the pastry disc, spacing evenly apart. Brush the strips lightly with more egg. Lay the remaining 5 pastry strips over, forming a lattice design. Brush lightly with more egg. Set the springform pan on a baking sheet.

Bake until the pastry is dark golden brown on top, about 1½ hours. Transfer the baking sheet to a rack and set aside to cool for 30 minutes. Resting prevents the cheese from oozing out when the torte is cut.

Do-ahead tip: The torte can be made a day ahead and reheated just before serving. Cover with foil and warm in a 350°F oven.

Make sure the layers are evenly distributed before folding the dough over the top. >

BREAKFAST ## simple buttermilk biscuits

For a recipe that you can make in no time, the rewards are amazing. These tender, flaky biscuits are an ideal accompaniment to soups and chowders. But my favorite way to eat them is in the morning, fresh from the oven, with soft butter and honey. It's pure perfection.

MAKES 10

- 3 cups all-purpose flour
- 3 tablespoons granulated sugar
- 4 teaspoons baking powder
- 1 teaspoon baking soda
- 1 teaspoon salt
- 6 ounces (1 ½ sticks) chilled unsalted butter, cut into pieces
- 1 cup chilled buttermilk
- 2 tablespoons unsalted butter, melted, for brushing tops of biscuits

Preheat the oven to 425°F. Line a baking sheet with parchment paper. Whisk the flour, sugar, baking powder, baking soda and salt in a large bowl to blend. Using your fingertips, rub the chilled butter into the dry ingredients until the mixture resembles a coarse meal. Add the buttermilk and stir with a spoon until the dough is completely and evenly moistened. Transfer the dough to a lightly floured surface and pat out the dough to ¾-inch thickness. Using a 2¾-inch round biscuit cutter, cut out about 8 biscuits. Gather the dough scraps together and press out the dough to ¾-inch thickness. Cut out additional biscuits for a total of 10.

Arrange the biscuits on the prepared baking sheet, spacing them evenly apart. Brush the biscuits with the melted butter. Bake until the biscuits are golden brown on top, about 18 minutes. Serve warm.

Do-ahead tip: The formed unbaked biscuits can be frozen in an airtight container for up to 2 weeks; do not thaw before baking. Bake according to the recipe, increasing the baking time a few extra minutes. The baked biscuits can be stored in an airtight container at room temperature for up to 2 days. Wrap them in foil and bake just until warm.

Zov's kitchen note: You can use any size biscuit cutter with this recipe.

BREAKFAST quince jam

Quince, a member of the rose family, looks like a cross between a pear and an apple, and is in season only from October to December. The yellow-skinned fruit has a beautiful sweet aroma and is quite tart when eaten raw, so it's much better cooked. It's perfect for jams because it has a huge amount of pectin, which makes things gel. This is one of my favorite jams, and so simple to make. The only trick is to cook the fruit until it's soft before adding the sugar. You can embellish the jam with apples, cinnamon or ginger. Play around with the ingredients and have fun.

MAKES FOUR 8-OUNCE JARS

Combine the water, lemon juice and lemon zest in a heavy, wide 5-quart pot. Working with 1 quince at a time, peel and quarter the quince. Using a large sharp knife, carefully cut the quarters to remove the cores. Cut the quince into ½-inch cubes and immediately place them in the lemon water to keep them from browning.

Bring the quince mixture to a boil over high heat. Reduce the heat to medium-low and simmer until the quince soften, about 20 minutes. Stir in the sugar and bring the mixture to boil, stirring to dissolve all of the sugar. Set a bowl of ice water and a pastry brush on the counter near the pot. While the quince cook, dip the brush into the ice water to moisten thoroughly and brush the water all along the inside walls of the pot to remove any sugar granules that are clinging to the side. Keep brushing the sides of the pot until the sugar is completely dissolved. Brushing the sides with ice water prevents the jam mixture from crystallizing. Lower the heat to medium-high and continue to cook uncovered, stirring occasionally, until the jam is thickened, about 35 minutes.

The jam will continue to thicken considerably when cooled, so do not allow it to thicken too much at this point. To test if the jam will be thick enough, drop a tablespoon of the hot jam onto a frozen plate and let cool. It should be firm but not hard. If it is too thin, continue cooking. If it is too firm, add some water to thin it to the desired consistency.

Ladle the hot jam into dry sterlizied jars, leaving about ¼-inch of room at the top. Cover and refrigerate for up to 2 weeks.

Do-ahead tip: To store longer, follow the canning instructions on page 86.

Zov's kitchen note: Quince cores are much harder than the cores of apples and pears, so they must be removed with a large, sharp knife, not with an apple corer.

2 ½ cups water
¼ cup fresh lemon juice
2 tablespoons lemon zest
6 fresh quince (about 3 pounds)
4 cups granulated sugar (about 2 pounds)

Special equipment:

four 8-ounce glass jars and canning tongs, both sterilized (for Sterilization and Canning Instructions, see page 86)

BREAKFAST: spanish omelet with manchego and cheddar cheese

Hearty and quite versatile, this omelet is ideal fare for virtually any meal, not just breakfast. It's made in a flash and can be prepared in various ways: scrambled, rolled, folded, flipped or stuffed. Add fresh asparagus, when in season, for a delicious variation.

SERVES 6

Heat the oil in a heavy, large saucepan over medium-high heat. Add the onion, mushrooms, celery, bell peppers, garlic, cumin and crushed red pepper. Cook until the vegetables are tender, stirring often, about 5 minutes. Add the fresh tomato and cook for 2 minutes, then add the canned tomatoes. Season with 1 teaspoon of salt and ½ teaspoon of black pepper. Decrease the heat to medium-low. Cook the sauce uncovered, stirring occasionally, until it becomes thick and chunky, about 30 minutes.

Whisk the eggs, milk and remaining ¾ teaspoon of salt in a large bowl to blend well. Melt ½ tablespoon of the butter in a 7-inch nonstick skillet over medium-low heat until bubbling. Pour about ½ cup of the egg mixture into the skillet and immediately begin lifting the edges of the omelet with a spatula to let the uncooked portion flow underneath, about 3 minutes. The omelet should still be moist on top. Reduce the heat to low and spoon ¼ cup of the sauce and 3 tablespoons each of the cheddar cheese and Manchego cheese down the center of the omelet. Cook 1 minute.

Using a spatula, fold ⅓ of the omelet over the filling, then slide the exposed third of the omelet onto a plate, and fold the omelet over onto itself. Top the omelet with 2 tablespoons of the remaining sauce and 1 tablespoon of each cheese. Let rest 1 minute before serving. Repeat to make 5 more omelets.

Do-ahead tip: The sauce can be covered and refrigerated for 1 week.

Zov's kitchen note: Adding diced potatoes to the filling is the traditional way of making a Spanish omelet. My version of the filling, without the potatoes, can do double-duty as a dip or as a topping for fish or chicken.

- 2 tablespoons olive oil
- 1 small red onion, finely chopped
- 3 ounces white mushrooms, chopped
- 1 celery stalk, finely chopped
- ½ green bell pepper, finely chopped
- ½ red bell pepper, finely chopped
- 1 tablespoon minced garlic
- ½ teaspoon ground cumin
- ½ teaspoon dried crushed hot red pepper
- 1 large tomato, finely chopped (with seeds)
- 1 14.5-ounce can diced tomatoes with juices
- 1¾ teaspoons kosher salt, divided
- ½ teaspoon freshly ground black pepper
- 12 large eggs
- ¼ cup whole milk
- 3 tablespoons unsalted butter, divided
- 1¼ cups shredded mild cheddar cheese
- 1¼ cups shredded Manchego cheese

BREAKFAST super easy fig jam

Every year I look forward to making my favorite fig jam, and for fig fans like myself, the season comes not a minute too soon. From mid-June through October the San Joaquin Valley and Coachella Valley become California's fig centers, where hundreds of varieties are harvested, including the popular Black Mission fig. Loaded with flavor, it has a slight chewy texture and is a tasty and nutritious treat all on its own, but even better as a sweet jam. I love it slathered over Gorgonzola cheese on a slice of baguette or served with an array of cheeses and thin crackers; or mix half a cup of mascarpone cheese with the fig jam to use as a spread on crackers. It also makes a terrific hostess gift around the holidays.

MAKES FIVE 8-OUNCE JARS

Combine the figs, sugar and lemon juice in a heavy pot over medium-low heat, stirring often, until the sugar liquefies, about 5 minutes. Set a bowl of ice water and pastry brush on the counter near the pot. While the figs cook, dip the brush into the ice water and brush all along the inside walls of the pot to remove any sugar granules that are clinging to the side. Keep brushing the sides of the pot until the sugar is completely dissolved. Brushing the sides with ice water prevents the jam mixture from crystallizing; if one granule of sugar clinging to the side of the pot gets into the jam, the whole batch of jam will crystallize.

Increase the heat to medium-high and continue cooking the jam, stirring often to prevent the jam from sticking to the bottom of the pot, until the mixture is thick, about 25 minutes. The jam will thicken considerably when cooled. To test if the jam will be thick enough, drop a tablespoon of the hot jam onto a frozen plate and let cool. It should be firm but not hard. If it is too thin, continue cooking. If it is too firm, add some water to thin it to the desired consistency.

Add the orange zest to the hot jam, then immediately ladle the hot jam into the dry sterilized jars, leaving about ¼-inch of room at the top. Cover and keep refrigerated for up to 2 weeks.

Do-ahead tip: To store longer, follow the canning instructions on page 86.

Zov's kitchen note: You can substitute fresh apricots for the figs or mix in fresh strawberries with the figs.

2 ½ pounds fresh Black Mission figs (unpeeled), stemmed, diced
2 ½ cups granulated sugar (about 1 ¼ pounds)
Juice of ½ lemon (about 2 tablespoons)
Zest of ½ orange

Special equipment:
five 8-ounce glass jars and canning tongs, both sterilized (for Sterlization and Canning Instructions, see page 86)

BREAKFAST ## ultimate cinnamon buns

This cinnamon roll is everything you dream it to be — soft, rich, buttery and so very comforting. The secret? No shortcuts or skimping on any of the good stuff. We have been making these breakfast treasures since we opened the bakery and they're still one of the most popular items on our menu. I guarantee they will disappear in a heartbeat.

MAKES 12 LARGE BUNS

Make the dough: Stir the sugar-water and yeast in a large bowl to blend. Set aside until the mixture is foamy, about 5 minutes. Using a heavy-duty stand mixer with the hook attachment, mix the flour, ¾ cup of sugar, salt and yeast mixture in the mixer bowl. Add the milk and egg yolks. Mix until the dough forms, about 2 minutes. Gradually add 4 ounces of the butter (1 stick), 1 tablespoon at a time, until well blended. Mix the dough until it is smooth and elastic and it slowly pulls away from the sides of the bowl, about 5 minutes. The dough should be a bit sticky, but if the dough is very sticky, add more flour, 1 tablespoon at a time, until it is just slightly tacky. Scrape down the sides of the bowl.

Dust a 17x14-inch rimmed baking sheet with flour, then turn the dough out onto the baking sheet. Using your hands, press the dough into a rectangle to cover the entire surface of the baking sheet. The dough should not stick to your hands when finished. Cover the dough with plastic wrap and refrigerate until cold, about 30 minutes. Resting the dough will help relax the gluten, making the dough more firm, and thus easier to roll out.

Turn the dough out onto a lightly floured work surface. Roll out the dough to an 18x13-inch rectangle. Position the dough so that one long side is closest to you. Brush away any excess flour. Spread the remaining 12 ounces (3 sticks) of softened butter over the left two-thirds of the dough, leaving a 1-inch border around the edge so that the butter will not ooze out. Fold the one-third unbuttered portion of the dough over the center third, then fold the remaining buttered third over the folded two-thirds, as is done for folding a letter. Return the dough to the baking sheet and refrigerate for 45 minutes.

Set the dough on the work surface so that the long edges of the dough are parallel to the edge of the work surface and so that the side with the seam is closest to you. Roll out the dough to a 17x11-inch rectangle. Fold one-third of the dough over the center third, then fold the remaining third over the folded two-thirds, as done previously. Place the dough on the baking sheet and refrigerate for 30 minutes. Repeat this rolling and folding 2 more times, refrigerating the dough for 30 minutes after each turn. »

Dough
½ cup warm water mixed with 1 teaspoon sugar
⅓ cup dry yeast
8 cups unbleached all-purpose flour, plus more for dusting
¾ cup granulated sugar
1 teaspoon fine-grained salt
2 cups whole milk, at room temperature
8 large egg yolks
16 ounces (4 sticks) unsalted butter, at room temperature, divided

Filling
Non-stick vegetable-oil cooking spray
6 ounces (1½ sticks) unsalted butter, at room temperature
2 cups (packed) golden brown sugar
⅓ cup ground cinnamon

Frosting
3 cups powdered sugar
8 ounces cream cheese
4 ounces (1 stick) unsalted butter, at room temperature
1 tablespoon whole milk

Assemble and bake the rolls: Preheat the oven to 350°F. Spray a 16x13-inch baking pan with 3½-inch-high sides with nonstick cooking spray and line the pan with parchment paper. Place the dough on the work surface with the long side nearest to you. Roll out the dough to a 17x11-inch rectangle. Using your hands, spread 6 ounces of butter (1½ sticks) over the dough, leaving a ½-inch border along the top edge of the dough.

Mix the brown sugar and cinnamon in a medium bowl, using your fingers to break up any sugar clumps. Sprinkle the cinnamon-sugar all over the dough, leaving a ¾-inch border along the top edge; smooth the cinnamon-sugar in an even layer with your hand, then gently press the cinnamon-sugar onto the dough to adhere.

Beginning with the long edge nearest to you, roll the dough into a very tight cylinder. Firmly pinch the seam to seal. Rotate the roll so that the seam side is down. Very gently stretch the roll to 18-inches in length; roll the cylinder and push in the ends to create an even diameter. Using a serrated knife, cut the cylinder with a sawing motion into 12 pieces, forming rolls that each weigh about 6 ounces. Place the rolls cut side down and side by side in the prepared pan.

Do-ahead tip: Store the cylinder of dough in the freezer for up to 2 months in an airtight container or freezer bag. Thaw before cutting. You can also freeze the cut rolls so that all you have to do is proof and bake them.

Cover the rolls with plastic wrap and place in a warm place until the rolls have doubled in size, about 40 minutes. Bake until the rolls are dark golden brown and the center rolls are cooked through, about 30 minutes. Transfer the pan to a cooling rack until the rolls are just warm, at least 1 hour.

Frost the rolls and serve: Using an electric mixer, beat the powdered sugar, cream cheese, butter and milk in a large bowl until light and fluffy. Spread the frosting over the warm rolls and serve.

Zov's kitchen note: I have also used dental floss instead of a serrated knife to cut the dough; it gives you a smoother cut. Make sure the rolls are warm but not hot when you frost them so that the frosting does not melt completely.

SOUPS

classic manhattan clam chowder **126**

coconut chicken chowder with lemongrass **128**

black bean soup with vegetables **130**

creamy potato-leek soup **132**

moroccan harira soup **134**

chicken and rice soup with lemon **136**

vegetable soup with tomato-basil pistou **138**

velvety cream of spinach and cauliflower soup **140**

tortilla soup with fresh corn, cilantro and lime **142**

SOUPS

There is nothing better on a cool fall day than a bowl of hot, steaming chicken soup filled with chunks of tender meat, fresh carrots, celery and soothing herbs. I don't know of one person who doesn't like soup. Maybe it's because soups are astonishingly versatile, taking on an amazing number of flavors, textures and even colors. Long appreciated for their homeopathic properties, soups satisfy a more basic need: They warm your body and soul. | I didn't realize how much people enjoyed soup until I opened Zov's Bistro in 1987. Our guests were always looking forward to our "soup of the day." And I am right there with them. As I was growing up, my mother often served hot tureens of Moroccan Harira with turmeric, chicken and rice, and hearty Vegetable Soup with Tomato-Basil Pistou. Here, I share those recipes along with other personal favorites. | In this chapter I will teach you how to choose the ideal soup for any occasion (almost all of these can be made ahead) and cook it flawlessly so that the smell alone will remind you of home. Honestly, there is no wrong occasion for soup. Both the Velvety Cream of Spinach and the Creamy Potato-Leek Soup work just as well in shot glasses at cocktail parties as they do at casual dinners. And when the weather turns cold, your family won't be able to resist steaming bowls of thick stew. All of these recipes can be modified with different vegetables and grains to fit your family's desires, but I'm confident you'll love them just the way they are. |

SOUPS classic manhattan clam chowder

This comforting chowder is even better the next day. For a meal that's pure heaven, serve with a full-bodied red wine and warm, crusty bread to soak up the broth. It's one of the most popular soups at our restaurants, and one that will have everyone lingering at the dinner table, asking for seconds.

SERVES 10 TO 15 (MAKES ABOUT 5 QUARTS)

Cook the bacon in a heavy 8-quart pot over medium-high heat until it is crisp and golden, stirring often, about 7 minutes. Add the celery, onion and bell peppers and sauté until the vegetables are limp and translucent, about 6 minutes. Add the garlic and cook another minute. Add the tomato paste and stir until well combined. Add the clam juice, water, crushed tomatoes and chopped tomatoes. Bring to a boil, then reduce the heat to medium-low. Add the potatoes, thyme, Worcestershire sauce, kosher salt, seasoned salt and black pepper.

Cover and simmer gently until the potatoes are tender when pierced with a skewer, about 45 minutes. Add the clams and chopped parsley.

Do-ahead tip: The chowder can be refrigerated for up to 4 days or frozen for up to 2 months. Transfer the chowder to five 1-quart containers, set the containers in a roasting pan and surround with ice. Set aside to cool, stirring occasionally. Cover the containers and store. Rewarm the soup in a covered pot over medium-low heat, stirring occasionally, just until it simmers.

Ladle the soup into deep bowls, top with parsley and serve.

Zov's kitchen note: Most of the ingredients can be prepared the night before, but dice the potatoes just before cooking, otherwise they will turn dark. I prefer Yukon Gold potatoes for their sweetness and high starch content. Applewood-smoked bacon is known for its smoky flavor and is available at most gourmet markets. Some seafood markets also carry fresh-shucked clams, which make an excellent substitute for canned clams.

How to peel tomatoes: Have you ever wondered how to peel a tomato without taking half of the tomato off with the skin? Here's a trick used by chefs everywhere that works like a charm. Slice a shallow x in the bottom end of the tomato (the end without the stem). Using a slotted spoon, plunge the tomato into boiling water for a few seconds and then transfer to a bowl of ice water. This will stop the tomato from cooking and loosen the skin. Remove from the ice water and peel the skin. The same technique can be applied to ripe peaches.

- 4 slices good-quality applewood-smoked bacon, chopped
- 3 celery stalks, finely chopped (about 1½ cups)
- 1 onion, finely chopped (about 1½ cups)
- ¾ cup chopped green bell peppers
- 5 garlic cloves, chopped
- 1 6-ounce can tomato paste
- 4 cups clam juice
- 2 cups water
- 1 28-ounce can whole tomatoes with juices, crushed
- 2 large tomatoes (about 1¾ pounds, peeled and chopped with seeds (see note)
- 5 cups diced peeled Yukon Gold potatoes (from 2 pounds)
- 3 tablespoons chopped fresh thyme
- 2 tablespoons Worcestershire sauce
- 1 tablespoon kosher salt
- 1 tablespoon seasoned salt (see Pantry and Produce)
- 1 teaspoon freshly ground black pepper
- 4 6½-ounce cans chopped clams with the juices
- ½ cup chopped fresh flat-leaf parsley, plus leaves for garnish

SOUPS: coconut chicken chowder with lemongrass

Elements of my favorite soups — corn chowder, chicken and mushroom and a Thai-style coconut soup — combine in this satisfying dish, resulting in a flavor that is inventive yet familiar. Don't be intimidated by the long ingredient list. Though a few bold flavors, like ginger and lemongrass, impart an Asian undertone, most of the ingredients are likely in your pantry. Believe me, this soup is worth the effort. It's one of the most popular soups at our restaurant.

SERVES 20 (MAKES ABOUT 8 QUARTS)

Heat the oil in a heavy 8-quart pot over medium-high heat. Add the onions, leeks, carrots, celery and mushrooms. Sauté until the vegetables are soft and the onions and leeks are translucent, about 10 minutes. Add the ginger, lemongrass, garlic and jalapeño and cook until all the liquid evaporates from the vegetables and the vegetables are tender and caramelized, about 10 minutes. Add the broth, coconut milk, corn and rice. Add the kosher salt, seasoned salt, black pepper, lemon pepper and crushed red pepper. Bring to a boil then reduce the heat to medium-low. Cover and simmer gently until the rice is tender and the flavors blend, stirring occasionally, about 30 minutes.

Add the chicken and cook until the chicken is just cooked through, about 5 minutes. Stir the lemon juice into the chowder. Season the chowder to taste with more salt and pepper.

Do-ahead tip: The chowder can be refrigerated for up to 4 days. Transfer the chowder to eight 1-quart containers, set the containers in a roasting pan and surround with ice. Set aside to cool, stirring occasionally. Cover the containers and store. Rewarm the chowder in a covered pot over medium-low heat, stirring occasionally, just until it simmers. If the chowder is too thick, add more broth or water to thin it to the desired consistency.

Ladle the chowder into deep bowls. Garnish with lime wedges and cilantro sprigs and serve.

Zov's kitchen note: Don't worry if the chowder looks curdled at the beginning. The coconut milk emulsifies at it cooks. This chowder is best for a large family meal or a party, as it does not freeze well.

- ⅓ cup olive oil
- 2 onions, chopped (about 3 cups)
- 3 leeks (white and pale green parts only), chopped (about 3 cups)
- 4 carrots, peeled and sliced diagonally (about 2 cups)
- 4 celery stalks, sliced diagonally (about 2 cups)
- 1½ pounds shiitake mushrooms, stemmed and sliced
- ¼ cup coarsely grated peeled fresh ginger
- ¼ cup finely chopped lemongrass (from bottom 4 inches of about 4 stalks, tough outer leaves discarded)
- 1 tablespoon minced garlic
- 1 jalapeño chile, seeded and minced
- 12 cups chicken broth
- 3 13.5-ounce cans unsweetened coconut milk
- 3 cups fresh or frozen corn kernels, thawed
- 1 cup uncooked long-grain rice
- 1 tablespoon kosher salt
- 1 tablespoon seasoned salt (see Pantry and Produce)
- 1 teaspoon freshly ground black pepper
- 1 teaspoon lemon pepper
- ½ teaspoon dried crushed hot red pepper
- 4 boneless skinless chicken breasts (about 2 pounds), thinly sliced across the grain
- 3½ tablespoons fresh lemon juice
- Lime wedges, for garnish
- Cilantro sprigs, for garnish

SOUPS: black bean soup with vegetables

This is a comfort soup if there ever was one. I'd never turn this down no matter what the season. Serve with Simple Buttermilk Biscuits (page 110).

SERVES 12 (MAKES ABOUT 5 QUARTS)

Heat the olive oil in a heavy 8-quart pot over medium-high heat. Add the onions, carrots, celery, zucchini, leek and garlic. Sauté until the vegetables are tender, about 10 minutes. Stir in the tomato paste and chopped tomatoes. Add the broth and the 6 cups of hot water. Stir in the dried beans and rice. Bring the mixture to a boil. Add the cilantro and parsley. Add the cumin, seasoned salt, kosher salt, black pepper, crushed red pepper and lemon pepper. Reduce the heat to medium-low. Cover and simmer gently until the beans are soft, stirring occasionally, about 2 hours.

Do-ahead tip: The soup can be refrigerated for up to 4 days or frozen for up to 2 months. Transfer the soup to five 1-quart containers, set the containers in a roasting pan and surround with ice. Set aside to cool, stirring occasionally. Cover the containers and store. Rewarm the soup in a covered pot over medium-low heat, stirring occasionally, just until it simmers.

Ladle the soup into bowls. Top with the sour cream, diced avocados, diced tomatoes and cilantro leaves.

Zov's kitchen note: If the soup gets too thick, you can thin it out with chicken broth or water, but make sure to adjust the seasoning. Adding liquid dilutes the flavor. It is important to simmer the soup on medium-low heat. Boiling the beans on high heat will cause the skins to separate. As a rule of thumb, one cup of dried beans yields about 2½ cups when cooked.

This soup is a great base for your favorite vegetables. I like it with jicama, or sautéed mushrooms, spinach or Swiss chard. Top the soup with Parmesan Croutons (page 308) for a nice crunch.

Soup

- ½ cup olive oil
- 2 large onions, chopped (about 3½ cups)
- 2 large carrots, peeled and thinly sliced (about 1 cup)
- 3 celery stalks, thinly sliced (about 1½ cups)
- 2 zucchini, thinly sliced diagonally (about 2 cups)
- 1 leek (white and pale green parts only), thinly sliced (about 1 cup)
- 6 garlic cloves, minced
- 1 6-ounce can tomato paste
- 4 plum tomatoes, seeded and chopped
- 6 cups chicken broth
- 6 cups hot water
- 2 cups dried black beans (about 1 pound)
- ½ cup uncooked long-grain rice
- ½ cup chopped fresh cilantro
- ½ cup chopped fresh flat-leaf parsley
- 1½ tablespoons ground cumin
- 1½ tablespoons seasoned salt (see *Pantry and Produce*)
- 1 tablespoon kosher salt
- 1 teaspoon freshly ground black pepper
- ½ teaspoon dried crushed hot red pepper
- ½ teaspoon lemon pepper

Garnishes

- Sour cream
- Firm but ripe avocados, peeled, pitted and diced
- Plum tomatoes, seeded, diced
- Cilantro leaves

SOUPS | creamy potato-leek soup

This is a rich and creamy soup that is delicious served hot or cold, and it tastes even better the next day.

SERVES 12 (MAKES ABOUT 3 QUARTS)

Melt 6 tablespoons of butter in a heavy 8-quart pot over medium heat. Add the celery and leeks. Cover and cook until the vegetables are tender but not brown, stirring often, about 10 minutes. Add the broth, milk and cream and bring to a boil. Stir in the potatoes and return to a simmer. Cover and simmer over low heat until the potatoes are fully cooked and tender, about 30 minutes. Add 1 tablespoon of the tarragon, 1 teaspoon kosher salt, seasoned salt and $\frac{1}{2}$ teaspoon white pepper.

Using a hand-held immersion blender, puree the soup in the pot until smooth. Season the soup to taste with more salt and white pepper, if necessary. Add the remaining 3 tablespoons of butter and blend until the butter is completely incorporated into the soup.

Do-ahead tip: The soup can be refrigerated for up to 4 days or frozen for up to 2 months. Transfer the soup to three 1-quart containers, set in a roasting pan and surround with ice. Set aside to cool, stirring occasionally. Cover the containers and store. Rewarm the soup in a covered saucepan over medium-low heat, stirring occasionally, just until it simmers.

Ladle the soup into small bowls. Garnish with tarragon leaves and serve with croutons or breadsticks.

Zov's kitchen note: This is a basic cream soup that you can make with broccoli, cauliflower or spinach. Just increase the liquid as necessary. For richer soup, add cream instead of milk or equal parts cream and milk. Adding the butter last keeps the soup from separating. I prefer russet potatoes or Yukon Golds for this recipe, as both have more starch and the best flavor.

---

9 tablespoons unsalted butter, divided
8 celery stalks, thinly sliced (about 4 cups)
4 leeks (white and pale green parts only), thinly sliced (about 4 cups)
4 cups chicken broth
2 $\frac{1}{2}$ cups whole milk
$\frac{1}{2}$ cup heavy cream
2 large russet potatoes (2 pounds total), peeled and cut into $\frac{1}{2}$-inch pieces (about 4 cups)
1 tablespoon fresh tarragon leaves, plus more for garnish
1 teaspoon kosher salt
1 teaspoon seasoned salt (see *Pantry and Produce*)
$\frac{1}{2}$ teaspoon freshly ground white pepper
Parmesan Croutons or breadsticks (optional; page 308)

SOUPS moroccan harira soup

The national soup of Morocco, Harira makes a fantastic and hearty one-pot meal. I was inspired to create this recipe when visiting North Africa, where it is traditionally eaten at sundown and often served with dense, dark bread. Though the long ingredient list may seem daunting, once you've prepped the components, the finished dish comes together with ease. For an authentic Middle Eastern feast, serve the soup with rustic artisanal bread, a plate of fresh herbs (cilantro, mint or chives), sliced feta cheese, string cheese and olives.

SERVES 8 TO 10 (MAKES ABOUT 5 QUARTS)

Heat an 8-quart pot over high heat until the first wisp of white smoke comes off of the pot. Add the oil, then the lamb, and cook until the meat is dark brown and all the liquid has evaporated, about 5 minutes. Add the onions and celery and cook until the vegetables are tender, about 5 minutes. Add the diced tomatoes, tomato paste and garlic. Stir until the tomato paste is well distributed among the vegetables. Stir in the broth. Add the lentils, rice and garbanzo beans. Bring to a boil, then reduce the heat to medium-low.

Simmer gently until the lentils and beans are soft and falling apart, stirring occasionally, about 45 minutes. Reduce the heat to medium-low. Add the chopped cilantro, mint, parsley, kosher salt, seasoned salt, cumin, granulated garlic, turmeric, lemon pepper, paprika and black pepper. Cover and simmer gently until the soup thickens slightly and the flavors blend, stirring often, about 45 minutes. Add the lemon juice to taste. Season the soup to taste with more spices, if desired.

Do-ahead tip: The soup can be refrigerated for up to 4 days or frozen for up to 2 months. Transfer the soup to five 1-quart containers, set the containers in a roasting pan and surround with ice. Set aside to cool, stirring occasionally. Cover the containers and store. Rewarm the soup in a covered saucepan over medium-low heat, stirring occasionally, just until it simmers. If the soup is too thick, add more broth to thin it to the desired consistency.

Ladle the soup into bowls, garnish with cilantro leaves and serve.

Zov's kitchen note: Serve with your favorite Pinot Noir or red Burgundy. Beef or chicken can be substituted for lamb, and 1/4 teaspoon of cayenne pepper can be added for a spicier kick. You can use either fresh garbanzo beans or canned in this recipe. The soup will thicken as it sits. To thin, add more liquid 1 cup at a time, making sure to adjust the seasoning accordingly.

---

3 tablespoons olive oil
8 ounces lean boneless leg of lamb, diced into pea-size pieces
1 large onion, finely diced (about 2 cups)
3 celery stalks, finely diced (about 1½ cups)
1 pound plum tomatoes, seeded and diced (about 1½ cups)
1 cup tomato paste
1½ tablespoons minced garlic
4½ quarts beef broth
1 cup uncooked green lentils
½ cup uncooked long-grain rice
2 cups cooked garbanzo beans (chickpeas)
1 bunch fresh cilantro, coarsely chopped (about 2 cups)
1 cup chopped fresh mint
1 cup chopped fresh flat-leaf parsley
1½ tablespoons kosher salt
1½ tablespoons seasoned salt (see Pantry and Produce)
3½ teaspoons ground cumin
1 tablespoon granulated garlic
1 tablespoon turmeric (see Pantry and Produce)
2 teaspoons lemon pepper
2 teaspoons paprika
½ teaspoon freshly ground black pepper
1 lemon, freshly squeezed
Cilantro leaves, for garnish

chicken and rice soup with lemon

My rendition of this classic starts with familiar flavors (chicken, carrots, celery) and then keeps going with thyme, lemon and garlic. It will fortify you on cold and rainy days, and help you feel better when you're under the weather. This is a thick and hearty soup, but you can thin it out by simply adding a few cups of chicken broth. Serve with crusty French bread or breadsticks.

SERVES 14 (MAKES ABOUT 5½ QUARTS)

Using a large, sharp knife, cut the chicken into 8 pieces (2 legs, 2 thighs, 2 wings, 2 breasts) and reserve the carcass. Place the chicken pieces and the carcass in a heavy 8-quart pot. Add 4½ quarts of water and bay leaves. Bring the water to a simmer, skimming off the foam that rises to the surface of the liquid. Lower the heat to medium-low and simmer gently until the chicken is just cooked through, about 45 minutes. Using tongs, transfer the chicken pieces to a large bowl and set aside until cool enough to handle. Discard the skin, bones and tendons, and shred the meat into bite-size pieces. Meanwhile, continue simmering the broth with the carcass.

Add the onions and garlic to the broth and simmer until the onions are translucent, about 8 minutes. Add the carrots, celery, rice, ½ cup of the parsley, thyme, 4 teaspoons of kosher salt and 2 teaspoons of seasoned salt to the broth. Cover and simmer gently over medium heat until the vegetables are tender and the rice is cooked, about 18 minutes. Remove the carcass (if desired, any meat from the carcass can be removed and added to the soup). Add the shredded chicken meat to the soup. Season the soup to taste with more kosher salt.

Do-ahead tip: The soup can be refrigerated for up to 4 days or frozen for up to 2 months. Transfer the soup to six 1-quart containers, set the containers in a roasting pan and surround with ice. Set aside to cool, stirring occasionally. Cover the containers and store. Rewarm the soup in a covered saucepan over medium-low heat, stirring occasionally, just until it simmers.

Squeeze the juice from 1 lemon into the soup. Ladle the soup into bowls. Garnish with the remaining ¼ cup of parsley and serve with lemon wedges.

1 4-pound whole chicken, rinsed, excess fat trimmed
4½ quarts water
2 bay leaves
2 onions, chopped (about 3 cups)
5 garlic cloves, minced
5 carrots, peeled and sliced diagonally (about 2½ cups)
5 celery stalks, sliced diagonally (about 2½ cups)
1 cup uncooked long-grain rice
¾ cup chopped fresh flat-leaf parsley, divided
2 tablespoons fresh thyme leaves, chopped
4 teaspoons kosher salt
2 teaspoons seasoned salt (see *Pantry and Produce*)
2 lemons

SOUPS: vegetable soup with tomato-basil pistou

This simple soup shows how easy it is to create culinary magic from beautiful produce and very little else. Fresh herbs and vegetables you already have on hand are transformed into a comforting starter or main course. The pistou, a garlicky basil sauce from Provence, is the secret ingredient. Usually the pistou is used as a topping, but I love swirling it into the soup for an extra layer of rich flavor. Accompany with crusty French bread or Parmesan Bruschetta (page 40).

SERVES 12 (MAKES ABOUT 5 QUARTS)

Heat the oil in a heavy, large pot over medium-high heat. Add the leeks, onion, carrots and celery. Sauté until the onions are translucent, about 10 minutes. Mix in the garlic and tomato paste. Add the water, potatoes, green beans, kidney beans, kosher salt, seasoned salt, lemon pepper and black pepper. Simmer gently until the vegetables are tender, about 1 hour. Add the pistou to the soup and return the soup to a simmer.

Do-ahead tip: At this point, the soup can be refrigerated for up to 4 days or frozen for up to 1 month. Transfer the soup to five 1-quart containers, set the containers in a roasting pan and surround with ice. Set aside to cool, stirring occasionally. Cover the containers and store. Rewarm in a covered pot over medium-low heat, stirring occasionally, just until it simmers.

Just before serving, add the vermicelli to the simmering soup and cook just until the vermicelli is tender, about 5 minutes. Remove any oil that accumulates on top of the soup. Add more hot water to thin the soup to the desired consistency, if necessary.

Ladle the soup into bowls. Garnish with shaved Parmesan cheese and basil sprigs, and serve.

Zov's kitchen note: Add whatever vegetables you like to this light and tasty soup. For a richer version, substitute chicken broth for the water. The soup will thicken the next day and the flavors will blend beautifully.

- ⅓ cup olive oil
- 2 leeks (white and pale green parts only), diced (about 2 cups)
- 1 large onion, chopped (about 2 cups)
- 4 carrots, peeled and diced (about 2 cups)
- 4 celery stalks, diced (about 2 cups)
- 4 garlic cloves, minced
- 2 tablespoons tomato paste
- 12 cups water
- 1 russet potato, peeled and cubed (about 3 cups)
- 2 cups diced green beans or 1 10-ounce package frozen green beans
- 1 15.5-ounce can kidney beans, rinsed and drained
- 2 tablespoons kosher salt
- 1 tablespoon seasoned salt (see *Pantry and Produce*)
- 1 teaspoon lemon pepper
- ½ teaspoon freshly ground black pepper
- Tomato-Basil Pistou (page 304)
- ¼ cup vermicelli noodles or fideos, broken up in pieces
- Shaved Parmesan cheese, for garnish
- Basil sprigs, for garnish

SOUPS: velvety cream of spinach and cauliflower soup

The richness of the soup comes from sautéing the vegetables in butter and olive oil, then simmering them in broth, milk and cream. Yukon Gold potatoes make the soup even more intensely creamy. This recipe makes an ample amount of soup, as I often serve it at parties, but it can be easily cut in half. It also freezes beautifully.

SERVES 20 (MAKES ABOUT 5 QUARTS)

Melt the butter and the olive oil in a heavy 8-quart pot over medium-high heat. Add the leeks, celery, onions and garlic. Reduce the heat to medium and cook until the vegetables are tender but not brown, stirring often, about 8 minutes. Add the cauliflower and potatoes. Stir in the broth, cream and water. Bring to a boil. Reduce the heat to low and simmer until the vegetables are very soft, stirring occasionally, about 30 minutes.

Add the spinach and thyme to the soup and continue cooking until the spinach wilts, about 2 minutes longer. Add the lemon pepper, kosher salt, seasoned salt and black pepper. Using a hand-held blender, puree the soup in the pot until smooth. Season the soup to taste with more salt and pepper.

Do-ahead tip: The soup can be refrigerated for up to 4 days or frozen for up to 2 months. Transfer the soup to five 1-quart containers, set in a roasting pan and surround with ice. Set aside to cool, stirring occasionally. Cover the containers and store. Rewarm the soup in a covered saucepan over medium-low heat, stirring occasionally, just until it simmers.

Ladle the soup into bowls and garnish with the toasted pumpkin seeds. Serve, passing a bowl of the croutons alongside.

Zov's kitchen note: When sautéing the vegetables, you can omit the butter and use only olive oil. Add 3 extra tablespoons to the pot. Nonfat milk, whole milk or half-and-half can be substituted for the cream. Just keep in mind the soup may not be as silky and rich. For a more colorful dish, try broccoli instead of cauliflower.

- 3 tablespoons unsalted butter
- 2 tablespoons olive oil
- 5 leeks (white and pale green parts only), thinly sliced (about 5 cups)
- 8 celery stalks, thinly sliced (about 4 cups)
- 4 cups chopped onions
- 3 tablespoons minced garlic
- 1 cauliflower head, cut into florets (about 1½ pounds)
- 3 small Yukon Gold potatoes (1 pound), peeled and diced
- 8 cups chicken broth
- 2 cups heavy cream
- 2 cups water
- 1 9-ounce bag fresh baby spinach
- 1 tablespoon fresh thyme leaves
- 2½ teaspoons lemon pepper
- 2 teaspoons kosher salt
- 1 teaspoon seasoned salt (see *Pantry and Produce*)
- 1 teaspoon freshly ground black pepper
- Pumpkin seeds, toasted, for garnish
- Parmesan Croutons (page 308)

tortilla soup with fresh corn, cilantro and lime

This classic tortilla soup relies on bold flavors of cumin, chili powder and jalapeño to enrich the tomato broth. The finished dish comes together in less than an hour, and is easily transformed into healthful, low-calorie main course by adding grilled, sliced chicken. A variety of toppings add a little excitement, making it especially fun to eat. Our customers must agree because this soup sells out by midday at our restaurants.

SERVES 10 (MAKES ABOUT 4 QUARTS)

Make the soup: Bring the chicken broth to a boil in a heavy, large pot over medium-high heat, then lower the heat to medium. In the meantime, blend the onions in the food processor until they are finely chopped. Add the whole tomatoes with their juices and tomato paste to the onions and blend until the tomatoes are finely diced (the mixture should remain slightly chunky). Add the tomato-onion mixture to the chicken broth and bring to a boil, about 5 minutes. Add the jalapeños, if using, garlic, seasoned salt, chili powder, cumin, kosher salt, oregano, lemon pepper and cayenne pepper. Stir in the torn tortillas and cilantro. Reduce the heat to medium-low. Cover and simmer gently until the onions and tomatoes become very tender and the tortillas break down completely, about 1 hour. Add the corn kernels. Cover and set aside for 30 minutes before serving to allow the flavors to marry.

Meanwhile, prepare the toppings: Heat the oil in a large frying pan over medium heat until it registers 350°F on a deep-fry thermometer. Working in 2 batches, fry the tortilla strips until crisp and golden, about 4 minutes. Using a slotted spoon, transfer the tortilla strips to a plate lined with paper towels to drain the excess oil. Set aside until ready to serve.

Do-ahead tip: The soup and fried tortilla strips can be made in advance. Transfer the soup to four 1-quart containers, set the containers in a roasting pan and surround with ice. Set aside to cool, stirring occasionally. Cover the containers and refrigerate for up to 4 days or freeze for up to 1 month. Rewarm the soup in a covered pot over medium-low heat, stirring occasionally, just until it simmers. Store the fried tortilla strips in an airtight container at room temperature for up to 4 days.

Ladle the soup into bowls and top with the diced avocados, cilantro, sour cream, queso fresco and fried tortilla strips. Serve with lime wedges.

Zov's kitchen note: Queso fresco is a Mexican cheese that's sold at Latin markets and some supermarkets. If you can't find it, use a good melting cheese such as fontina or Monterey Jack. Not a fan of spice? Just omit the jalapeño and cayenne pepper.

Soup

- 8 cups chicken broth
- 2 onions, coarsely chopped (about 3 cups)
- 2 28-ounce cans whole tomatoes with juices
- 3 tablespoons tomato paste
- 2 jalapeño chiles, minced with seeds (optional)
- 4 garlic cloves, minced
- 1½ tablespoons seasoned salt (see *Pantry and Produce*)
- 1 tablespoon chili powder
- 2 teaspoons ground cumin
- 2 teaspoons kosher salt
- 1 teaspoon dried oregano
- 1 teaspoon lemon pepper
- ¼ teaspoon cayenne pepper
- 4 6-inch corn tortillas, torn
- 1 bunch chopped fresh cilantro (about 2 cups)
- 3 cups fresh or frozen corn kernels, thawed

Toppings

- 2 cups canola oil
- 8 6-inch tortillas, very thinly sliced
- 2 large firm but ripe avocados, peeled, pitted and diced
- 1 cup fresh cilantro leaves
- ½ cup sour cream
- 1½ cups crumbled queso fresco (see note)
- 3 limes, cut into wedges

SALADS

cabbage salad with bulgur **148**

black bean and avocado salad **150**

barley salad with summer vegetables and feta cheese **152**

wedge salad with apple smoked bacon and maytag blue cheese **154**

tomato and watermelon salad with feta cheese **156**

beet salad with watercress, spinach and fennel **158**

summer corn salad with avocados and celery **160**

cauliflower and broccoli salad with red wine-dijon vinaigrette **162**

tuscan tomato salad (panzanella) **164**

SALADS

One of my favorite things to do is to stroll through the meandering walkways of a neighborhood farmers' market. The narrow stalls are filled with tables piled high with the freshest vegetables, nuts and preserves. I love watching people approach the stands, admiring heads of crisp lettuce, bundles of asparagus or bright glossy red apples. They run their fingers over the produce, checking for freshness, or bring it to their nose to smell the sweet, ripe fruit. | There is nothing more inspiring to me than local, organic produce and no better way to appreciate it than in a delectable salad. Salads aren't limited to the basic components of leafy greens and tomatoes; they can combine onions, beans, beets, peppers and many other ingredients in surprising ways. Salads are also a delicious way to showcase fruits, nuts, cheeses, grains and pasta. | From special events to picnic lunches, salads fit nearly every occasion, either as a nutritious side or a light entrée. In this chapter, you will learn how to incorporate a variety of fresh ingredients into scrumptious, easy-to-make salads that you can mix and match with other recipes from this book. | And the best way to source those ingredients is to take a trip to your local farmers' market, where you can see for yourself the spectacular selection of fruits and vegetables, and the differences in quality and freshness over supermarket produce. I'll show you how a few enhancements and unique twists add incredible crunch and flavor. |

SALADS | cabbage salad with bulgur

Ripe, juicy tomatoes, fresh-squeezed lemon juice, and mint brighten this recipe and play wonderfully with the crunchiness of the cabbage. This healthful, low-fat salad is hearty enough for a vegetarian lunch but works just as well as a summery side.

MAKES 6 MAIN COURSE SERVINGS; 8 TO 10 SIDE-DISH SERVINGS

Place the bulgur in a large bowl. Scatter the tomatoes over the bulgur in the bowl, then layer the green onions, red onion, mint and lastly, the cabbage. It is important to first cover the bulgur with the tomatoes, as their juices help soften the bulgur. Sprinkle the Aleppo pepper, black pepper and salt over the layered salad. Drizzle the olive oil and then the lemon juice over the salad. Let the salad sit until the bulgur softens, about 30 minutes.

Do-ahead tip: At this point, the salad can be covered and refrigerated for up to 12 hours. Do not toss the salad before refrigerating or the cabbage will become limp.

Just before serving, toss the salad, then let it sit for 10 minutes to allow the flavors to blend. Toss the salad again and serve immediately.

Zov's kitchen note: You can substitute chopped Roma tomatoes for the teardrop tomatoes. For a complete meal, add grilled sliced steak, chicken or grilled or poached salmon.

½ cup fine-grade bulgur (#1) (see *Pantry and Produce*)
3 cups small teardrop tomatoes or cherry tomatoes (about 1 pound), halved
½ cup thinly sliced green onions
½ cup finely chopped red onion
1 cup fresh mint leaves, thinly sliced
5 cups thinly sliced green cabbage (from 1 head)
1 teaspoon Aleppo pepper (optional) (see *Pantry and Produce*)
1 teaspoon freshly ground black pepper
1 teaspoon kosher salt
6 tablespoons extra-virgin olive oil
6 tablespoons fresh lemon juice (from about 2 lemons)

SALADS: black bean and avocado salad

This colorful salad is packed with protein and veggies, and goes well with just about any grilled entrée, from salmon to steak to chicken. The vibrant flavors of sun-ripened vegetables intensify as the salad sits, making this a wonderful choice for potlucks or summer picnics. Try adding fresh, sweet corn when the season rolls around.

MAKES 10 SIDE-DISH SERVINGS

Make the dressing: Whisk all of the ingredients in a small bowl to blend.

Meanwhile, make the salad: Soak the beans in a large bowl of water for 1 hour. Drain the soaking liquid. Place the beans in a heavy large pot and add enough cold water to cover the beans by 1 inch. Bring to a simmer over medium-high heat, then reduce the heat to medium-low and simmer gently until the beans are tender but still hold their shape, about 1 hour. Drain and scatter the beans over a large baking sheet to cool.

Heat 2 tablespoons of olive oil in a heavy, large sauté pan over medium-high heat. Add the mushrooms and sauté 1 minute. Add the shallots and garlic and sauté until the mushrooms are soft, about 2 minutes. Set aside to cool.

Do-ahead tip: At this point, the dressing, beans and sautéed mushrooms can be made ahead. Refrigerate the dressing in a tightly-sealed jar for up to 5 days. Let stand at room temperature until the olive oil liquefies, about 20 minutes, before shaking to blend. Cover and refrigerate the beans and mushrooms separately for up to 2 days.

Toss the cooled beans, sautéed mushrooms, celery, tomatoes, bell peppers, red onion, green onions and jalapeños in a large bowl. Add cilantro and mint to the salad. Drizzle the salad with dressing and toss gently to coat. Add diced avocados and toss again. Transfer the salad to a bowl and garnish with cilantro sprigs, avocado slices and lime wedges. Serve immediately.

Zov's kitchen note: One cup of dried beans yields about 2½ cups when cooked. Though I much prefer dried beans, you can use canned beans instead. Make sure to drain and rinse the beans before using.

Lemon-lime dressing
- 5 tablespoons fresh lemon juice (from about 2 lemons)
- 3 tablespoons fresh lime juice (from about 2 limes)
- ¼ cup olive oil
- 1 tablespoon seasoned salt (see *Pantry and Produce*)
- 2 teaspoons ground cumin
- ½ teaspoon freshly ground black pepper
- 1 teaspoon kosher salt

Salad
- 2 cups dried black beans
- 2 tablespoons olive oil
- 8 ounces cremini mushrooms, sliced
- 3 tablespoons minced shallots
- 2 garlic cloves, minced
- 5 celery stalks, thinly sliced (about 2½ cups)
- 3 tomatoes, seeded and diced, or 3 cups teardrop tomatoes, cut in half
- 1 red bell pepper, thinly sliced
- 1 yellow bell pepper, thinly sliced
- ½ small red onion, thinly sliced
- 5 green onions, thinly sliced (about 1 cup)
- 2 medium jalapeño chiles, seeded and minced
- ½ cup coarsely chopped fresh cilantro
- ¼ cup thinly sliced fresh mint
- 3 firm but ripe avocados, peeled and pitted; 2 diced and 1 thinly sliced
- Cilantro sprigs, for garnish
- Lime wedges, for garnish

SALADS: barley salad with summer vegetables and feta cheese

Not just any old summer salad, this is one of my all-time favorites. It's nutritious, filling and has a surprisingly delicious nutty flavor that just makes people happy. Since this salad is so easy to pull together, it's a good one to have on hand for a snack or for last-minute picnics and potlucks. Serve with grilled chicken, steak or as a vegetarian main course.

MAKES 6 MAIN COURSE SERVINGS; 8 TO 10 SIDE-DISH SERVINGS

Prepare the salad: Put the barley in a heavy medium saucepan and add enough water to cover the barley by 2 inches. Bring the water to a boil over high heat. Reduce the heat to medium-low, cover and simmer gently until the barley is tender, about 18 minutes. Drain well, then toss the barley in a large bowl with the oil to coat. Cool completely.

Toss the barley with the bell peppers, cucumber, zucchini, green onions, red onion, teardrop tomatoes, mint and sun-dried tomatoes.

Prepare the dressing: Whisk the lemon juice, oil, seasoned salt, kosher salt, crushed red pepper and black pepper in a medium bowl to blend.

Do-ahead tip: At this point, the barley salad and dressing can be covered separately and refrigerated for up to 4 hours. Bring the dressing to room temperature before continuing.

Pour the dressing over the barley salad and toss to coat. Transfer the salad to a serving bowl, garnish with the walnuts and feta cheese and serve.

Zov's kitchen note: For a heartier version, mix in 1 cup of drained cooked garbanzo beans.

Salad

- 8 ounces pearl barley (about 1¼ cups) (see *Pantry and Produce*)
- 1 tablespoon extra-virgin olive oil
- 1 red bell pepper, cut into medium dice
- 1 yellow bell pepper, cut into medium dice
- 1 small cucumber, peeled, seeded and sliced into half-moons
- 1 small zucchini, cut into medium dice
- 3 green onions, thinly sliced diagonally
- ½ small red onion, thinly sliced
- 1 cup teardrop tomatoes, cut in half
- ½ cup fresh mint, thinly sliced
- ½ cup thinly sliced drained sun-dried tomatoes (packed in oil)

Dressing

- 6 tablespoons fresh lemon juice
- 3 tablespoons extra-virgin olive oil
- 2 teaspoons seasoned salt (see *Pantry and Produce*)
- 1 teaspoon kosher salt
- ¾ teaspoon dried crushed hot red pepper
- 1 teaspoon freshly ground black pepper
- ¾ cup walnuts, toasted and coarsely chopped
-  ½ cup crumbled feta cheese

SALADS ## wedge salad with applewood-smoked bacon and maytag blue cheese

Homemade Blue Cheese Dressing (page 294) and high-quality ingredients take this old classic to new heights. I add radishes for crunch and a nice peppery bite. Tangy Maytag blue cheese, crumbled over the salad right before serving, is the finishing touch.

MAKES 8 SIDE-DISH SERVINGS

Cook the bacon in a large sauté pan over medium heat until crisp, stirring often, about 8 minutes. Using a slotted spoon, transfer the bacon to a plate lined with paper towels to drain the excess oil.

Arrange 2 lettuce wedges on each of 8 plates. Spoon some of the dressing over the wedges (placing the dressing on the lettuce first prevents the ingredients from falling off). Top with the bacon, red onions, radishes, then the tomatoes and chives. Drizzle again with more dressing and top with crumbled blue cheese. Sprinkle with freshly ground black pepper and serve immediately.

Zov's kitchen note: This salad lends itself to improvisation. Instead of iceberg, try Bibb lettuce or hearts of romaine. Replace regular radishes with Daikon, a large Asian radish with a slightly sweet, spicy flavor. Roma, beefsteak or heirloom tomatoes are all great substitutes for teardrop tomatoes; cut them in wedges or coarsely chop them and sprinkle over the salad. Maytag blue cheese, however, is one ingredient I wouldn't substitute. It's a superior blue cheese handcrafted in Iowa.

12 slices applewood-smoked bacon, cut crosswise into strips
2 heads iceberg lettuce, each cut into 8 wedges
Blue Cheese Dressing (page 294)
1 small red onion, sliced paper thin
7 radishes, thinly sliced
1¼ cups teardrop tomatoes, cut in half
¼ cup chopped fresh chives
3 ounces Maytag blue cheese
Freshly ground black pepper

SALADS: tomato and watermelon salad with feta cheese

You will be surprised at how well watermelon and feta work together. Salty, sweet and refreshing, every bite bursts with flavor. This salad is truly a keeper, and an inventive way to make the most of summer produce. I love using heirloom tomatoes when I can find them. Serve with grilled fish or grilled steak.

MAKES 6 SIDE-DISH SERVINGS

Make the vinaigrette: Whisk the vinegar, salt and pepper in a medium bowl to blend. Gradually whisk in the oil to blend well. Set aside.

Do-ahead tip: The vinaigrette can be made up to 1 week ahead. Store in a tightly sealed jar and refrigerate. Let the vinaigrette stand at room temperature until the olive oil liquefies, about 20 minutes, before shaking to blend.

Make the salad: Cut the cucumber in half lengthwise, then, using a spoon, scrape out the seeds. Cut the cucumber halves crosswise into thin half-moon slices. Using a mandoline, cut the onion into 1-inch-long paper-thin slices. Toss the sliced cucumber, onion, tomatoes, watermelon, bell pepper, cheese and mint in a large bowl with enough vinaigrette to coat. Serve immediately.

Zov's kitchen note: Feta is traditionally a Greek sheep's milk cheese, but I prefer the French variety for its mild and creamy taste. Always store tomatoes at room temperature; place them in a decorative basket in your kitchen. Refrigeration can make them pulpy and dull their flavor. Do not cut or slice the tomatoes too far ahead of time or they will oxidize and turn acidic.

Vinaigrette
- ¼ cup red wine vinegar
- 1 teaspoon kosher salt
- ¼ teaspoon freshly ground black pepper
- ½ cup extra-virgin olive oil

Salad
- 1 small cucumber, peeled
- ½ small red onion
- 3 heirloom tomatoes (about 12 ounces total), cut into bite-size chunks
- 3½ cups peeled seeded bite-size watermelon chunks
- 1 red bell pepper, cut into bite-size chunks
- 7 ounces French feta cheese, cut into ½-inch cubes (see note)
- 1 cup fresh mint leaves, thinly sliced

SALADS beet salad with watercress, spinach and fennel

No other vegetable can match the beet's subtle sweetness and ruby intensity — and it contains powerful cancer-fighting nutrients. Here's a beautiful salad with a lovely balance of flavors and textures. The soft, buttery beets are a delicious foil for tangy goat cheese and crunchy pine nuts. This works well as a main course for a luncheon or as a first course for an elegant dinner party. Beets do take some time to cook, but it's well worth the effort. Just watch out for stained hands. I always wear plastic disposable gloves whenever I touch cooked beets.

MAKES 4 MAIN COURSE SERVINGS; 6 SIDE-DISH SERVINGS

Make the vinaigrette: Whisk the first 7 ingredients in a large bowl to blend. Gradually add the olive oil, whisking until emulsified. Set aside.

Prepare the salad: Place the red beets in 1 saucepan and the yellow beets in another saucepan. Add enough water to both saucepans to cover the beets by 2 inches. Bring the water to a boil, then reduce the heat to medium. Simmer until the beets are easily pierced with a knife, about 25 minutes. Trim the ends and slip the skins off the beets under running water. Keep the red beets separate from the yellow beets so that they do not discolor. Cut each beet into 12 wedges. Set aside to cool to room temperature.

Do-ahead tip: The vinaigrette and beets can be prepared in advance. Refrigerate the vinaigrette in a tightly sealed jar for up to 1 week. Let stand at room temperature until the oil liquefies, about 20 minutes, before shaking to blend. Refrigerate the red and yellow beets separately in airtight containers for up to 3 days.

Just before serving, toss the watercress, spinach and all but ½ cup of the fennel slices in a large bowl with enough vinaigrette to coat. Mound the watercress mixture in the center of 6 large pasta bowls or onto 6 large plates.

Toss the yellow beets and red beets in separate bowls with enough vinaigrette to coat. Arrange the beets decoratively atop the salads. Coarsely crumble the goat cheese over the salads. Sprinkle with pine nuts and tomatoes. Garnish with the remaining fennel slices and serve immediately.

Zov's kitchen note: This is a great vinaigrette to have on hand, as it complements almost any salad with citrus in it. Make sure to slice the fennel paper-thin, and keep the slices in water so they stay crisp. Serve the beets at room temperature so they soak up as much dressing as possible. Feta cheese can be substituted for goat cheese.

Sherry-orange vinaigrette

½ cup orange juice
⅓ cup Sherry wine vinegar
2 tablespoons honey
1 tablespoon minced shallots
1 teaspoon Dijon mustard
1½ teaspoons kosher salt
½ teaspoon freshly ground black pepper
¾ cup olive oil

Salad

3 medium red beets, scrubbed
3 medium yellow beets, scrubbed
3 7-ounce bunches hydroponic watercress, stems trimmed (see *Pantry and Produce*)
1 6-ounce bag fresh baby spinach
2 fennel bulbs, sliced paper-thin, divided
7 ounces goat cheese
½ cup pine nuts, toasted
1 pint red teardrop tomatoes, cut in half

SALADS summer corn salad with avocados and celery

The perfect idea for a summer picnic: sensational corn salad. Put the bounty of the garden to good use in this colorful make-ahead dish. Fresh herbs add pizzazz, and for even more flavor, toss in grilled zucchini, eggplant or mushrooms. Make sure to use good quality extra-virgin olive oil. The salad is a delicious side to Greek-Style Chicken Kebabs (page 232) and Barramundi with Preserved Lemons and Chickpeas (page 174).

MAKES 12 SIDE-DISH SERVINGS

Bring a large pot of water to a boil over high heat. Add the corn and cook until the yellow color brightens and the corn is crisp-tender, about 2 minutes. Remove from the water and set aside to drain and cool. Using a sharp knife, cut the kernels off the cobs, trying to stay as close to the cob as possible. You should have about 5 cups of corn kernels.

Combine the corn kernels, cucumber, bell peppers, celery, green onions, red onion, basil and mint in a large bowl.

Do-ahead tip: At this point, the salad can be covered and refrigerated for up to 8 hours.

Add the olive oil, vinegar, lime juice, 1 teaspoon of the kosher salt, seasoned salt, crushed red pepper and ½ teaspoon of black pepper to the corn mixture. Toss gently to coat. Scatter the diced avocados and ½ cup of the tomatoes over the salad and toss again to coat. Season to taste with more kosher salt and pepper.

Transfer the salad to a serving dish. Garnish with the avocado slices, remaining tomatoes and parsley. Serve immediately.

Zov's kitchen note: You can use any kind of fresh tomato that you like. Though Roma, beefsteak and teardrop tomatoes are available year-round, heirloom tomatoes reach their peak in July and would be a beautiful addition to the salad. Frozen corn can stand in for fresh. Add chopped and seeded jalapeño for extra heat.

- 5 ears fresh yellow corn, shucked
- 1 cucumber, peeled, seeded and diced
- 1 red bell pepper, diced
- 1 yellow bell pepper, diced
- 2 celery stalks, thinly sliced diagonally (about 1 cup)
- 5 green onions, thinly sliced diagonally (about 1 cup)
- ¾ cup finely chopped red onion
- ½ cup thinly sliced fresh basil
- ⅓ cup thinly sliced fresh mint
- ⅓ cup extra-virgin olive oil
- 3 tablespoons rice vinegar
- 2 tablespoons fresh lime juice
- 1 teaspoon kosher salt
- 1 teaspoon seasoned salt (see *Pantry and Produce*)
- ½ teaspoon dried crushed hot red pepper
- ½ teaspoon freshly ground black pepper
- 3 firm but ripe avocados, pitted and peeled; 2 diced and 1 sliced
- 1 cup teardrop tomatoes, cut in half, divided
- 2 tablespoons coarsely chopped fresh flat-leaf parsley

SALADS | cauliflower and broccoli salad with red wine-dijon vinaigrette

This fantastic salad is too good to be limited to only one season. So think of it as an ideal side for any time of the year. You will never have to tell your family to eat their vegetables again. It works especially well as part of a potluck or cookout, since it's so simple to make, and is a nice complement to chicken or beef kebabs. Try adding your favorite vegetables.

MAKES 6 TO 8 SIDE-DISH SERVINGS

Char the bell peppers over a gas flame until the skin is blistered and blackened all over, turning often, about 8 minutes. Immediately place the charred peppers in a plastic bag and set aside until you can remove the skin easily, about 15 minutes. Peel the peppers and remove the membrane and seeds. Slice the peppers and set aside.

Preheat a grill pan (medium-high heat). Brush olive oil all over the zucchini and season with salt and pepper. Grill the zucchini until charred with grill marks, about 4 minutes per side. Cut the grilled zucchini crosswise and on a diagonal into ½-inch-thick slices; set aside to cool.

Cook the cauliflower florets in a large pot of boiling water for 2 minutes. Using a slotted spoon, transfer the cauliflower florets to a colander to drain, then arrange the florets on a baking sheet to cool. Add the broccoli florets to the same pot of boiling water and cook just until they become bright green, about 1 minute. Drain the broccoli then arrange it on another baking sheet to cool.

Toss the cauliflower, broccoli, grilled zucchini, roasted red peppers, red onion and oregano in a large bowl with enough vinaigrette to coat. Season to taste with salt and pepper. Transfer the salad to a bowl and serve.

Do-ahead tip: This salad is best served the day it is made, but if you like your vegetables marinated, you can toss the salad with the vinaigrette and refrigerate it overnight.

- 2 red bell peppers
- 2 teaspoons olive oil
- 1 large zucchini, halved lengthwise
- Sea salt and freshly ground black pepper
- 1 head cauliflower (about 2 pounds), cut into florets, stems removed
- 1 head broccoli (about 1 pound), cut into florets, stems removed
- 1 small red onion, thinly sliced
- 3 tablespoons chopped fresh oregano
- Red Wine-Dijon Vinaigrette (page 302)

SALADS | tuscan tomato salad (panzanella)

Classic panzanella is the perfect way to showcase beautiful summer tomatoes. This easy bread salad is colorful, refreshing and satisfying all at once. The secret is to use the ripest tomatoes and best ingredients possible, including the olive oil. Serve with steak, chicken or fish.

MAKES 8 SIDE-DISH SERVINGS

Preheat the oven to 375°F. Place the bread cubes in a single layer over a large baking sheet and bake until toasted and very pale golden, about 6 minutes.

Combine the oil, vinegar, lemon juice, capers, salt, anchovies, garlic, and black pepper in a glass jar. Seal with the lid and shake the dressing vigorously until well blended.

Combine the cucumber, onion, bell peppers, mozzarella, parsley, basil and olives in a large bowl.

Do-ahead tip: The toasted bread, dressing and vegetables can be prepared 1 day ahead. Store the toasted bread in an airtight container at room temperature. Cover the dressing and vegetables separately and refrigerate. Bring the dressing to room temperature before continuing.

Add the tomatoes and half of the dressing to the vegetable mixture and toss to coat. Add the toasted bread and toss with enough of the remaining dressing to coat. Let stand until the bread absorbs some of the vinaigrette, tossing occasionally, about 10 minutes. Toss the salad with more dressing as desired and serve.

Zov's kitchen note: Anchovy paste can be used in place of anchovy filets. Store fresh tomatoes at room temperature for optimal flavor.

- ½ loaf day-old crusty French bread (about 10 ounces), cut into 1-inch cubes (about 4 cups)
- ½ cup good-quality extra-virgin olive oil
- ⅓ cup good-quality red wine vinegar
- ¼ cup fresh lemon juice
- 2 tablespoons drained capers
- 1½ tablespoons kosher salt
- 1 tablespoon minced anchovy fillets (see note)
- 1 tablespoon minced fresh garlic
- 1 teaspoon freshly ground black pepper
- 1 hothouse cucumber, quartered lengthwise then cut crosswise into chunks
- 1 red onion, halved and thinly sliced
- 1 red bell pepper, cut into ¾-inch chunks
- 1 yellow bell pepper, cut into ¾-inch chunks
- 8 ounces water-packed buffalo mozzarella cheese, drained and cut into ½-inch cubes
- 2 cups fresh flat-leaf parsley leaves (not chopped)
- 1 cup fresh basil leaves, torn into pieces
- ½ cup pitted kalamata olives, cut in half
- 4 heirloom tomatoes (about 1¼ pounds), cut into chunks

SEAFOOD

grilled halibut with mango salsa, cilantro and mint **170**

shrimp with cannellini beans and basil **172**

barramundi with preserved lemons and chickpeas **174**

pan-seared scallops with tarragon mushroom sauce **176**

spicy grilled salmon with fresh herbs and ginger **180**

spicy shrimp curry bowl **182**

seared ahi with edamame **184**

mediterranean bouillabaisse with pearled couscous **186**

stuffed trout with tahini sauce **188**

SEAFOOD

I have always loved Southern California, living so close to the ocean and smelling the salty air that blows in from the Pacific on a warm summer afternoon. Shortly after getting married, one my favorite memories is of my husband and I walking with his family to the pier in Newport Beach, where local fisherman would display wonderfully succulent, fresh-caught rock cod, sea bass, red snapper and halibut. The fishermen would wield their knives with the swiftness and skill of ancient samurai and fillet the fish right in front of me. | We would take home the fresh fish and I would grill, sauté and fry it many different ways, creating incredible meals where the fish would just melt in your mouth like butter, leaving you begging for more. | Seafood is one of the world's healthiest foods, and the fatter the fish, the higher it is in brain-boosting omega-3s. For fillets, the simplest of preparations — covered in a saucepan and paired with fresh vegetables — is sometimes the only enhancement it needs. But in this chapter, I have included recipes for preparing all types of seafood in a number of delicious ways. Some might think that shopping for the ingredients might be too much trouble, but these fast and simple recipes prove that nothing could be further from the truth. The ingredients are all easy to come by. Making grilled halibut with tropical mango salsa is a snap. And the trout stuffed with spicy jalapeños, cayenne pepper and nuts is not as intimidating as it sounds. The recipes here take fresh fish to new heights, while making quick work of dinner. |

SEAFOOD: grilled halibut with mango salsa, cilantro and mint

In this popular recipe, vibrant mango salsa jazzes up halibut.

SERVES 4

Make the salsa: Using a sharp paring knife, cut the peel and all of the white pith from the grapefruit, then cut the segments away from the membranes. Cut each grapefruit segment into 3 pieces. Combine the grapefruit pieces, mangoes, avocado, bell pepper, jalapeño, cilantro, mint, red onion and green onion in a large bowl. Add the lime juice, vinegar, lemon juice, ½ teaspoon of salt and ¼ teaspoon of black pepper. Toss gently to combine.

Do-ahead tip: This salsa is best eaten immediately, but it can be covered and refrigerated for up to 4 hours before serving.

Prepare the halibut: Preheat the oven to 400°F. Place the pistachios in a shallow dish. Season the halibut on both sides with salt and pepper and brush with 1 tablespoon of the olive oil. Dredge the halibut in the pistachios to coat lightly on both sides, then shake off the excess.

Brush the remaining 1 tablespoon of oil over a ridged grill pan set over medium-high heat. Grill the halibut until it is brown and crisp and grill marks form on both sides but it is still raw in the center, about 3 minutes per side. Place the fish on a baking sheet and bake in the oven until it is just cooked through and flakes when pierced with a fork, about 5 minutes longer.

Place each halibut fillet in the center of 4 plates and spoon the mango salsa over the fish. Garnish with the cilantro sprigs and serve with lime wedges.

Zov's kitchen note: A good substitute for halibut is sea bass or mahi mahi.

Salsa
- 1 pink or red grapefruit
- 2 mangoes, peeled, pitted and diced
- 1 firm but ripe avocado, peeled, pitted and diced
- ½ red bell pepper, diced
- 1 jalapeño chile, finely chopped
- 2 tablespoons chopped fresh cilantro
- 2 tablespoons chopped fresh mint
- 1 tablespoon finely diced red onion
- 1 tablespoon green onion, sliced paper-thin
- 3 tablespoons fresh lime juice
- 2 tablespoons rice vinegar
- 1 tablespoon fresh lemon juice
- ½ teaspoon kosher salt, plus more for seasoning
- ¼ teaspoon freshly ground black pepper, plus more for seasoning

Halibut
- ⅔ cup shelled raw unsalted pistachios, finely ground
- 4 6- to 7-ounce halibut fillets
- 2 tablespoons olive oil, divided
- Cilantro sprigs, for garnish
- 4 lime wedges

SEAFOOD shrimp with cannellini beans and basil

This is one of those standby recipes that you can whip up in less than 15 minutes. It's a fabulous entrée for an elegant luncheon, or a bridal or baby shower. It's also a terrific side dish on a buffet table.

SERVES 4

Heat ¼ cup of the oil in a heavy large skillet over high heat. Add the shrimp and sprinkle with ½ teaspoon of salt and ¼ teaspoon of black pepper; cook for about 1½ minutes, tossing frequently. Using a slotted spoon, transfer the shrimp to a bowl and cover to keep warm.

Stir the garlic and serrano chile into the same skillet over medium heat. Add the beans, chopped parsley, lemon juice, and remaining ½ teaspoon of salt and ¼ teaspoon of black pepper. Cook until the beans are heated through, about 1 minute. Add the tomatoes and basil and toss until the tomatoes are just warmed through, stirring constantly, about 30 seconds. Do not overcook or the tomatoes will become mushy. Season to taste with salt and pepper.

Transfer the bean mixture to a platter and arrange the cooked shrimp on top of the beans. Garnish with parsley sprigs and lemon wedges and drizzle with extra-virgin olive oil. Serve immediately or at room temperature.

- ¼ cup extra-virgin olive oil, plus more for drizzling
- 20 large shrimp, peeled and deveined
- 1 teaspoon kosher salt, divided
- ½ teaspoon freshly ground black pepper, divided
- 4 garlic cloves, thinly sliced
- 1 serrano chile, thinly sliced into rings
- 3 cups canned cannellini beans, rinsed and drained (from 2 14-ounce cans)
- ¼ cup chopped fresh flat-leaf parsley
- 1 tablespoon fresh lemon juice
- 3 plum tomatoes, seeded and cut into medium dice
- ½ cup fresh basil leaves, thinly sliced or finely chopped
- Flat-leaf parsley sprigs, for garnish
- Lemon wedges, for garnish

SEAFOOD barramundi with preserved lemons and chickpeas

Many of us are discovering the sweet, buttery flavor of barramundi, one of Australia's finest eating fish. Preserved Lemons (page 296) bring a bright salty-citrus note to this dish. To me, preserved lemons are one of the best-kept secrets of North African cuisine. It's a quick and simple way of adding incredible flavor. Here, all you have to do is brown the delicate fillets until crisp and golden, then scent the sauce with the citrus confit. The tomatoes and cumin also add fragrant flavor to the sauce.

SERVES 6

Season the fish on both sides with salt and pepper. Lightly dredge the fish in flour to coat completely, then shake off the excess flour.

Heat 2 heavy, nonstick, 12-inch skillets over medium-high heat. When the skillets are hot, add 3 tablespoons of the olive oil and 1 tablespoon of butter to each skillet and cook until the butter is melted and hot. Place 3 fish fillets in each skillet (skin side down, if using fish with the skin on) and cook until a golden crust forms on both sides of the fish, about 5 minutes per side. If using fish fillets with the skin on, press on the fillets as they cook to ensure the skin browns evenly. When turning the fish over, turn it away from you to avoid any splattering, and while the fish cooks, gently shake the skillet for the first few seconds to ensure the fish doesn't stick to the skillet. Transfer the fish to a warm plate and tent with foil to keep warm while preparing the topping.

Discard the oil from 1 skillet, then wipe the skillet with a paper towel. Heat 3 tablespoons of the olive oil in this skillet over medium-high heat until the oil shimmers. Add the cumin seeds and stir until fragrant, about 10 seconds. Add the garbanzo beans, 1/2 teaspoon of salt and 3 tablespoons of water and cook until the chickpeas are just warmed through, about 3 minutes. Stir in the tomatoes and cook just until heated through, about 3 minutes. Add the chopped cilantro, parsley and preserved lemons and season to taste with more salt, if needed, and pepper.

Divide the couscous among 6 dinner plates. Place the fish on the couscous and spoon the tomato and chickpea mixture over the fish. Garnish with harissa and cilantro sprigs and drizzle with the remaining tablespoon of olive oil at the table.

Zov's kitchen note: Serve the harrisa in small, individual ramekins alongside the fish. If you are using a fish with skin, remember to cook with the skin down first. Striped sea bass, salmon and halibut can stand in for barramundi.

6 6- to 7-ounce barramundi fillets with or without skin
1/2 cup all-purpose flour
10 tablespoons (about) extra-virgin olive oil, divided
2 tablespoons unsalted butter
1/4 teaspoon cumin seeds
1 1/2 cups canned garbanzo beans (chickpeas), drained and rinsed
1/2 teaspoon kosher salt
4 large ripe tomatoes (about 1 1/2 pounds), seeded and diced
1/4 cup chopped fresh cilantro
1/4 cup chopped fresh flat-leaf parsley
1/4 cup chopped Preserved Lemons (page 296)
3 cups cooked Couscous with Preserved Lemon, Aleppo Pepper and Pine Nuts (page 250)
6 tablespoons Harissa (page 310), for garnish
Cilantro sprigs, for garnish

SEAFOOD pan-seared scallops with tarragon mushroom sauce

This is an elegant yet simple main course. Scallops are very tender and have a mild, sweet taste, so the less you fuss with them, the better. The trick is to quickly sear them in a hot pan so the outside gets a crisp, brown crust and the inside remains tender and creamy. Serve with Creamy Angel Hair Pasta (page 264). These scallops are also lovely atop Sautéed Swiss Chard with Lemon and Pine Nuts (page 248) or on a simple bed of watercress, as it's served here.

SERVES 4

Mix 3 tablespoons of the butter, shallots, garlic and chopped tarragon in a small bowl to blend. Set aside to use later in the pan sauce.

Remove the membrane from the side of the scallops and discard. Pat the scallops dry and sprinkle with ½ teaspoon each of salt and pepper. Heat a heavy 12-inch stainless-steel skillet over medium-high heat until hot but not smoking. Add 1½ tablespoons of the oil, then arrange half of the scallops in the hot pan. There should be enough room between the scallops so they sizzle rather than steam. If your pan is not large enough to hold the scallops without crowding, sear them in more batches. Cook the scallops until they are brown and caramelized on each side, about 2 minutes per side. The scallops are done when they feel barely firm to the touch, and are faintly opalescent in the very center. Make sure you do not overcook scallops as they can become tough. Transfer the scallops to a plate and cover with foil to keep them warm. Repeat with the remaining scallops, adding 1 more tablespoon of oil to the skillet.

Make the sauce: Heat the remaining 2 tablespoons of oil with 1 tablespoon of butter in the same skillet over medium-high heat. Add the mushrooms and season with salt and pepper. Sauté until tender and almost golden, about 5 minutes. Transfer the mushrooms to a plate and set aside. »

- 4 tablespoons unsalted butter, at room temperature, divided
- 2 tablespoons minced shallots
- 1 tablespoon minced garlic
- ½ teaspoon finely chopped fresh tarragon
- 20 large sea scallops (1½ pounds) (see note)
- ½ teaspoon kosher salt
- ½ teaspoon freshly ground black pepper
- 4½ tablespoons olive oil, divided
- 6 ounces cremini mushrooms, thinly sliced
- 4 ounces shiitake mushrooms, stemmed and thinly sliced
- 1 cup dry white wine
- 1 cup chicken broth
- ⅓ cup heavy cream
- 2 cups watercress, tough stems trimmed
- Tarragon sprigs, for garnish

Add the wine and broth to the same pan and bring to a boil over high heat. Boil uncovered, stirring occasionally, until the liquid reduces by half, about 8 minutes. Add the cream and any accumulated juices from the scallops. Boil until the sauce reduces and thickens slightly, about 2 minutes. Reduce the heat to low and stir in the shallot-butter mixture. Stir the mushrooms into the sauce and cook until heated through. Season to taste with salt and pepper.

Mound the watercress in the center of 4 large plates. Arrange the scallops on top of the watercress, then spoon the mushroom sauce over. Garnish with tarragon sprigs and serve.

Zov's kitchen note: When shopping for scallops, look for ones that are ivory or cream-colored, or even as dark as light tan; a stark, bleached white scallop can be a sign of heavy phosphate treatment. There should be little or no milky liquid in the tray, another sign of heavy soaking. The best dry-packed scallops are often a bit sticky. A fishy or sour smell indicates spoilage.

You can find cremini at most supermarkets. Choose mushrooms that are firm with tightly closed caps. >

SEAFOOD: spicy grilled salmon with fresh herbs and ginger

The dining scene is changing as more people travel around the world seeking out new tastes and culinary adventures. Here is a delicious example of the complex flavors found in authentic Asian cooking, as it represents the five basic tastes: sweet, sour, salty, pungent and bitter. It sounds intimidating, but it's not. This dish can be prepared in less than a half hour. In fact, it's a great last-minute recipe for casual get-togethers. Bistro Potato Gratin (page 254) is the perfect complement.

SERVES 6

Preheat the barbecue (high heat). Stir the cilantro, mint, soy sauce, lime juice, ginger, chili sauce, water, garlic, vinegar, Thai chiles, black pepper and salt in a medium bowl to blend.

Place the salmon fillets in a 13x9x2-inch dish. Spoon 6 tablespoons of the sauce over the salmon and let stand 5 minutes. Turn the salmon over and spoon 5 tablespoons of the remaining sauce over the salmon; let stand 5 minutes. Reserve the remaining sauce to serve with the salmon.

Brush the grill rack with oil to keep the salmon from sticking. Grill the salmon until char marks form on the bottom, about 4 minutes. Using a wide spatula, turn the fillets over and grill until the salmon is still pink in the center, about 4 minutes. The salmon will continue to cook as it sits. Let rest 5 minutes before serving.

Transfer the salmon fillets to a platter or individual plates. Garnish with lemon wedges, radishes and chives. Serve the reserved sauce alongside.

Zov's kitchen note: This versatile sauce goes with a variety of dishes, and also works well as a dip. I love using it as a basting sauce for flank steak, rib-eye or any protein that requires Asian flair. It's great on chicken and other types of meaty fish as well.

- ½ cup chopped fresh cilantro
- ⅓ cup chopped fresh mint
- 5 tablespoons soy sauce
- ¼ cup fresh lime juice
- ¼ cup minced peeled fresh ginger
- ¼ cup Thai sweet chili sauce
- 2 tablespoons water
- 1½ tablespoons minced garlic
- 1 tablespoon balsamic vinegar
- 2 Thai red chiles, minced
- 1 teaspoon freshly ground black pepper
- ½ teaspoon kosher salt
- 6 6-ounce skinless salmon fillets

Garnishes
- 1 lemon, cut into 6 wedges
- 6 radishes, thinly sliced
- 2 tablespoons chopped fresh chives

SEAFOOD spicy shrimp curry bowl

This spicy shrimp bowl is made largely with ingredients that you probably have on hand. It's one of the most flavorful dishes at our cafés, and so easy to make at home.

SERVES 4 TO 6

Heat the oil in a heavy, large skillet over medium-high heat. Stir in the garlic, shallots and ginger. Add the bell peppers, red onion and carrots. Increase the heat to high. Toss and cook for 4 minutes, or until the vegetables are crisp-tender. Add the shrimp and zucchini and cook for about 2 minutes. Add the curry sauce and basil. Cook and toss until the sauce is reduced, about 3 minutes. Add crushed red pepper, if using, to taste.

Divide the rice among 4 to 6 serving bowls. Spoon the curry over the rice and garnish with cilantro leaves.

Zov's kitchen note: If you substitute chicken or pork for the shrimp, cut the meat into 1-inch pieces. Instead of rice, try tossing the mixture with one pound of linguini or rice noodles cooked according to package directions. You will need an extra cup of curry sauce, and more if necessary, to thoroughly coat the noodles.

- 3 tablespoons olive oil
- 1 tablespoon minced garlic
- 1 tablespoon minced shallot
- 1 tablespoon minced peeled fresh ginger
- 1 small green bell pepper, thinly sliced
- 1 small red bell pepper, thinly sliced
- 1 small yellow bell pepper, thinly sliced
- 1 small red onion, thinly sliced (about 1 cup)
- 2 carrots, peeled and thinly sliced diagonally (about 1 cup)
- 1½ pounds extra-large shrimp, peeled and deveined
- 1 zucchini, halved lengthwise then thickly sliced diagonally (about 1 cup)
- ½ cup Curry Sauce (page 299)
- ¼ cup fresh basil, thinly sliced
- Dried crushed hot red pepper (optional)
- 2 to 3 cups Jasmine Rice Pilaf with Vermicelli (page 262) or white rice
- Cilantro leaves, for garnish

SEAFOOD seared ahi with edamame

Make sure you purchase sushi-grade ahi from a trusted and knowledgeable source. The fish should be very fresh and pink in color. I like my ahi on the rare side, but it's just as delicious done medium or medium-rare. This is a fantastic, healthful main-course salad.

SERVES 6

Make the vinaigrette: Whisk the vinegar, garlic, kosher salt, seasoned salt and black pepper in a medium bowl to blend. Gradually whisk in the oil.

Make the salad: Bring a large saucepan of water to a boil. Add the green beans and cook just until they turn bright green, about 2 minutes. Immediately transfer the beans to a large bowl of ice water. Let stand until cold. Drain the beans well and pat completely dry. Cut the green beans diagonally into 2-inch-long pieces.

Do-ahead tip: The vinaigrette and all the beans can be refrigerated for up to 1 day. Store separately in airtight containers; bring the vinaigrette to room temperature and whisk to blend before using.

Heat 1 tablespoon of oil in a heavy, large sauté pan over medium-high heat. Add the mushrooms, salt and pepper, and sauté until tender and golden, about 8 minutes. Set aside to cool.

Preheat the barbecue or an indoor grill pan (medium-high heat). Place the sesame seeds on a plate. Brush the remaining 3 tablespoons of oil over both sides of the tuna and season with salt and pepper, and then dip the tuna into the sesame seeds to coat. Grill the tuna until grill marks appear but the tuna is still rare in the center, about 1½ minutes on each side. Set aside.

Toss the green beans, mushrooms, edamame beans, kidney beans, tomatoes, onion, bell peppers, green onions, cilantro, basil and jalapeño in a large bowl with enough of the vinaigrette to coat. Mound the salad on plates and top with the tuna and avocados. Serve immediately.

Zov's kitchen note: The on't adhere to the beans if they are not dried thoroughly. For an Asian twist, try sesame soy dressing for this salad instead of the red wine vinaigrette.

Red wine vinaigrette
¼ cup red wine vinegar
2 garlic cloves, minced
1 teaspoon kosher salt
1 teaspoon seasoned salt (see *Pantry and Produce*)
½ teaspoon freshly ground black pepper
½ cup extra-virgin olive oil

Salad
2 cups fresh green beans
4 tablespoons olive oil, divided
12 ounces cremini mushrooms, thickly sliced
½ teaspoon kosher salt
½ teaspoon freshly ground black pepper
½ cup sesame seeds
6 ahi tuna fillets (each about 6 ounces and 1-inch thick)
3 cups frozen shelled edamame beans, thawed and patted dry
2 cups canned kidney beans, rinsed, drained and patted dry
3 tomatoes, seeded and diced
1 small red onion, thinly sliced (about 1 cup)
1 red bell pepper, thinly sliced
1 yellow bell pepper, thinly sliced
4 green onions, diagonally sliced (about ¾ cup)
1 cup chopped fresh cilantro
½ cup thinly sliced fresh basil
1 jalapeño chile, seeded and finely chopped
2 avocados, peeled, seeded and sliced

SEAFOOD mediterranean bouillabaisse with pearled couscous

At the restaurant I call this dish Seafood Tagine, but it's really more like that classic Provençal stew, bouillabaisse. Since my cooking is rooted in Eastern Mediterranean cuisine, I couldn't help but add pearl couscous for a nontraditional twist. It adds lovely texture to the stew. The key to bouillabaisse is to use the freshest seafood you can find. Serve with dry white wine and crusty French bread to soak up the broth. What a way to celebrate with friends!

SERVES 8

Add the couscous to a large pot of boiling salted water and boil for about 5 minutes (do not overcook the couscous at this point, as it will continue cooking in the bouillabaisse). Drain well and toss the couscous with 2 tablespoons of the olive oil.

Do-ahead tip: Cover the couscous and refrigerate for up to 1 day.

Heat the remaining 4 tablespoons of olive oil in a heavy, large, wide pot over medium heat. Stir in the garlic and shallots. Add the shrimp and sauté until almost cooked through, about 2 minutes. Using tongs, transfer the shrimp to a bowl and set aside. Removing the shrimp prevents them from overcooking.

Add the clams and mussels to the pot and toss to coat with the garlic and shallots. Add the clam juice, wine, salt, black pepper and crushed red pepper and bring to a boil over high heat. Add the tomato sauce and cook until most of the mussels and clams have opened, about 5 minutes. Add the sea bass, cooked shrimp and couscous to the sauce and cook until the fish is just cooked through and all the clams and mussels open, about 2 minutes. Discard any clams and mussels that do not open. Stir in the butter.

Divide the bouillabaisse among 8 large pasta bowls and garnish with parsley. Serve with lemon wedges and bruschetta.

Zov's kitchen note: If you have extra time, wrap the sea bass in brined grape leaves to give it a nice tangy flavor. Look for pearled couscous (also called Israeli couscous) at Middle Eastern markets, Trader Joe's, natural foods stores and specialty foods stores. If you can't find clam juice, substitute chicken broth. When choosing fresh clams and mussels, make sure the shells are completely closed when you purchase them as well as when you add them to the pot. Remember to discard any clams or mussels that do not open once cooked.

- 8 ounces pearled couscous
- 6 tablespoons olive oil, divided
- 3 tablespoons minced garlic
- 3 tablespoons minced shallots
- 16 jumbo shrimp, peeled and deveined
- 16 Manila clams, scrubbed and debearded
- 16 mussels (preferably green-lipped), scrubbed
- 2 cups clam juice
- 1½ cups dry white wine
- 2 teaspoons kosher salt
- 1½ teaspoons freshly ground black pepper
- ⅛ teaspoon dried crushed hot red pepper
- 6 cups Tomato-Basil Sauce (page 308)
- 1 pound sea bass, cut into 16 pieces
- 2 tablespoons unsalted butter
- Chopped fresh flat-leaf parsley, for garnish
- 12 lemon wedges
- Parmesan Bruschetta (page 40)

SEAFOOD: stuffed trout with tahini sauce

This recipe is one of my family treasures. For the stuffing, spicy jalapeño and cayenne pepper are combined with cilantro and garlic. This unique preparation yields a flavor that is nothing short of amazing. You may think it calls for too much garlic, but you'd be surprised; the garlic doesn't overpower the other flavors. This makes a wonderful buffet item, as it can be served at room temperature. Serve with Jasmine Rice Pilaf with Vermicelli (page 262).

SERVES 6

Preheat the oven to 400°F. Line a heavy, large, rimmed baking sheet with aluminum foil. Brush 2 tablespoons of the oil all over the foil.

Pulse the pine nuts, pistachios, almonds and walnuts in a food processor until they are medium fine; do not pulverize the nuts into a fine powder, as the stuffing should retain a fine crunch. Transfer the nuts to a medium bowl. Stir in the onion, 1 of the chopped tomatoes, chopped cilantro, garlic and jalapeño, then stir in the coriander, cumin, 1 teaspoon of salt, black pepper and cayenne pepper. Add the lemon juice, then slowly add the remaining ¼ cup of olive oil while stirring to blend.

Sprinkle the trout inside and out with salt. Spoon the nut mixture into the trout cavities, dividing equally. Fold the trout to enclose the filling.

Do-ahead tip: The trout can be prepared up to this point 8 hours ahead. Cover and refrigerate.

Bake the trout until the flesh flakes easily, about 20 minutes. Let the trout rest for 5 minutes. Using a sharp knife, carefully remove the skin, fins and any visible bones from the fish.

Using a spatula, carefully transfer the fish to a serving platter. Garnish with cilantro sprigs and the remaining chopped tomato. Drizzle the tahini sauce over the fish and serve with lemon wedges and more sauce alongside.

Zov's kitchen note: Sea bass, rock cod, John Dory and coho salmon are all good substitutes for the trout in this impressive dish. Instead of individual rainbow trout, you can stuff a large whole fish that weighs up to 3 pounds. Another option is to stack two filets together, with the filling in between, and bake. Just pour the tahini sauce over the fish before serving.

- 2 tablespoons plus ¼ cup olive oil
- ⅓ cup pine nuts
- ⅓ cup shelled raw unsalted pistachios
- ⅓ cup slivered almonds
- ⅓ cup walnuts
- 1 small onion, finely chopped (about 1 cup)
- 2 tomatoes, seeded and cut into small dice, divided
- 1 cup chopped fresh cilantro
- 15 garlic cloves, minced
- 1 jalapeño chile, seeded and finely chopped
- 1 teaspoon ground coriander (see *Pantry and Produce*)
- 1 teaspoon ground cumin
- 1 teaspoon kosher salt, plus more for seasoning
- 1 teaspoon freshly ground black pepper
- ½ teaspoon cayenne pepper
- ½ cup fresh lemon juice
- 6 10-ounce whole rainbow trout, boned, cleaned and heads removed (6 to 7 ounces when cleaned)
- Cilantro sprigs, for garnish
- 1½ cups Tahini Sauce (page 304)
- 6 lemon wedges

MEATS

beef and eggplant tagine **194**

beef brochettes with garlic-thyme marinade **196**

beef short ribs with horseradish-yogurt sauce **198**

beef tenderloin with spinach, leeks and goat cheese **200**

beef stroganoff with mushrooms and green onions **202**

grilled skirt steak with zahtar and fresh lime **204**

braised green beans with beef and tomatoes **206**

greek burgers with baby arugula and feta cheese **208**

lamb stew with swiss chard **210**

spicy ground meat kebabs **212**

pork tenderloin with sour cherry sauce **214**

meat and potato casserole **216**

tamarind pork kebabs with ginger and soy **218**

zov's favorite meatloaf **220**

MEATS

When I was younger and dreamed of America, I often dreamed of the tall skyscrapers in New York, of the Statue of Liberty with her green tint, standing in the harbor as a beacon of help and, finally, of the spur-wearing cowboys from the Wild West. I remembered watching Western movies with rough-riding legends like John Wayne and Clint Eastwood. They were usually seated around a glowing campfire, hunched over a deep bowl of hardy beef stew packed with carrots and potatoes, or eating a thick, juicy steak on a tin plate out on the ranch. Besides the boots, hats and scruff, one other thing these rough, masculine men had in common was their carnivorous appetites. Although today's men have traded in their leather vests for ties, and pistols for briefcases, they still have those bottomless appetites for meat. | No matter how much you try to persuade your husband, boyfriend, brother or son that too much red meat is bad for their health and that they should put down their dripping hamburger and pick up a handful of steamed edamame beans, they will always crave traditional meat and potatoes. | In this chapter, I have designed several recipes that are full of flavor, satisfying and, most importantly, man-friendly. | One of my personal favorites is my homemade meatloaf seasoned with fresh rosemary, thyme and Parmesan cheese and cooked in a unique way that ensures a crispy crust all around. I also especially love the Beef Short Ribs with Horseradish-Yogurt Sauce and the Tamarind Pork Kebabs with Ginger and Soy. | These recipes are sure to please everyone, but will have the men in your life bringing over their friends just so they can try some of your famous meat dishes. |

MEATS: beef and eggplant tagine

This dish was inspired by my visits to ethnic markets around the world, where bold colors, interesting textures and aromas truly stir the senses. A tagine is a classic Moroccan stew that bursts with flavor yet is easy to prepare, which makes it perfect for a family or large crowd. Here, a tomato broth is the backdrop for tangy turmeric and sour grapes, my two secret ingredients. Sour grapes resemble baby green grapes and are a great flavor enhancer for soups and stews. Serve with a light salad.

SERVES 6 TO 8

Preheat the oven to 350°F. Cut the eggplants crosswise into 1-inch-thick slices, then quarter each slice. Toss the eggplant pieces with ¼ cup of oil in a large bowl to coat. Arrange the eggplant pieces in a single layer on a rimmed, heavy, large baking sheet. Roast the eggplant pieces until they are medium brown, about 30 minutes. Maintain the oven temperature.

Meanwhile, preheat a heavy, wide ovenproof pot over high heat just until the first wisp of white smoke appears. Add the remaining ¼ cup of oil to the pot and immediately add the beef. Cook until the meat is browned, about 8 minutes. If your pot is not wide enough to hold the beef in a single layer without crowding, brown the meat in two batches. Add the onions and garlic to the meat and cook until the onions are soft and translucent, stirring constantly so the meat does not stick to the pot, about 5 minutes. Add the pureed tomatoes, water, tomato paste, sour grapes, if using, salt, turmeric and pepper. Bring the mixture to a simmer, then reduce the heat to medium-low. Stir the roasted eggplant pieces into the stew. Return the stew to a simmer.

Cover the stew and transfer the pot to the oven. Cook the stew until the meat is tender and the eggplant is very soft, about 1½ hours. Sprinkle with chopped parsley and serve with rice pilaf, polenta or couscous.

Do-ahead tip: Refrigerate for up to 2 days. Cool completely, cover and store. Rewarm, covered, over medium heat, stirring occasionally until heated through, adding a bit of water if needed to loosen the sauce.

Zov's kitchen note: Sour grapes are sold at Persian and Middle Eastern markets. Lamb shoulder or chicken thighs can stand in for the beef chuck.

This tagine can be cooked in a slow cooker instead of an oven. After adding the roasted eggplant and bringing the stew to a simmer, transfer to a slow cooker and cook at least 6 hours until the meat becomes tender. For a variation, use zucchini and mushrooms instead of eggplant. Or mix in one cup of cooked garbanzo beans when adding the roasted eggplant pieces.

- 3 medium eggplants (about 3¼ pounds total)
- ½ cup olive oil, divided
- 3 pounds boneless beef chuck, trimmed of excess fat and cut into 1½-inch cubes
- 2 large onions, thinly sliced (about 3½ cups)
- 3 tablespoons minced garlic
- 1 28-ounce can whole tomatoes (with juices), pureed in food processor
- 2 cups water
- 1 6-ounce can tomato paste
- ½ cup sour grapes (optional; see note)
- 1½ tablespoons kosher salt
- 2 teaspoons turmeric (see *Pantry and Produce*)
- 1½ teaspoons freshly ground black pepper
- ½ cup chopped fresh flat-leaf parsley, for garnish
- Jasmine Rice Pilaf with Vermicelli (page 262), polenta or couscous

MEATS: beef brochettes with garlic-thyme marinade

Easier than the sophisticated title might lead you to believe, these satisfying skewers are great for a last-minute dinner. They go well with Black Bean and Avocado Salad (page 150), Jasmine Rice Pilaf (page 262) or Tuscan Tomato Salad (page 164). Or serve them on a bed of Cabbage Salad with Bulgur (page 148). Round out the meal with crusty French bread.

SERVES 6

Whisk the olive oil, parsley, thyme, lemon juice, mustard, salt, Aleppo pepper, black pepper and garlic in a large bowl to blend. Add the beef cubes and toss until all the beef is well coated. Cover and set aside for at least 30 minutes or cover and refrigerate for up to 4 hours; let the chilled mixture stand at room temperature for 30 minutes before grilling to ensure the meat cooks evenly.

Spray the barbecue with grilling nonstick spray and then preheat the barbecue (high heat). Thread the beef onto 6 metal skewers. Grill the meat, turning the skewers as needed, for about 10 minutes, or until evenly browned on all sides and cooked to medium doneness.

Transfer the skewers to a platter and serve with lemon wedges and tzatziki or Greek-style yogurt on the side.

Zov's kitchen note: Instead of tenderloin of beef, you can use flat iron steak from the shoulder top blade or sirloin steak. It's important to bring the meat to room temperature before putting it on the grill to ensure even cooking. If you are using wooden skewers, be sure to soak them in cold water for 30 minutes to prevent them from burning.

- 3 tablespoons olive oil
- 2 tablespoons chopped fresh flat-leaf parsley
- 2 tablespoons chopped fresh thyme
- 2 tablespoons fresh lemon juice
- 1 tablespoon Dijon mustard
- 1½ teaspoons kosher salt
- 1 teaspoon Aleppo pepper (see *Pantry and Produce*)
- 1 teaspoon freshly ground black pepper
- 3 garlic cloves, minced
- 2 pounds trimmed beef tenderloin, cut into 1½- to 2-inch cubes
- Grilling nonstick spray
- Lemon wedges
- Tzatziki Sauce (page 303) or Greek-style yogurt

MEATS beef short ribs with horseradish-yogurt sauce

Long and low is the preferred cooking method for short ribs, a cut of meat that is succulent and also economical. It is in the pot roast family, otherwise known to me as heaven on a plate. Short ribs epitomize the pleasures of braised beef, with meat so tender it falls off the bone. Here, they get a deeper richness with blended spices and full-bodied red wine, which combine with the essences of browned beef during the slow-cooking process. Serve with Creamy Mashed Potatoes (page 266), Couscous with Preserved Lemon (page 250) or rice pilaf.

SERVES 8

Preheat the oven to 350°F. Sprinkle the short ribs with salt and pepper, then dust them with the flour to coat lightly. Heat a large Dutch oven over medium-high heat. Add the oil to the Dutch oven. Then, working in batches, add the short ribs and cook until they are browned on all sides, about 3 minutes per side. Do not crowd the short ribs in the pot or they will steam and not brown properly. Transfer the short ribs to a bowl and set aside.

Add the onion, carrots, celery, fennel and garlic to the Dutch oven and cook until the vegetables are caramelized, stirring often, about 8 minutes. Stir in the tomato paste. Stir in the beef broth and wine, scraping up the browned bits on the bottom of the pot. Add the figs, if using, thyme, rosemary, sage, if using, bay leaves and jalapeño. Bring to a boil, stirring and mixing well. Return the short ribs to the pot, pressing to submerge them in the cooking liquid. Grate the zest of 1 lemon into the mixture. Cover and bake in the oven until the meat is fork-tender and begins to fall off the bone, about 3 hours.

Transfer the short ribs to a plate and tent with foil to keep warm. Discard the rosemary, thyme and bay leaves. Spoon off any excess oil that has accumulated on top. Using an immersion blender, blend the liquid in the pot until the vegetables are pureed and the liquid is slightly thickened. The braising liquid becomes a delicious sauce that has the consistency of thin gravy. Bring to a simmer over high heat. Reduce the heat to medium-low and return the short ribs to the sauce. Cook until the ribs are heated through, about 2 minutes.

Arrange the short ribs on plates and spoon the sauce over the ribs. Top with dollops of horseradish-yogurt sauce. Grate the zest from the remaining lemon over the ribs and garnish with parsley and chives. Serve, passing extra yogurt sauce alongside.

Zov's kitchen note: Pull apart leftover meat and add it to Bolognese Sauce (page 300), serve with pasta or on sliders. I also love it in a baguette sandwich with sautéed peppers and 2 tablespoons of braising liquid.

- 8 meaty beef short ribs (each 4-inches long and 2½-inches thick; about 5½ pounds total)
- 1 tablespoon kosher salt
- 1 tablespoon freshly ground black pepper
- 2 tablespoons all-purpose flour
- ¼ cup olive oil
- 1 large onion, finely chopped (about 2 cups)
- 3 carrots, peeled and finely chopped (about 1½ cups)
- 2 celery stalks, finely chopped (about 1 cup)
- 1 fennel bulb, thinly sliced
- 2 tablespoons minced garlic
- 3 tablespoons tomato paste
- 6 cups good-quality beef broth
- 2 cups dry red wine
- ¼ cup dried Black Mission figs, coarsely chopped (optional)
- 6 thyme sprigs
- 3 rosemary sprigs
- 2 sage leaves (optional)
- 3 bay leaves
- 1 tablespoon chopped jalapeño chile
- 2 lemons, divided
- Horseradish-Yogurt Sauce (page 298)
- 2 tablespoons finely chopped fresh flat-leaf parsley, for garnish
- 2 tablespoons finely chopped fresh chives, for garnish

MEATS: beef tenderloin with spinach, leeks and goat cheese

Here is an elegant way to present beef. Butterflying is quite simple and can be done quickly, but you can also have your butcher do it for you. Round out the meal with Couscous with Preserved Lemon (page 250), Cauliflower and Broccoli Salad (page 162), Creamy Mashed Potatoes (page 266) or Bistro Potato Gratin (page 254).

SERVES 6 TO 8

Heat a large skillet over medium-high heat. Add 2 tablespoons of the olive oil, leeks, mushrooms and garlic and cook until the leeks and mushrooms are tender and the liquid has evaporated, stirring often, about 5 minutes. Add the spinach and sauté until tender and the liquid evaporates, about 3 minutes. Season the spinach mixture with thyme, 1 teaspoon of the salt and ½ teaspoon of the pepper. Stir in the goat cheese and pine nuts until the cheese is melted and creamy. Set aside to cool while you prepare the beef.

Do-ahead tip: Refrigerate the filling for up to 2 days.

Butterfly the beef tenderloin by cutting the tenderloin lengthwise down the center and about two-thirds of the way through the beef. Lay the tenderloin open on a work surface. Using a mallet, pound the beef to ¼- to ½-inch thickness.

Season the beef with salt and pepper, then spread the filling mixture down the center of the tenderloin. Roll the beef around the filling in a tight cylinder, then continue rolling as you would a jelly roll to enclose the filling. Using butcher string, tie and secure the beef in 2-inch intervals. Refrigerate for at least 1 hour or up to 8 hours.

Preheat the oven to 425°F. Heat a large roasting pan over medium-high heat. Add the remaining ¼ cup of olive oil to the hot pan, then immediately lay the beef in the pan and quickly brown on all sides, about 2 minutes per side. Transfer the beef to a rack set on a heavy large baking sheet. Roast for about 35 minutes for medium-rare. Transfer the beef to a cutting board and let rest for 15 minutes.

Using a large, sharp knife, cut the tenderloin crosswise into slices and transfer to plates. Spoon the sauce over the beef and serve.

- 2 tablespoons plus ¼ cup olive oil
- 1 leek (white and pale green parts only), thinly sliced (about 1 cup)
- 4 ounces cremini mushrooms, thinly sliced (about 1½ cups)
- 2 tablespoons minced garlic
- 9 ounces fresh baby spinach
- 1½ tablespoons chopped fresh thyme
- 1 teaspoon kosher salt, plus more for seasoning
- ½ teaspoon freshly ground black pepper, plus more for seasoning
- 8 ounces fresh goat cheese, room temperature
- ¼ cup toasted pine nuts
- 1 3-pound whole beef tenderloin, trimmed
- Red Wine Sauce (page 302)

MEATS: beef stroganoff with mushrooms and green onions

So simple and satisfying, this Russian dish became one of the quintessential comfort foods of the '60s, and is one of my all-time favorites for a last-minute dinner party or hearty family meal. Serve over Jasmine Rice Pilaf (page 262) or buttered noodles.

SERVES 6

Ingredients

- 2½ pounds beef tenderloin, well trimmed of fat and sinew
- 3 tablespoons olive oil
- 4 tablespoons (½ stick) unsalted butter, divided
- 1½ pounds cremini mushrooms, thickly sliced
- 8 green onions (white and green parts), chopped (about 1½ cups)
- ¼ cup finely chopped shallots or white onions
- 1 tablespoon minced fresh garlic
- 1 teaspoon kosher salt
- ½ teaspoon freshly ground black pepper
- 2 tablespoons Dijon mustard
- ¼ teaspoon cayenne pepper
- 3 tablespoons all-purpose flour
- 4 cups beef broth
- 1½ cups sour cream
- Jasmine Rice Pilaf with Vermicelli (page 262)

Instructions

Using a large, sharp knife, cut the beef into ⅓-inch-thick strips that are 2-inches long and 1-inch wide. Pat the beef strips dry with paper towels, then season them with salt and pepper.

Heat a large, deep stainless-steel frying pan (not nonstick) over high heat until the pan is very hot and a wisp of white smoke comes off of the pan. Add 1½ tablespoons of oil and 1 tablespoon of butter to the hot pan. Immediately add half of the beef strips to the pan in a single layer and cook just until brown on the outside but still very rare in the center, about 1 minute per side. Transfer the beef strips to a rimmed baking sheet and keep warm. Repeat with 1½ tablespoons of oil, 1 tablespoon of butter and the remaining beef.

Melt the remaining 2 tablespoons of butter in the same pan over medium-high heat. Add the mushrooms, green onions, shallots and garlic and sauté until the mushrooms soften, about 5 minutes. Continue cooking until the liquid from the mushrooms evaporates, scraping the pan bottom to loosen any bits, about 10 minutes. Add 1 teaspoon of salt, ½ teaspoon of black pepper, the mustard and cayenne pepper. Sprinkle the flour over the mixture and stir until well incorporated. Stir in the beef broth. Simmer over medium-high heat until the sauce is smooth and thickens slightly, stirring often, about 15 minutes. Add the beef strips and any accumulated beef juices to the skillet.

In a small bowl, mix the sour cream with a fork until creamy. Slowly add the sour cream to the sauce, stirring until all the sour cream is incorporated. Bring the mixture to a boil, stirring constantly.

Spoon the rice pilaf onto 6 plates, top with stroganoff and serve immediately.

Zov's kitchen note: I prefer beef tenderloin for this recipe. Cuts like sirloin or top round aren't as tender and juicy, and can even be tough if cut the wrong way (cut thin slices across the grain if you choose to substitute).

Be very careful when adding the cold sour cream to the hot sauce. To prevent curdling, add it very slowly to help temper the sauce.

MEATS: grilled skirt steak with zahtar and fresh lime

Skirt steak has become popular in recent years thanks in no small part to fajitas, the delicious Southwestern dish in which it stars. When I grill skirt steak, I use zahtar, a North African spice blend; it brings wonderful nutty and smoky flavors to the dish. Lime juice, the other main ingredient, provides a bright contrast, and should be squeezed on each piece right before eating. Though skirt steak is incredibly simple and quick to prepare, you must watch it carefully on the grill so it doesn't overcook. Serve with Perfect Guacamole (page 64), roasted red peppers and caramelized onions. A black bean salad would also be a terrific accompaniment. The steaks need to marinate for at least two hours, so plan accordingly.

SERVES 6 TO 8

Mix 3 tablespoons of the olive oil, soy sauce, mustard, granulated garlic, cumin, turmeric, salt, crushed red pepper and black pepper in a medium bowl to blend. Rub the meat generously with the marinade. If the meat looks too dry, add more oil 1 tablespoon at a time. Lay the meat on a baking sheet. Cover with plastic wrap and refrigerate for at least 2 hours.

Do-ahead tip: The steaks can marinate for up to 2 days; keep them covered and refrigerated.

Spray the barbecue with grilling nonstick spray, then preheat the barbecue (high heat). Sprinkle the zahtar all over the steaks. Grill until the steaks are slightly charred with grill marks and still pink in the center, about 1½ minutes per side. The steaks become tough if overcooked, so make sure the heat is high and you don't cook them more than 2 minutes per side.

Transfer the steaks to a work surface, tent with foil and let stand for 3 minutes; the steaks will continue to cook as they sit. Cut the steaks across the grain into thin strips. Arrange on a platter and serve with lime wedges.

Zov's kitchen note: Skirt steak is a boneless cut of beef from the lower part of the brisket. If skirt steak is not available, substitute flap steak, a similar cut that is sold in Latin markets. Instead of barbecuing, the steaks can be cooked indoors on an oiled grill pan over medium-high heat.

- 3 tablespoons (or more) olive oil
- 3 tablespoons soy sauce
- 1 tablespoon Dijon mustard
- 1 tablespoon granulated garlic
- 1 teaspoon ground cumin
- 1 teaspoon ground turmeric (see *Pantry and Produce*)
- 1 teaspoon kosher salt
- ½ teaspoon dried crushed hot red pepper
- ½ teaspoon freshly ground black pepper
- 3 pounds skirt steak
- Grilling nonstick spray
- ⅓ cup zahtar (see *Pantry and Produce*)
- 1 lime, cut into 6 or 8 wedges

MEATS braised green beans with beef and tomatoes

Serve with fluffy steamed rice, rice pilaf or couscous.

SERVES 6 TO 8

Heat the oil with the butter in an 8-quart pot over medium-high heat. Add the ground beef, onions, mushrooms and garlic and cook until the meat is brown and the onions are translucent, stirring constantly and scraping the bottom of the pot occasionally to ensure the mixture does not stick or scorch, about 12 minutes. Reduce the heat to medium. Stir in the green beans. Cover and continue cooking, stirring occasionally, until the green beans are bright green, about 8 minutes.

Add the broth, potatoes, stewed tomatoes and tomato paste to the meat mixture and stir until the sauce is blended. Bring the mixture to a simmer and then reduce the heat to medium-low. Cover and continue cooking until the beans and potatoes are tender, stirring occasionally, about 40 minutes. Stir in the seasoned salt, kosher salt, lemon pepper and black pepper. Continue cooking, uncovered, until the sauce coats the spoon and is reduced slightly, stirring often, about 3 minutes. Add the cilantro. Transfer the mixture to a deep bowl and serve.

Do-ahead tip: This dish can be made up to 2 days ahead. Cool, then cover and refrigerate. Rewarm in a covered sauté pan over medium heat, until heated through, stirring often and adding water by the tablespoon to loosen the sauce as needed.

- 3 tablespoons olive oil
- 1 tablespoon unsalted butter
- 8 ounces lean ground beef
- 1 large onion, chopped (about 2 cups)
- 4 ounces white mushrooms, thickly sliced (about 1½ cups)
- 3 tablespoons minced garlic
- 2 pounds fresh green beans cut into 1½-inch lengths
- 2 cups vegetable broth or water
- 3 medium russet potatoes, peeled and cut into 1-inch chunks
- 1 14½-ounce can Italian-style stewed tomatoes, chopped (with juices)
- 1 6-ounce can tomato paste
- 1½ teaspoons seasoned salt (see *Pantry and Produce*)
- 1 teaspoon kosher salt
- 1 teaspoon lemon pepper
- ½ teaspoon freshly ground black pepper
- 1 cup chopped fresh cilantro

MEATS: greek burgers with baby arugula and feta chesse

For a new twist on the Greek burger, I mix lamb and pork together. Pork gives the patty texture and helps keep it moist and succulent. The heat from the Aleppo pepper and the smokiness from the cumin add another interesting layer of flavor. The burger is further enhanced with the delicious combination of tangy feta cheese and sun-dried tomatoes. All of these flavors complement each other so well. Instead of burgers, you can shape the meat mixture into kebabs on flat metal skewers and grill them. This style of preparation is known in Morocco as brochettes de kefta.

MAKES 8 BURGERS

Prepare the patties: Mix all the ingredients in a large bowl. Form the mixture into eight 1-inch-thick patties. Place the patties on a baking sheet, then cover and refrigerate for 30 minutes.

Do-ahead tip: The patties can be wrapped individually and refrigerated overnight or frozen in an airtight container for up to 1 month. Thaw the patties in the refrigerator for 24 hours before using.

Prepare the burgers: Prepare the barbecue (medium-high heat). Rub the grill rack with the oil. Grill the patties until they are nicely charred on the outside, turning once, about 5 minutes per side for medium-rare. Grill the hamburger buns until warm and toasty, about 30 seconds.

Meanwhile, toss the arugula, feta cheese, sun-dried tomatoes and red onions in a small bowl. Spread some sauce on each bun bottom, top with a cooked patty, then with the arugula mixture. Spread more sauce on each bun top and set the tops on the burgers. Serve immediately.

Zov's kitchen note: Beef or turkey can stand in for the lamb. Serve with Summer Corn Salad (page 160) or Bistro Potato Gratin (page 254).

- 1 pound ground lamb
- 1 pound ground pork
- 1 onion, finely grated (about 1 cup)
- 2 tablespoons Aleppo pepper (see *Pantry and Produce*)
- 1 tablespoon Dijon mustard
- 1 tablespoon dried oregano
- 1 tablespoon granulated garlic
- 1 tablespoon tomato paste
- 2 teaspoons ground cumin
- 1 teaspoon freshly ground black pepper
- 1 teaspoon ground coriander (see *Pantry and Produce*)
- 1 teaspoon kosher salt
- 1 teaspoon seasoned salt (see *Pantry and Produce*)
- 1 tablespoon olive oil
- 8 burger buns, split
- 3 cups (lightly packed) baby arugula leaves
- 1 cup crumbled feta cheese
- 1 cup drained sun-dried tomatoes (packed in oil), coarsely chopped
- ½ cup thinly sliced red onion
- Chile-Lime Chipotle Sauce (page 303)

MEATS: lamb stew with swiss chard

Aleppo pepper, with its mild heat and deep flavor, adds a nice twist to stews and soups. I also love Swiss chard and use it in many of my dishes. Packed with vitamins, this leafy vegetable is a member of the beet family (but without the beets), and is widely used in Middle Eastern cooking. The leafy portion is always green, while the stalk can be white, yellow or red. This delicious stew is so comforting and easy to make. Try it over couscous, Jasmine Rice Pilaf (page 262) or noodles. If you own a slow cooker, this is the perfect time to pull it out.

SERVES 6

Pat the lamb dry with paper towels, then sprinkle with salt and pepper. Toss the lamb in a large bowl with the flour to coat lightly. Heat the oil in a heavy, large pot over high heat. Working in 2 batches, add the lamb to the pot and cook just until lightly brown, about 7 minutes for each batch. Using a slotted spoon, transfer the lamb to a bowl.

Add the onions, ginger, garlic, cumin, cayenne, coriander and Aleppo pepper to the same pot. Stir until the onions soften, about 6 minutes. Stir in the beef broth, scraping up the brown bits from the bottom of the pot. Return the lamb and any accumulated juices to the pot. Bring the mixture to a simmer. Decrease the heat to medium-low. Cover partially and simmer very gently until the lamb is tender, stirring occasionally, about 1½ hours.

Add the Swiss chard and garbanzo beans to the stew. Simmer uncovered over medium heat until the liquid reduces and forms a sauce and the lamb is very tender, stirring occasionally, about 30 minutes.

Spoon the stew into bowls, top each with a dollop of Greek-style yogurt, and garnish with cilantro.

Do-ahead tip: The stew improves overnight. Refrigerate in an airtight container for up to 4 days. Rewarm in a covered pot over medium heat.

Zov's kitchen note: Wondra flour thickens the stew without a heavy flour taste. For extra intensity, add 1 cup of chopped cilantro or mint.

- 2½ pounds lean boneless leg of lamb, cut into 1½-inch cubes
- 1½ teaspoons salt
- ½ teaspoon freshly ground black pepper
- 3 tablespoons Wondra flour
- ¼ cup olive oil
- 1 pound yellow onions, chopped
- 3 tablespoons minced peeled fresh ginger
- 2 tablespoons minced garlic
- 2 teaspoons ground cumin
- 1 teaspoon cayenne pepper
- 1 teaspoon ground coriander (see *Pantry and Produce*)
- ½ teaspoon Aleppo pepper (see *Pantry and Produce*)
- 7½ cups beef broth
- 1 bunch Swiss chard, coarsely chopped
- 3 cups canned garbanzo beans, rinsed and drained
- 2 cups Greek-style yogurt, for topping
- Cilantro leaves, for garnish

MEATS spicy ground meat kebabs

These delectable kebabs are molded by hand around flat metal skewers and cooked over an open fire or gas grill. They are typical fare in Eastern European countries. Serve them right off the grill with warm pita bread and rice pilaf. Roasted Red Pepper and Eggplant Sauce (page 311) on the side adds zing, while creamy yogurt tames the heat. Look for 8-inch flat-sided metal skewers at cookware stores. By using flat skewers, the meat won't turn or slip as it does with conventional ones. The meat mixture needs to chill for two hours before grilling, so start the recipe ahead.

SERVES 6 (MAKES 12 KEBABS)

Using your hands, gently mix the beef, lamb, pork, onion, garlic, soda water, Aleppo pepper, salt, black pepper, mint, thyme and cayenne pepper in a large bowl to blend. Cover and refrigerate for 2 hours to allow the flavors to blend.

Knead the mixture once again. Press 1/3 cup of the meat mixture (about 3½ ounces) into a 4-inch-long sausage around the center of 1 metal skewer. Repeat to form 12 kebabs total.

Do-ahead tip: The kebabs can be formed 2 days ahead. Arrange the kebabs on a baking sheet, cover with plastic wrap and refrigerate.

Preheat the barbecue (high heat) or a grill pan (medium-high heat). Lightly coat the kebabs with oil. Grill the kebabs until they are brown on all sides and cooked through, turning often, about 12 minutes. Serve immediately with the sauce, yogurt and warm pita bread.

Zov's kitchen note: You can omit the beef and just use pork and lamb, but I prefer using all three meats for a moist and tender result. Adding soda water to the kebab mixture produces lighter, fluffier kebabs.

½ pound ground beef
½ pound ground lamb
½ pound ground pork
1 yellow onion, grated (about 1 cup)
3 garlic cloves, minced
¼ cup soda water
1 tablespoon Aleppo pepper or hot paprika (see *Pantry and Produce*)
1 teaspoon kosher salt
1 teaspoon freshly ground black pepper
¾ teaspoon dried mint
¾ teaspoon dried thyme
½ teaspoon cayenne pepper
Canola oil
Roasted Red Pepper and Eggplant Sauce (page 311)
1 cup Greek-style yogurt or sour cream
Pita bread, warmed

Special equipment:
twelve flat metal skewers

MEATS: pork tenderloin with sour cherry sauce

This is one of the most popular entrées at our restaurant. The pork needs to marinate in the brine for four hours, so plan ahead. Serve with Ultimate Risotto (page 280) or Butternut Squash Bread Pudding (page 260).

SERVES 6 TO 8

Squeeze the juice of the lemon into a 2 1/2-gallon resealable plastic bag. Add the next 8 ingredients, then the water and stir to dissolve the sugar. Add the pork, then seal the bag and marinate for at least 4 hours or overnight.

Preheat the oven to 350°F. Remove the pork from the brine and pat dry. Sprinkle the Moroccan spice mix all over the pork tenderloins. Heat 3 tablespoons of canola oil in a heavy large skillet over medium-high heat. Add the pork and cook until brown on all sides, about 6 minutes. Transfer the pork to a baking sheet and roast in the oven until a meat thermometer registers 160°F for medium doneness, about 20 minutes.

Let the pork rest at room temperature for 5 minutes, then thinly slice the tenderloins crosswise. Serve with sour cherry sauce.

Sour Cherry Sauce: Heat the oil in a heavy large saucepan over medium heat. Add the garlic and shallots, and sauté until tender, about 2 minutes. Stir in the Marsala. Increase the heat to medium-high and simmer for 2 minutes. Stir in three-fourths of the cherries and all of the broth. Bring the mixture to a boil. Reduce the heat to medium and simmer uncovered until the cooking liquid reduces by half and thickens slightly, stirring occasionally, about 35 minutes. Stir in the remaining cherries. Remove from the heat. Stir in the butter one piece at a time until well blended. Season the sauce to taste with salt and pepper. *Serves 6 to 8.*

Moroccan Spice Mix: Stir all the ingredients in a small bowl to blend. Transfer to an airtight container and freeze indefinitely. *Makes 3/4 cup.*

Zov's kitchen note: Sprinkle extra spice mix on soups, salads, seafood or chicken. You can also use the brine for turkey, chicken or other cuts of pork. Instead of slices, try making pork kebabs. Simply remove the tenderloins from the brine, pat dry, cut into 1 1/2-inch cubes, thread onto skewers and grill. Serve with Couscous with Preserved Lemon (page 250).

Brine
- 1 lemon, cut in half
- 1/2 cup kosher salt
- 1/2 cup granulated sugar
- 1/4 cup whole garlic cloves, peeled
- 3 bay leaves
- 1 teaspoon whole black peppercorns
- 1/2 teaspoon dried crushed hot red pepper
- 4 rosemary sprigs
- 4 thyme sprigs
- 3 quarts cold water
- 2 pork tenderloins (each 1 1/2 pounds)
- 2 tablespoons Moroccan Spice Mix
- 3 tablespoons canola oil

Sour cherry sauce
- 2 tablespoons olive oil
- 2 tablespoons minced garlic
- 3 tablespoons minced shallots
- 1 1/2 cups Marsala wine
- 1 pound fresh or frozen pitted tart cherries, thawed if frozen
- 1 3/4 cups beef stock or broth (from one 14-ounce can)
- 4 tablespoons (1/2 stick) chilled unsalted butter, cut into 1/2-inch pieces

Moroccan spice mix
- 3 tablespoons paprika
- 2 tablespoons dried thyme
- 2 tablespoons ground cumin
- 1 tablespoon grated nutmeg
- 1 tablespoon ground black pepper
- 1 tablespoon ground ginger
- 2 teaspoons ground cinnamon
- 1 teaspoon cayenne pepper
- 1 teaspoon ground allspice

MEATS meat and potato casserole

This is one of those hearty, warming dinners that you will crave on a rainy day or whenever you are really hungry. I get the most out of every ingredient by layering flavors, which intensify even more the second day. Round out the menu with Jasmine Rice Pilaf (page 262) and sautéed green beans. If you're feeling adventurous, substitute eggplant for the potatoes. For a smaller portion, divided the recipe in half and bake in an oval dish.

SERVES 6 TO 8

Preheat the oven to 375°F. Coat a 13x9x2-inch baking dish with 1 tablespoon of the oil. Toss the bread cubes with the half-and-half in a large bowl to coat. Set aside until the bread is very soft and all of the liquid is absorbed, about 10 minutes. Puree the onion pieces and garlic in a food processor.

Add the pureed onion and garlic, and then the next 6 ingredients to the bread mixture. Using your hands, mix just until thoroughly blended.

Peel the potatoes and slice into ¼-inch-thick rounds. To prevent the slices from discoloring, submerge them in cold water until you assemble the dish.

Lay 1 potato slice on the work surface. Press 1½ ounces of the meat mixture atop the potato slice to cover. Top with another potato slice, then more meat mixture. Repeat stacking the potatoes and meat mixture until you have about 4 layers of each. Lay the stack on its side in the baking dish. Repeat stacking the meat and potatoes and lining the baking dish with the stacks, forming 3 rows total (each row will consist of about 13 to 15 slices of potatoes stacked between 13 to 15 meat patties).

Brush the tops with the remaining 1 tablespoon of olive oil. Bake uncovered until juices form, about 30 minutes. Remove the dish from the oven and carefully pour off the juices and oil that have accumulated (you should have about ½ cup of juices and oil). Return the dish to the oven and continue baking until the tops of the potatoes and meat are golden brown, about 10 minutes.

Meanwhile, whisk the water and tomato paste in a small saucepan to blend and bring to boil over high heat. Pour the tomato sauce over the meat and potatoes. Cover the dish tightly with aluminum foil. Bake until the potatoes are tender and cooked all the way through, about 30 minutes. Uncover and continue baking until the sauce reduces by about one-third, about 40 minutes. Let stand 10 minutes to cool slightly, then serve.

Do-ahead tip: Cover and refrigerate any leftover casserole for up to 2 days. Rewarm in the microwave until heated through.

2 tablespoons olive oil, divided
1⅔ cups (about 2½ ounces) cubed day-old white bread
½ cup half-and-half
1 large onion, peeled and quartered
3 large garlic cloves, peeled
2½ pounds ground beef (22% fat)
½ cup chopped fresh flat-leaf parsley
3 large eggs
2½ teaspoons freshly ground black pepper
2½ teaspoons kosher salt
1½ teaspoons seasoned salt (see *Pantry and Produce*)
6 large russet potatoes (8 to 10 ounces each)
3 cups water
1 6-ounce can tomato paste

MEATS: tamarind pork kebabs with ginger and soy

Tamarind is a concentrate that is extracted from the tamarind pod. Its sweet-and-sour flavor brightens up stews, sauces and marinades. It's also used as a glaze for grilled foods. Serve these kebabs with fruit chutney and cooling Tzatziki Sauce (page 303) on the side. Cabbage Salad with Bulgur (page 148) or skewers of zucchini, red pepper and onion are also nice accompaniments.

SERVES 6

Stir the coriander seeds in a heavy, small sauté pan over medium-low heat until fragrant and toasty, about 5 minutes. Transfer the seeds to a clean coffee grinder or mortar and coarsely grind them.

Whisk the ground coriander, ¼ cup of oil, lemon juice, ginger, garlic, soy sauce, tamarind, crushed red pepper and salt in a large bowl to blend. Stir in the cilantro. Add the pork and toss to coat with the marinade. Cover and refrigerate for 1 hour.

Spray the barbecue or indoor grill pan with grilling nonstick spray and then preheat the barbecue (medium-high heat). Pour off the marinade from the pork and pat the pork with paper towels to remove any excess marinade. Thread the pork on 6 long metal skewers, leaving only a slight space between each piece. Lightly brush the pork with oil. Grill the pork, turning occasionally, until it is cooked through, tender, and lightly charred all over, about 14 minutes. Serve with tzatziki.

Zov's kitchen note: Tamarind paste, also called tamarind concentrate, is sold at Indian and Middle Eastern markets. Try the same seasonings and technique with other meats as well. If you are using wooden skewers, be sure to soak them in cold water for 30 minutes to prevent them from burning.

- 2 teaspoons coriander seeds (see *Pantry and Produce*)
- ¼ cup olive oil, plus more for brushing
- 2 tablespoons fresh lemon juice
- 2 tablespoons grated peeled fresh ginger
- 2 tablespoons minced garlic
- 2 tablespoons soy sauce
- 2 tablespoons tamarind paste (see note)
- 1 teaspoon dried crushed hot red pepper
- 1 teaspoon kosher salt
- ⅓ cup chopped fresh cilantro
- 2½ pounds pork tenderloin, cut into 2-inch cubes
- Grilling nonstick spray
- Tzatziki Sauce (page 303)

MEATS zov's favorite meatloaf

Too often meatloaf is soggy and ends up sitting in an unappealing pool of grease. Not my version. I bake my meatloaf on a rack set on top of a baking sheet, instead of a loaf pan, so a delicious golden brown crust forms on all sides. Lining the baking sheet with foil makes cleaning up a snap. Top with Crispy Onion Rings (page 34) and serve Creamy Mashed Potatoes (page 266) on the side.

SERVES 6

Position the oven rack in the middle of the oven, then preheat the oven to 350°F. Line a heavy, large baking sheet with foil. Place a cooling rack on top of the baking sheet. Spray the cooling rack with nonstick cooking spray.

Toss the bread cubes with the half-and-half in a large bowl to coat. Set aside until the bread is very soft and all of the liquid is absorbed, about 10 minutes. Add the ground beef, parsley, shallots, Parmesan, tomato paste, eggs, oregano, thyme, pepper, salt, rosemary and seasoned salt. Using your hands, mix just until all of the ingredients are thoroughly blended, being careful not to overmix, which may cause the meatloaf to be tough.

Form the meat mixture into a 9x4-inch oval loaf. Set the meatloaf atop the prepared rack on the baking sheet. Bake for about 1 hour or until an instant-read meat thermometer registers 160°F when inserted into the center of the meatloaf. Don't worry if it looks pink; the tomato paste gives it this color. Let the meatloaf rest for 15 minutes (this will help keep the meatloaf moist). Using a large, sharp knife, cut the meatloaf into thick slices, then transfer the slices to plates. Spoon the mushroom sauce over the meatloaf and serve.

Mushroom sauce: Heat 2 tablespoons of butter with the oil in a large sauté pan over medium-high heat. Add the mushrooms and cook until browned, stirring occasionally, about 5 minutes. Add the shallots, garlic and oregano and sauté until the shallots are tender and the garlic is fragrant, about 1 minute. Add the flour and mix well for 1 minute. Slowly add the hot broth, whisking until incorporated. Bring to a simmer. Continue to simmer for 2 minutes or until the sauce has thickened. Add the black pepper, salt and seasoned salt. Add the remaining 2 tablespoons butter and stir until well incorporated. The sauce should have the consistency of a creamy soup. Makes 3 cups.

Zov's kitchen note: A mix of wild mushrooms gives this sauce an earthy flavor. Avoid using common white mushrooms since they tend to release a lot of liquid when sautéed, which prevents them from browning properly.

Nonstick cooking spray
1 cup (about 1½ ounces) cubed day-old white bread
⅓ cup half-and-half
1½ pounds ground beef (22% fat)
⅓ cup chopped fresh flat-leaf parsley
⅓ cup finely chopped shallots
⅓ cup grated Parmesan cheese
⅓ cup tomato paste
2 whole large eggs
1 tablespoon chopped fresh oregano
2 teaspoons chopped fresh thyme
1½ teaspoons freshly ground black pepper
1½ teaspoons salt
1 teaspoon chopped fresh rosemary
1 teaspoon seasoned salt (see *Pantry and Produce*)

Mushroom sauce
4 tablespoons unsalted butter, divided
1 tablespoon olive oil
12 ounces fresh assorted mushrooms (such as cremini, enoki and stemmed shiitake), sliced
3 tablespoons finely chopped shallots
2 teaspoons finely chopped garlic
1 teaspoon chopped fresh oregano
2 tablespoons all-purpose flour
2 cups beef broth, heated
¼ teaspoon freshly ground black pepper
¼ teaspoon salt
¼ teaspoon seasoned salt

POULTRY

asian noodle chicken salad with toasted sesame seeds **226**

grilled ginger–lime chicken thighs with harissa **228**

fusilli pasta salad with rotisserie chicken **230**

greek-style chicken kebabs with lemon and oregano **232**

harisah (pelted wheat porridge with chicken) **234**

oven-fried parmesan chicken fingers **236**

chicken tagine with currants **238**

parmesan-crusted chicken salad with poached pears and candied walnuts **240**

spaghetti with turkey meatballs and marinara sauce **242**

POULTRY

After a long day of work, picking the kids up from school, dropping one off at soccer practice and the other at ballet (and remembering to pick them up), the last thing on your mind is dinner. The minute you walk in the door, the kids are chasing the dog around the kitchen, the phone is ringing off the hook and the dryer is buzzing. As you stand there, trying to remember where you left your brain, and who that other kid is running around with your two children, someone from down the hall yells, "Hey, Mom, what's for dinner?" Dinner? You hadn't even thought that far. | Quick, simple, kid-friendly, nutritious: That is your dinner challenge, and that is where the versatility of poultry comes in. Poultry is the original convenience food, low in fat and delicious whether grilled, poached, pan-seared or baked. This chapter is filled with amazingly delightful recipes like Asian Noodle Chicken Salad with Toasted Sesame Seeds or Greek-Style Chicken Kebabs with Lemon and Oregano. Even on your most hectic evenings, do not fear, for a recipe is near. Oven-Fried Parmesan Chicken Fingers is the quintessential kid-friendly dinner. It is quick and simple, and you won't be hovering over a pan of hot oil. With this recipe, and many more, you will be able to get the kids to the table, do the laundry, and perhaps even take a moment to breathe. |

POULTRY: asian noodle chicken salad with toasted sesame seeds

If you crave Asian chicken salad like I do, this is a recipe you'll want to keep. It's quick and delicious — especially if you use a roast chicken from the supermarket deli — and great for a luncheon since most of the ingredients can be prepared a day ahead. But what makes it really delightful is the balance among the crunchiness of the cabbage and peanuts, the sweetness of the red pepper and the spiciness of the chili sauce in the vinaigrette. The flavors work together beautifully. It is one of my all-time favorites. Toss with vinaigrette just before serving.

SERVES 6 TO 8

Cook the pasta in a large pot of boiling water for just 1½ minutes (do not cook any longer). Drain the pasta in a colander, but do not rinse it. Toss the pasta in the colander with the olive oil to coat. Scatter the pasta over a large baking sheet and set aside to cool.

Stir the sesame seeds in a heavy, small sauté pan over medium heat until they are golden, about 5 minutes. Set aside to cool.

Do-ahead tip: The pasta can be cooked up to 2 days ahead; store in an airtight container and refrigerate. Store the sesame seeds in an airtight container at room temperature for up to 2 weeks.

Toss the cooled pasta, toasted sesame seeds, cabbage, lettuce, chicken, celery, bell pepper, cucumber, red onion, green onions, cilantro and mint in a large bowl with enough vinaigrette (about 1½ cups) to coat. Mound the salad on 6 to 8 plates or in a large serving bowl. Sprinkle with the peanuts and serve with lime wedges.

Zov's kitchen note: Add 1 grated carrot for color, if desired. It might seem like there is a lot of salad, but the greens usually shrink after the dressing is added. I like to save half of the salad without the dressing in my refrigerator and snack on it when I'm hungry. Drizzle with dressing right before eating. The cut vegetables will keep up to 3 days.

- 8 ounces angel hair pasta, broken in thirds
- 2 tablespoons extra-virgin olive oil
- ¼ cup sesame seeds
- ½ head Napa cabbage, thinly sliced
- ½ head romaine lettuce, thinly sliced
- 3 cups pulled roasted chicken meat (from 1 whole rotisserie chicken)
- 2 celery stalks, thinly sliced diagonally (about 1 cup)
- 1 red bell pepper, seeded and cut into matchstick-size strips
- ½ English hothouse cucumber, halved, seeded and thinly sliced into half-moons
- ½ small red onion, thinly sliced (about ½ cup)
- 5 green onions, sliced diagonally (about 1 cup)
- 1 cup coarsely chopped cilantro leaves
- 1 cup fresh mint leaves, torn by hand
- Ginger-Sesame Vinaigrette (page 298)
- ¾ cup roasted peanuts, coarsely chopped
- 6 to 8 lime wedges

POULTRY: grilled ginger-lime chicken thighs with harissa

Chicken thighs are economical, moist, tender — and one of my favorite ways to eat poultry. The meat simply has more flavor than chicken breasts. I prefer the bone-in variety over boneless because it cooks quickly and produces the juiciest results. Harissa in the marinade takes this dish to another level. The end result is not only healthful, but it's surprisingly exotic and delicious. Serve with Beet Salad with Watercress (page 158), Bulgur Pilaf with Tomatoes (page 284) or Cauliflower and Broccoli Salad (page 162). Couscous with Preserved Lemon (page 250) and a simple green salad would also be nice accompaniments.

SERVES 6

Spray the barbecue or grill pan with grilling nonstick spray, then preheat the barbecue (high heat). Preheat the oven to 400°F. Remove all of the gristle and fat from the chicken thighs and set aside.

Puree the lime juice, ginger, green onions, harissa, garlic, shallots, oil, salt and pepper in a food processor until it forms a loose paste. Toss the chicken with half of the paste (about ½ cup) in a large bowl to coat completely.

Do-ahead tip: Cover and refrigerate the paste for up to 4 hours.

Grill the chicken thighs until grill marks appear but the thighs are still raw in the center, about 2 minutes per side. Return the chicken to the same bowl and toss with the remaining paste, making sure it is completely coated. Arrange the chicken thighs, skin side up, on a heavy, large baking sheet and roast them in the oven until tender and cooked through, about 35 minutes.

Transfer the chicken to a platter and garnish with cilantro leaves and lime wedges. Serve immediately.

Zov's kitchen note: Do not marinate the chicken for more than 4 hours in the lime mixture or the chicken will get too acidic. Leaving the skin on will keep it moist. If you're concerned about fat, you can always take the skin off after grilling. Just before serving, squeeze lime on the chicken to refresh the taste. Use leftovers in pulled chicken sandwiches. Pile chicken onto crispy baguettes and top with tomatoes, avocados, Swiss cheese and lettuce.

Grilling nonstick spray
8 to 10 chicken thighs with skin and bones (about 3 pounds)
¼ cup plus 2 tablespoons fresh lime juice
¼ cup grated peeled fresh ginger
4 green onions, finely chopped (about 1 cup)
3 tablespoons Harissa (page 310)
2 tablespoons minced garlic
2 tablespoons minced shallots
2 tablespoons olive oil
1½ tablespoons kosher salt
1 teaspoon freshly ground black pepper
Cilantro leaves, for garnish
Lime wedges, for garnish

POULTRY: fusilli pasta salad with rotisserie chicken

Here's a satisfying pasta salad that's easy to make and travels well. Fresh vegetables add crunch, giving this dish extra texture and taste. Its crowd-pleasing flavor makes it a natural for picnics, buffets and showers. I find it's especially nice at outdoor gatherings.

SERVES 10 TO 12

Make the vinaigrette: Whisk all the ingredients together in a bowl (do not worry about blending the oil and vinegar). Set the vinaigrette aside.

Prepare the salad: Bring a large pot of salted water to a boil over high heat. Add the green beans and cook just until they turn bright green, about 1 minute. Immediately transfer the green beans to a large bowl of ice water and set aside just until they are cool. (Reserve the boiling salted water.) Drain the beans and pat completely dry.

Meanwhile, return the salted water to a boil. Add the pasta and cook until tender but still firm to the bite, stirring occasionally, about 8 minutes. Add the corn kernels, then drain the pasta and corn and transfer them to a large bowl (do not rinse). Toss the pasta and corn with the oil, then cool to room temperature.

Toss the cooled pasta and corn with the green beans, chicken, red pepper, zucchini, celery, green onions, red onion, carrot and mint.

Do–ahead tip: At this point, the pasta salad and vinaigrette can be covered separately and refrigerated for up to 4 hours. Bring the vinaigrette to room temperature before continuing.

Toss the pasta salad with the vinaigrette to coat. Transfer the salad to a serving bowl or platter, then top with the teardrop tomatoes and parsley.

Zov's kitchen note: This recipe makes great use of leftover chicken. If you don't have fresh corn, you can use frozen. The undressed salad can be prepared up to 2 days ahead, but once you add the vinaigrette, it should be eaten within a day.

Vinaigrette

¾ cup drained sun-dried tomatoes (packed in oil), finely chopped
½ cup olive oil
⅓ cup red wine vinegar
¼ cup finely chopped shallots
3 tablespoons capers, plus 2 tablespoons brine
3 tablespoons finely chopped fresh flat-leaf parsley
3 tablespoons fresh lemon juice
1 tablespoon Dijon mustard
1 tablespoon kosher salt
1 teaspoon dried crushed hot red pepper
1 teaspoon freshly ground black pepper

Salad

8 ounces green beans, trimmed and cut into 1-inch pieces
1 pound fusilli pasta
2 ears fresh corn, shucked (about 1½ cups of kernels)
2 tablespoons olive oil
1 pound roasted chicken meat (skin and bones discarded), hand pulled
1 red bell pepper, cut into matchstick-size strips
1 medium zucchini, thinly sliced diagonally (about 1 cup)
1 celery stalk, thinly sliced diagonally (about ½ cup)
3 green onions, thinly sliced diagonally (about ½ cup)
1 small red onion, sliced paper thin
1 large carrot, peeled and coarsely shredded
⅔ cup chopped fresh mint
Teardrop tomatoes, for garnish
Fresh flat-leaf parsley, for garnish

POULTRY

greek-style chicken kebabs with lemon and oregano

This dish has it all. It's quick, easy, economical, and most importantly, absolutely delicious! It's the kind of recipe that will impress your family. I like to serve the kebabs with pita bread and an assortment of condiments such as Tomato-Cucumber Relish (page 309), grilled onions and Greek-style yogurt. In the unlikely event that you'll have leftovers, try the chicken in a pita sandwich with chopped tomatoes, fresh mint, a sprinkle of sumac and a drizzle of yogurt sauce.

SERVES 4 TO 6

Mix the olive oil, oregano, lemon juice, garlic, shallots, salt, Aleppo pepper and black pepper in a large bowl to blend. Add the chicken and toss to coat. Cover and refrigerate for at least 1 hour and up to 2 days.

Preheat the barbecue (medium-high heat). Thread the chicken strips onto 12-inch-long metal skewers, folding each strip in half as you skewer it. Grill the kebabs, turning them as needed, until they are cooked through and evenly charred on all sides, about 12 minutes total. Serve immediately.

Zov's kitchen note: Chicken thighs are much more succulent and tender than chicken breasts or drumsticks. To make spearing the meat as easy as possible, purchase the boneless, skinless variety. If you are using wooden skewers, be sure to soak them in cold water for 30 minutes to prevent them from burning.

¼ cup olive oil

2 tablespoons chopped fresh oregano

2 tablespoons fresh lemon juice

1 tablespoon minced garlic

1 tablespoon minced shallots

2 teaspoons kosher salt

1 teaspoon Aleppo pepper (see *Pantry and Produce*)

½ teaspoon freshly ground black pepper

2 pounds boneless, skinless chicken thighs, halved lengthwise into 2-inch-wide strips

POULTRY: harisah (pelted wheat porridge with chicken)

Every region has a different name for this traditional Armenian porridge. Some call it kash, others call it harisah. And there is no final word on the recipe; every mother or grandmother makes a harisah that is believed to be the best, and each makes them differently. But one thing is certain: All versions are beloved by Armenians throughout the world. Here is my rendition, a low-calorie version that also makes a nutritious breakfast.

SERVES 8 TO 12

Remove any excess fat from the chicken. Rinse the chicken and remove the giblets, liver and neck. Combine the chicken, 4½ quarts of water, onions, bay leaves and 2 tablespoons of salt in an ovenproof 8-quart pot. Bring the water to a simmer over high heat, then reduce the heat to medium-low. Cover and simmer gently for 1½ hours.

Remove the pot from the heat. Using tongs, remove the chicken from the broth and place it on a baking sheet until cool enough to handle.

Preheat the oven to 325°F. Remove and discard the skin and bones from the chicken. Add the chicken meat and the pelted wheat to the broth. Bring the mixture to a simmer. Cover the pot and transfer to the oven. Cook, simmering, until the wheat and chicken are very tender, the broth is absorbed, and the mixture has thickened to the consistency of thick oatmeal, stirring occasionally, about 4 hours. Stir in 2 teaspoons cumin, 1 teaspoon Aleppo pepper, lemon pepper and seasoned salt. Cover and set aside for 30 minutes.

Remove the bay leaves. Using an electric mixer or whisk, mix the porridge in the pot until it is the consistency of cream of wheat, about 5 minutes. It should resemble a thick porridge; the wheat should be barely visible.

Do-ahead tip: At this point, the porridge can be refrigerated for up to 3 days. Transfer to four 1-quart containers, set the containers in a roasting pan and surround with ice. Set aside to cool, stirring occasionally. Cover the containers and store. Rewarm the porridge over medium heat, stirring often and adding more water to thin it to the desired consistency.

Melt the butter in a heavy, small saucepan over medium heat. Ladle the porridge into bowls, drizzle 1 tablespoon of the melted butter over each serving, sprinkle with ground cumin and Aleppo pepper, and serve.

Zov's kitchen note Don't worry if the porridge thickens the next day. The wheat expands quite a bit, exerting starches that absorb extra liquid. To thin it out, mix in more broth or water to reach the desired consistency.

- 1 whole chicken, 4½ to 5 pounds
- 4½ quarts water
- 2 large onions, coarsely chopped (about 3½ cups)
- 3 bay leaves
- 2 tablespoons kosher salt
- 1 24-ounce package pelted wheat (about 3¼ cups) (see *Pantry and Produce*)
- 2 teaspoons ground cumin, plus more for serving
- 1 teaspoon Aleppo pepper, plus more for serving (see *Pantry and Produce*)
- 1 teaspoon lemon pepper
- 1 teaspoon seasoned salt (see *Pantry and Produce*)
- 4 to 6 ounces (1 to 1½ sticks) unsalted butter

POULTRY | oven-fried parmesan chicken fingers

These chicken fingers are baked, not fried, for a healthier version of the kid-approved classic. They are delicious served with ranch dressing, and make a great snack, appetizer or main course. For a colorful presentation, place the chicken fingers in a serving bowl or on a platter and top with Italian parsley sprigs, lemon wedges or tomato wedges. Serve the dressing in a decorative bowl on the side.

SERVES 4 TO 6

Position the oven racks in the upper and lower thirds of the oven and preheat the oven to 475°F. Spray 2 large baking sheets with cooking spray.

Using the flat side of a meat pounder or a rolling pin, gently pound the chicken breasts between sheets of plastic wrap to about ½-inch thick. Cut the chicken lengthwise into 1-inch-wide strips.

Stir the butter, salt and pepper in a shallow dish. Mix the panko and Parmesan in another shallow dish. Working with 1 strip at a time, dip the chicken strips in butter, and then dredge them in the panko mixture, pressing firmly to help the crumbs adhere. Arrange the coated chicken strips in a single layer, spacing evenly apart on the prepared baking sheets.

Do-ahead tip: The chicken can be coated 3 hours ahead. Cover and refrigerate until ready to bake.

Bake the chicken strips, switching the position of the pans halfway through baking, until the chicken is golden and cooked through, about 15 minutes total. Serve warm or transfer the baking sheets to cooling racks and set aside until the chicken has cooled to room temperature (the crust will firm up as it cools). Serve ranch dressing alongside.

- Nonstick vegetable-oil cooking spray
- 4 skinless, boneless chicken breast halves (about 1½ pounds total)
- 6 tablespoons (¾ stick) unsalted butter, melted
- 1 teaspoon kosher salt
- ½ teaspoon freshly ground black pepper
- 2 cups panko (Japanese breadcrumbs) or crushed Ritz crackers
- 1 cup freshly grated Parmesan cheese
- Ranch dressing, for dipping

POULTRY: chicken tagine with currants

Of all my visits to Morocco throughout the years, one chicken tagine stands out in my mind, and I have re-created that dish here. This version is a little fiery, thanks to jalapeños, and calls for dark meat, which stays moist when simmered. To serve, fill a bowl with rice, top with chicken and then the sauce. I like to sprinkle the tagine with toasted almonds, but it's just as good without.

SERVES 4 TO 6

Preheat the oven to 350°F. Mix the flour, 1 teaspoon salt and ½ teaspoon pepper in a pie plate. Sprinkle the chicken thighs on both sides with 1½ teaspoons salt and 1¼ teaspoons pepper. Dredge the chicken in the flour and tap off any excess flour.

Heat 2 tablespoons of the oil in a large, ovenproof pot over medium heat. Working in 2 batches, cook the chicken until golden brown on all sides, about 8 minutes per batch. Transfer the chicken to a plate.

Do-ahead tip: The chicken can be browned at least 3 hours ahead and refrigerated.

Discard the oil from the pot and wipe the pot clean. Heat 2 tablespoons of the oil in the pot over medium heat. Add the onion, bell peppers, carrots, garlic, ginger and jalapeño. Sauté until the vegetables are tender, about 8 minutes. Mix in the currants, if using, cumin and turmeric. Stir in the fresh diced tomatoes, canned tomatoes and tomato paste. Add the chicken broth. Nestle the chicken thighs into the tomato mixture, cover with a tight-fitting lid and bake for 35 minutes. Uncover and continue to bake until the chicken falls away from the bones, about 15 minutes. Season the tagine to taste with salt and pepper.

Do-ahead tip: The tagine can be refrigerated for up to 2 days. Transfer to a casserole dish and set aside to cool, stirring occasionally. Cover and store. Rewarm the tagine in a covered pot over medium-low heat, stirring occasionally, until the chicken pieces are hot in the center.

Stir the parsley into the tagine. Transfer the chicken to plates, spoon the sauce over the chicken and serve.

Zov's kitchen note: An added bonus of this stew is that it tastes even better the next day. To intensify the flavor, try adding olives, Harissa (page 310) and Preserved Lemons (page 296) or lemon zest.

- ½ cup all-purpose flour
- 2½ teaspoons kosher salt, divided
- 1¾ teaspoons freshly ground black pepper, divided
- 12 chicken thighs with skin and bone, excess skin and fat trimmed
- 4 tablespoons canola oil, divided
- 1 large onion, thinly sliced (about 1¾ cups)
- 1 red bell pepper, thinly sliced
- 1 yellow bell pepper, thinly sliced
- 2 large carrots, peeled and sliced diagonally (about 1 cup)
- 3 tablespoons minced garlic
- 3 tablespoons minced peeled fresh ginger
- 1 jalapeño chile, minced with seeds
- ⅓ cup currants or raisins (optional)
- 1 tablespoon ground cumin
- 1 tablespoon ground turmeric (see *Pantry and Produce*)
- 5 ripe tomatoes, diced with seeds
- 1 15-ounce can diced tomatoes with juices
- 1 6-ounce can tomato paste
- 2 cups chicken broth
- ¾ cup chopped fresh flat-leaf parsley

POULTRY

parmesan-crusted chicken salad with poached pears and candied walnuts

Fresh greens, poached pears and candied walnuts come together in a bright-tasting salad that becomes a sophisticated main course with the addition of chicken paillard. The lovely balance of flavors will wow your guests, but no one will guess how easy it is to make. This basic recipe should be in every cook's repertoire. Choose tender greens such as mâche, Boston lettuce or red leaf lettuce, which are available year-round at farmers' markets. You can also use pre-packaged baby greens.

SERVES 4

Prepare the chicken: Blend the panko, Parmesan, parsley, ½ teaspoon of salt and ½ teaspoon of black pepper in a food processor until the mixture resembles coarse flour. Set aside.

Pound each chicken breast between 2 sheets of plastic wrap to about ¼-inch thickness. Sprinkle the chicken breasts with salt and pepper, then dip the chicken in the panko mixture to coat completely, patting firmly to adhere. Set aside.

Do-ahead tip: Wrap the coated chicken breasts with plastic wrap and refrigerate for up to 1 day.

Divide the oil and butter between 2 large frying pans set over medium-high heat and cook until the butter foams and sizzles. Lay 2 chicken pieces in a single layer in each pan and cook until they are brown on both sides and just cooked through, about 2 minutes per side. Transfer the chicken to a plate and tent with foil to keep warm.

Assemble the salad: Toss the lettuces with enough balsamic vinaigrette to coat and mound the lettuces high in the center of 4 plates. Sprinkle with the onion and surround with the tomatoes and poached pears. Slice the chicken breasts into strips and arrange them atop the salads. Coarsely crumble the cheese over the salads and top with the candied walnuts. Serve immediately.

Zov's kitchen note: We make our own candied walnuts at the restaurant, and it is a lengthy and tricky process. For the home cook, I recommend using store-bought candied walnuts or pecans, which are available at most supermarkets. Instead of teardrop tomatoes, you can use 2 plum (Roma) tomatoes, each cut into 8 wedges.

Chicken

- ⅔ cup panko (Japanese breadcrumbs)
- ½ cup freshly grated Parmesan cheese
- ¼ cup chopped fresh flat-leaf parsley
- ½ teaspoon kosher salt
- ½ teaspoon freshly ground black pepper
- 4 5- to 6-ounce boneless, skinless chicken breasts
- 4 tablespoons olive oil
- 4 tablespoons unsalted butter

Salad

- 8 ounces mixed baby lettuce leaves
- ¾ cup (about) Balsamic Vinaigrette (page 294)
- 1 small red onion, sliced paper-thin
- 1 cup teardrop tomatoes, cut in half
- 4 halved Simple Poached Pears (page 362), each quartered lengthwise
- 4 ounces goat cheese or blue cheese
- ¾ cup candied walnuts or candied pecans

POULTRY: spaghetti with turkey meatballs and marinara sauce

This is what I call a "feel-good favorite." It is like a big hug served in a bowl! Classic spaghetti noodles are tossed with a savory Marinara (page 306), and topped with meatballs and freshly grated Parmesan. Serve with a green salad and Parmesan Bruschetta (page 40).

SERVES 12

Make the meatballs: Preheat the oven to 450°F. Line 2 large, rimmed baking sheets with parchment paper. Crumble the ground turkey into a large bowl. Add the next 15 ingredients, including the crushed red pepper, if using. Using your hands, lightly work the mixture together, making sure not to overmix, which can cause the meatballs to be tough. Using about 2 ounces of the meat mixture for each, form the mixture into 2½-inch round meatballs, making about 36 meatballs total. As you form each meatball, dip your hands in cold water so that the mixture doesn't stick to your hands, and make sure you roll compact meatballs so they will not crack while baking. Set the meatballs on the prepared baking sheets, spacing evenly apart.

Bake the meatballs until they are golden brown and firm to the touch, rotating the pans from top to bottom halfway through, about 20 minutes.

Do-ahead tip: At this point, the meatballs can be refrigerated for up to 2 days in an airtight container or frozen for up to 2 months in a freezer bag. Cool the meatballs completely before storing.

Prepare the spaghetti and serve: Bring the marinara sauce to a simmer in an 8-quart pot. Add the meatballs and simmer for about 20 minutes.

Meanwhile, cook the spaghetti in another large pot of boiling salted water until tender but still firm to the bite, stirring often, about 8 minutes. Drain the pasta and return it to the pot. Spoon some of the sauce over the hot spaghetti and toss to coat. Transfer the pasta to plates. Top with the meatballs and more sauce, garnish with parsley and Parmesan, and serve.

Zov's kitchen note: If you are not a fan of ground turkey, substitute lean ground beef. To fry the meatballs, pour canola oil into one or two large frying pans to a depth of about ¾ inch. Heat the oil over medium-high heat until it sizzles when a piece of a meatball is dropped in. Working in batches, add the meatballs to the hot oil, leaving plenty of room between the meatballs and taking care not to overcrowd the pan. Fry the meatballs until they are browned all over and cooked through.

- 3 pounds ground turkey
- 2 cups panko (Japanese breadcrumbs)
- 1 6-ounce can tomato paste
- 4 large eggs
- ½ cup finely chopped fresh flat-leaf parsley, plus more for garnish
- ½ cup minced shallots
- ½ cup freshly grated Parmesan cheese, plus more for serving
- 2 tablespoons minced garlic
- 1 teaspoon chopped fresh thyme
- 1 teaspoon dried basil
- 1 teaspoon dried oregano
- 1 teaspoon finely chopped fresh rosemary
- 1 teaspoon freshly ground black pepper
- 1 teaspoon kosher salt
- 1 teaspoon seasoned salt (see *Pantry and Produce*)
- ½ teaspoon dried crushed hot red pepper (optional)
- Marinara Sauce (page 306)
- 2 pounds spaghetti

SIDE DISHES

sautéed swiss chard with lemon and pine nuts **248**

couscous with preserved lemon, aleppo pepper and pine nuts **250**

butter beans with pancetta and leeks **252**

bistro potato gratin **254**

cannelloni stuffed with cheese **256**

holiday creamed corn **258**

butternut squash parmesan bread pudding **260**

jasmine rice pilaf with vermicelli **262**

creamy angel hair pasta with tomatoes and gorgonzola cheese **264**

creamy mashed potatoes **266**

cheese enchiladas **268**

lentil patties with tomato and cucumber **270**

garlic roasted cauliflower with parsley and thyme **272**

tuscan eggplant parmesan **274**

spanish rice pilaf **278**

ultimate risotto with fresh peas, mushrooms and corn **280**

bulgur pilaf with tomatoes **284**

zov's silky macaroni and cheese **286**

SIDE DISHES

Too often sides are an afterthought. But a well-executed side dish can heighten the entire dining experience. In fact, many of the sides in this chapter can stand on their own, as I often integrate vegetables and starches into a single dish. Armenian and Mediterranean homes cooks are handy at creating integrated recipes that are bold, balanced and tasty. Dishes like Bulgur Pilaf with Tomatoes or Butter Beans with Pancetta and Leeks can double as light entrées, but won't steal the spotlight when served with a main course. | The side dishes in this chapter are especially wonderful when served family style. I always serve four to five sides at a large gathering, and just one or two with smaller groups. Guests enjoy having a choice. All of these recipes can be at least partially prepared ahead of time, so you'll have more time to enjoy with friends and family. | Of course, these recipes work for traditional every-night dinners too, and can be served with a variety of grilled, pan-fried or braised meats. The recipes in this chapter show just how easily sides can enliven any meal. |

SIDE DISHES: sautéed swiss chard with lemon and pine nuts

I love all parts of Swiss chard, from the crinkly leaves to the colorful, crunchy stems. A member of the beet family, its mild earthy flavor is similar to spinach, and it's also one of the world's healthiest foods, rich in iron and vitamins A and C. I love tossing the raw leaves into salads. Chopped raw stems are delicious, too, and can range in color from dark green and ruby red (the most common) to gold, pink and orange (the "rainbow" variety). If you can't find rainbow chard, red or green chard works just as well in this recipe. Serve with kebabs or any grilled protein.

SERVES 6

- 2 bunches rainbow Swiss chard (about 1½ pounds total), rinsed
- 3 tablespoons olive oil
- 2 tablespoons minced shallots
- 1 tablespoon minced garlic
- ½ teaspoon kosher salt
- ½ teaspoon freshly ground black pepper
- ¼ teaspoon dried crushed hot red pepper
- ½ lemon
- ½ cup toasted pine nuts

Trim the stem ends of the chard. Cut out the center vein and the stems from the chard leaves. Coarsely chop the leaves and stem pieces.

Heat the oil in a deep 12-inch frying pan over medium heat. Add the shallots and garlic and cook just until fragrant, about 1 minute. Add the chard stem slices and cook until they are crisp-tender, stirring often, about 8 minutes. Stir in the salt, black pepper and crushed red pepper. Add half of the chard leaves and toss to coat with the oil mixture. As the chard cooks and begins to wilt, add the remaining chard leaves. Continue cooking until the chard wilts but still has a vibrant green color, about 3 minutes. Make sure you do not overcook the chard. Drain any excess liquid, if necessary.

Transfer the chard to a serving platter and squeeze the lemon over the chard. Sprinkle with pine nuts and serve.

Zov's kitchen note: Swiss chard leaves are very tender and cook quickly. The stems, however, take longer to cook, so add them to the pan first, before adding the leaves. For extra flavor, sprinkle with ¼ cup of grated Parmesan cheese. Chard's slightly bitter undertone is particularly delicious in soups and stews. If you can't find it, spinach is a good substitute.

SIDE DISHES couscous with preserved lemon, aleppo pepper and pine nuts

This is a great all-purpose side dish that goes well with any protein. Apart from its versatility, this couscous is easy to make — the entire dish comes together in less than twenty minutes — and provides a refreshing (and delicious) break from ordinary rice or potatoes. Try it as a fluffy bed for stews and grilled kebabs.

SERVES 6

Melt the butter in a heavy, large saucepan over medium-high heat until it foams. Add the shallots and garlic and cook until the shallots are soft and translucent, about 2 minutes. Add the harissa, ginger, preserved lemons, Aleppo pepper, salt and pepper, then the broth. Bring to a boil. Remove the saucepan from the heat and stir the couscous into the broth mixture. Cover and let rest for 5 minutes, or until the couscous has absorbed the broth.

Fluff the couscous with a fork. Mix in the pine nuts and lemon zest. Divide the couscous among 6 plates or spoon it into a serving bowl. Garnish with the parsley and serve with the lemon wedges.

- 4 tablespoons unsalted butter (½ stick)
- 1 cup finely chopped shallots
- 1 tablespoon minced garlic
- 1 tablespoon Harissa (page 310)
- 1 tablespoon minced peeled fresh ginger
- 1 tablespoon minced Preserved Lemons (optional; page 296)
- 1 teaspoon Aleppo pepper (see *Pantry and Produce*)
- ½ teaspoon kosher salt
- ½ teaspoon freshly ground pepper
- 2 cups chicken broth or vegetable broth
- 2 cups couscous
- ½ cup toasted pine nuts
- 1 teaspoon grated lemon zest
- 2 tablespoons chopped fresh flat-leaf parsley
- 6 lemon wedges

SIDE DISHES: butter beans with pancetta and leeks

A few years back, my friend Cathy Thomas organized a fabulous culinary tour of Tuscany, and all I can remember from that trip are these beans. Our group consisted of 15 people, and to this day, whenever we all get together these beans are the topic of conversation. The recipe comes from a woman named Lucy, who converted a 500-year-old farmhouse into a bed-and-breakfast called Villa Lucia. Lucy used to live in Orange County, where she owned and operated two restaurants and a catering business, but once she discovered Tuscany on vacation she fell in love. Villa Lucia has many modern amenities, but the Old World charm is alive and well, especially in the kitchen. Lucy makes her own olive oil and plucks vegetables from her garden to make dinner for her guests. And then there are her prize-winning beans. So simple and delicious, they may be the best you have ever tasted. Serve alongside meat, fish or chicken, or with couscous as a vegetarian addition to a buffet.

SERVES 6

- 2 tablespoons extra-virgin olive oil
- 3 ounces pancetta, finely diced
- 3 fresh sage leaves, torn into pieces
- 3 large leeks (white and pale green parts only), halved lengthwise, thinly sliced crosswise (about 3 cups)
- ½ teaspoon dried crushed hot red pepper
- 2 14-ounce cans butter beans (fagioli bianchi di spagna; see note)
- 1 tomato, diced
- ½ teaspoon (about) kosher salt

Heat the oil in large sauté pan over medium-high heat. Add the pancetta and sage leaves and sauté until the pancetta is crisp and brown, about 4 minutes. Add the leeks and crushed red pepper. Sauté until the leeks start to soften, about 3 minutes. Reduce the heat to medium-low and cook gently until the leeks are tender but not brown, about 8 minutes. Add the beans with their liquid. Bring to a boil over high heat. Reduce the heat to medium-low and simmer gently until the juices reduce slightly, about 12 minutes. Add the tomatoes and cook just until they are warmed through, about 1 minute. Canned beans are packed in varying amounts of liquid. If the pan becomes too dry, add a little water or chicken broth to loosen the bean mixture. Season with ½ teaspoon salt and more crushed red pepper, if desired.

Do-ahead tip: The beans can be made up to 3 days ahead. Cool completely, then cover and refrigerate. Rewarm over medium heat, stirring often, until the beans are heated through.

Zov's kitchen note: I prefer not to use dry beans. Lucy used canned beans in her recipe and I think it's amazing just the way it is. A butter bean — named for its buttery texture — is a type of dried lima bean that is large, white and flat. You can find them at gourmet stores and many supermarkets. Cannellini beans are a good substitute. To wash leeks, rinse them under cold running water once they have been cut in half lengthwise. Make sure to wash away the grit and dirt between each layer.

I like to garnish this dish with fried sage leaves. It's easy to do: Heat some oil in a skillet and fry the whole leaves for a couple of minutes, until crisp.

SIDE DISHES: bistro potato gratin

Here's a great new way to spruce up ordinary potato gratin. Parmesan, thyme and shallots flavor this easy side dish, which pairs well with grilled fish, chicken or steak. Assemble ahead and bake just before serving.

SERVES 6

Preheat the oven to 375°F. Oil six 8-ounce ramekins and set the ramekins on a baking sheet. Place the potatoes in a large pot of water and bring to a boil. Boil the potatoes until they are soft but still holding their shape, about 15 minutes. Drain and transfer the potatoes to a baking sheet to cool.

Heat 2 tablespoons of olive oil in a heavy, small sauté pan over medium heat. Add the shallots and sauté until the shallots are tender, about 1 minute.

Toss the potatoes, shallots, cream, ½ cup of the Parmesan, parsley, thyme, salt and pepper in a large bowl until well combined. Spoon the potato mixture into the prepared ramekins, dividing equally.

Do-ahead tip: Each of the prepared ramekins can be covered and refrigerated for up to 2 days.

Bake until the tops are lightly browned, about 25 minutes. Remove the ramekins from the oven and sprinkle the remaining Parmesan over the potatoes, dividing equally. Continue baking until the cheese creates a crust on top, about 15 minutes.

Zov's kitchen note: If assembling ahead, submerge the peeled potatoes in cold water for about 30 minutes to prevent them from turning dark. If pressed for time, you can bake this dish the day before and reheat before serving. But for a fresher taste, I prefer to assemble in advance and bake as needed.

- 3½ pounds russet potatoes, peeled and cut into ½-inch cubes (see note)
- 2 tablespoons olive oil
- ½ cup minced shallots
- 2 cups heavy cream
- ½ cup plus 6 tablespoons freshly grated Parmesan cheese
- ⅓ cup chopped fresh flat-leaf parsley
- 1 tablespoon chopped fresh thyme
- 3½ teaspoons kosher salt
- 1 teaspoon freshly ground black pepper

SIDE DISHES: cannelloni stuffed with cheese

I have been making this dish for my family for more than a decade, and I'm including it here by popular demand. Few stuffed pastas are as adored as this traditional cannelloni, which is made with an Italian crepe-like pasta called crespelle and filled with three types of cheese. As it bakes, small chunks of mozzarella melt with ricotta and Parmesan to create an ooey-gooey goodness that's downright addictive.

SERVES 9

Make the tomato sauce: Heat the oil in a heavy medium saucepan over medium-high heat. Add the onions and garlic and sauté until the onions soften, about 5 minutes. Add the whole tomatoes with their juices and the next 7 ingredients. Stir in the water and smash the tomatoes with a fork. Bring to a boil, then reduce the heat to medium-low. Cover and simmer, stirring occasionally, until the tomatoes break down, about 1 hour.

Meanwhile, make the crespelle: Using an electric mixer, beat the flour, water, eggs and salt in a medium bowl just until a smooth batter forms. Strain the batter into another bowl. Let the batter stand for at least 30 minutes or cover and refrigerate for up to 1 day.

Heat an 8-inch nonstick skillet over medium heat. Spray the skillet with cooking spray. Pour 3 tablespoons of batter into the center. Quickly rotate the skillet to evenly coat the bottom. Cook until the top is dry but the bottom is not brown, about 1 minute. Loosen the crespella from the pan then slide onto a wire rack to cool (do not turn over to cook the second side). Repeat to form 18 crespelle total, stacking them between sheets of wax paper. Cool.

Make the cannelloni: Preheat the oven to 350°F. Spoon 1½ cups of the tomato sauce into each of two 13x9x2-inch baking dishes.

Mix the ricotta, mozzarella, ½ cup of Parmesan, eggs, parsley, salt and pepper in a large bowl until light and fluffy. Spoon about ¼ cup of the filling down the center of each crespella and roll up. Place 9 assembled cannelloni, seam side down, in a single layer in each dish. Spoon 1 cup of tomato sauce over the cannelloni in each dish then sprinkle with the remaining ½ cup of Parmesan.

Do-ahead tip: Store in an airtight container and refrigerate for up to 2 days or freeze for up to 1 month. Thaw in the refrigerator before baking.

Bake uncovered until the filling is hot and the sauce is bubbly, about 30 minutes, or 45 minutes if the cannelloni have been chilled.

Tomato sauce
- ⅓ cup olive oil
- 1 onion, finely chopped (about 1½ cups)
- 1 garlic clove, chopped
- 1 28-ounce can whole tomatoes (with juices)
- 1 6-ounce can tomato paste
- 2 tablespoons chopped fresh flat-leaf parsley
- 1 tablespoon kosher salt
- 1 tablespoon granulated sugar
- 1 teaspoon dried basil
- ¾ teaspoon dried oregano
- ¼ teaspoon freshly ground black pepper
- 1½ cups water

Crespelle
- 1½ cups all-purpose flour
- 1½ cups water
- 6 large eggs, at room temperature
- ¼ teaspoon kosher salt
- Nonstick vegetable-oil cooking spray

Cheese filling
- 2 16-ounce containers part-skim ricotta cheese
- 8 ounces mozzarella cheese, finely diced
- 1 cup freshly grated Parmesan cheese, divided
- 2 large eggs
- 1 tablespoon chopped fresh flat-leaf parsley
- 1 teaspoon kosher salt
- ¼ teaspoon freshly ground black pepper

SIDE DISHES: holiday creamed corn

For me, one of the highlights of Thanksgiving and Christmas is this rich and velvety creamed corn. Holiday dinners at the restaurant are never complete without it. In fact, it's the most requested recipe by our customers. So easy and delicious, it is a classic accompaniment to Christmas prime rib, but also goes well with steaks, grilled chicken or fish.

SERVES 8

Cook the corn kernels in a pot of boiling water until tender, about 3 minutes. Drain and set aside.

Melt the butter in a large saucepan over medium heat. Add the shallots and garlic and cook until softened, about 1 minute. Stir in the corn kernels, 2 tablespoons of the sugar, thyme, salt and pepper. Stir in the cream and 1 cup of the milk. Bring the mixture to a simmer, about 8 minutes. Simmer, stirring occasionally, until the corn is crisp-tender, about 5 minutes. Make sure the corn is cooked and tender before adding the cornstarch.

Mix the cornstarch and the remaining ½ cup of cold milk in a small bowl until it is dissolved. Pour the cornstarch mixture into the corn mixture and cook, stirring rapidly, until the mixture is thickened, about 2 minutes. Add more sugar to sweeten the creamed corn, if desired.

Transfer the creamed corn to a serving dish, garnish with parsley and serve.

Do-ahead tip: Cover and refrigerate for up to 2 days. Rewarm in a heavy, large saucepan, covered, over medium-low heat, stirring occasionally.

Zov's kitchen note: In place of fresh corn, you can substitute two 16-ounce packages of frozen corn. Wash the frozen corn under hot running water, drain it and proceed with the recipe.

It is imperative to use cold milk when diluting cornstarch. If the milk is not cold, the cornstarch will never dissolve and the creamed corn will be lumpy.

- 7 large ears of corn, kernels cut from cob, about 6 cups (or frozen, thawed; see note)
- 2 tablespoons unsalted butter
- 2 tablespoons minced shallots
- 1 garlic clove, minced
- 2 tablespoons (or more) granulated sugar
- 1 teaspoon minced fresh thyme
- 1½ teaspoons kosher salt
- ½ teaspoon freshly ground black pepper
- 1½ cups heavy cream
- 1½ cups cold whole milk, divided
- 2 tablespoons cornstarch
- Chopped flat-leaf parsley, for garnish

SIDE DISHES: butternut squash parmesan bread pudding

Mention bread pudding, and most people think dessert. But this savory side is just as delicious, and has the same luscious, creamy texture that makes the sweet version so appealing. The velvety texture comes from soaking the bread until all of the custard is absorbed. Butternut squash lends a sweet, nutty flavor, and is a perfect partner for Pork Tenderloin with Sour Cherry Sauce (page 214).

Serves 8

Preheat the oven to 450°F. Coat a 13x9x2-inch baking dish or eight 10-ounce ramekins with olive oil.

Peel, seed and cut the butternut squash into ½- to ¾-inch cubes (you should have about 3½ cups). Toss the squash in a large bowl with 1½ tablespoons olive oil to coat. Arrange the squash in a single layer on a heavy, large baking sheet. Roast for 10 minutes. Stir the shallots and remaining 1 tablespoon of oil into the squash. Continue roasting until the squash and shallots are just tender, about 7 minutes longer. Set aside. Decrease the oven temperature to 350°F.

Whisk together the eggs, chicken stock, cream and milk in a large bowl to blend. Stir in the cheddar cheese, Parmesan, thyme, kosher salt, seasoned salt and black pepper. Stir in the squash and cubed brioche. Let rest for 30 minutes, or until the bread soaks up most of the liquid. Transfer the mixture to the prepared baking dish or ramekins.

Do-ahead tip: At this point, the bread pudding can be covered and refrigerated for up to 1 day.

Place the baking dish or ramekins in a roasting pan that is at least 1½ to 2 inches high. Transfer the pan to the oven and add enough hot water to the roasting pan to come halfway up the sides of the baking dish or ramekins. Bake until the pudding is golden brown on top and just set in the middle, about 50 minutes if using ramekins and 55 minutes if using a baking dish. Using oven mitts, carefully remove the roasting pan from the oven. The water in the roasting pan will be very hot, so take caution not to spill any water on yourself or inside the bread pudding. Serve immediately.

Zov's kitchen note: The hot-water bath provides a constant, steady heat source and ensures even, slow cooking. After the pudding has baked, some of the water will have evaporated, but some will remain, so be careful not to tip the roasting pan when you take it out of the oven.

- 1⅓ pounds butternut squash
- 2½ tablespoons olive oil, divided
- ½ cup minced shallots
- 5 large eggs
- 2 cups chicken stock
- 2 cups heavy cream
- 2 cups whole milk
- 2 cups grated cheddar cheese
- ½ cup freshly grated Parmesan cheese
- 2 teaspoons dried thyme
- 1½ teaspoons kosher salt
- 1½ teaspoons seasoned salt (see *Pantry and Produce*)
- ½ teaspoon freshly ground black pepper
- 1 1-pound loaf of brioche bread, cut into ½-inch cubes

jasmine rice pilaf with vermicelli

Here's a rice pilaf that is so versatile it may soon become a staple in your kitchen. It is in mine. I pair it with grilled and roasted meats and fish, but I don't limit it to the role of side dish. It also makes a great Asian salad. Just toss in chopped celery, onions, cilantro, mushrooms, sugar snap peas, ginger or whatever vegetables you have on hand, and finish it with a dressing made from garlicky soy sauce and toasted sesame oil. Play around with the ingredients and see what happens.

SERVES 4 TO 6

½ cup vermicelli or fideo noodles
6 tablespoons (¾ stick) unsalted butter
1 cup jasmine rice (see note)
1 teaspoon salt
½ teaspoon ground black pepper
1¾ cups vegetable broth
¼ cup water

Preheat the oven to 350°F. Arrange the vermicelli on a heavy baking sheet. Bake the vermicelli until they are golden brown, stirring occasionally to ensure even browning, about 5 minutes. Set the vermicelli aside.

Melt the butter in a heavy, medium saucepan over medium-low heat. Stir in the rice and toasted vermicelli. Stir in the salt and pepper. Add the broth and water. Increase the heat to high and bring the liquid to a boil. Cover and simmer gently over low heat until the rice is tender and the liquid is absorbed, about 20 minutes (do not stir the rice as it cooks). Remove the saucepan from the heat. Fluff the rice with a large fork. Transfer to a bowl and serve.

Zov's Kitchen Note: Good pilaf begins with good-quality rice. Not only do I love the fragrant aroma of jasmine rice, it also works particularly well in pilafs because its long grains don't get sticky when cooked. Jasmine rice is sold at most supermarkets, but I recommend buying it at Asian markets, where it's likely to be fresher, less expensive and available in bulk. If you can't find it, use basmati or another long-grain white rice.

For a variation, rinse 10 ounces of frozen soybeans (edamame) and add them and ¼ cup of chopped fresh dill to the rice mixture just before adding the broth. The soybeans do not need to be thawed.

For a buffet, double the recipe and mound the pilaf on a platter and sprinkle with ⅓ cup each toasted pine nuts, diced dried apricots, golden raisins and toasted slivered almonds. Unsalted pistachios and dried currants also make good additions.

SIDE DISHES: creamy angel hair pasta with tomatoes and gorgonzola cheese

Gorgonzola is a rich, blue-veined cheese that is made from cow's milk. It has a strong, slightly pungent flavor and melts quickly, making it perfect for creamy pasta or vegetable sauces. This easy dish comes together in less than 20 minutes. For a more elegant meal, add large sautéed shrimp. You will definitely wow your guests.

SERVES 4 TO 6

Heat ¼ cup of the oil in a deep, large, nonstick frying pan over high heat. Add the garlic and shallots and cook until tender, about 1 minute. Reduce the heat to medium-low. Add the tomatoes, salt, black pepper and crushed red pepper and cook until the tomatoes break down, stirring often, about 12 minutes. Add the cheese and stir until most of it has melted, then add the cream and bring the sauce to a simmer.

Meanwhile, bring a large pot of salted water to a boil over high heat. Stir in the pasta and cook for just 1½ minutes to soften the pasta slightly. Using a pasta spoon with tines, lift the pasta from the boiling water and transfer it to a large bowl. Toss the pasta with the remaining 2 tablespoons of oil. Reserve the cooking liquid in the pot.

Add the Swiss chard and pasta to the sauce and toss well to coat, adding enough reserved cooking liquid to moisten as desired.

Divide the pasta among individual bowls, garnish with the basil leaves and serve immediately.

Zov's kitchen note: For extra flavor, chop some pancetta and sauté over low heat to render the fat. Then add the garlic and shallots. Any kind of blue cheese works in this recipe. Linguini can stand in for angel hair, but no matter what type of pasta you use, make sure to serve it immediately.

- ¼ cup plus 2 tablespoons olive oil
- 3 tablespoons minced garlic
- 2 tablespoons chopped shallots
- 1 28-ounce can whole tomatoes, drained and coarsely chopped
- 1 teaspoon kosher salt
- 1 teaspoon freshly ground black pepper
- ¾ teaspoon dried crushed hot red pepper
- 1½ cups crumbled Gorgonzola cheese (about 7 ounces)
- 1 cup heavy cream
- 10 ounces dried angel hair pasta or thin spaghetti
- 3 cups thinly sliced Swiss chard (center vein and stems removed)
- Basil leaves, for garnish

creamy mashed potatoes

Mashed potatoes are one of the easiest dishes to make but one of the hardest to perfect. The trick to that fluffy, creamy texture we all love is to promptly remove the potatoes from the water after they've cooked to avoid waterlogging. If the potatoes sit in water, they will release their starch, and in turn, become flavorless, slimy and mushy. Instead, drain the potatoes immediately after cooking and keep them almost dry until you're ready to mash with a ricer or food mill. Be careful not to overwork the potatoes, as this will result in that dreaded gluey texture. Follow these steps and you will never go wrong.

SERVES 4

2 pounds Yukon Gold potatoes, peeled and cut into 1-inch-thick slices
1 cup heavy cream
6 tablespoons unsalted butter, cut into pieces (¾ stick)
¼ cup freshly grated Parmesan cheese (optional)
1 teaspoon kosher salt
⅛ teaspoon ground white pepper

Place the potatoes in a colander and rinse under cold running water, tossing for 10 seconds. Transfer the potatoes to a deep pot, add enough water to cover the potatoes by 1 inch, and bring to a boil over high heat. Reduce the heat to medium and cook until the potatoes are tender, about 25 minutes.

Meanwhile, heat the cream and butter in a small saucepan over medium heat until the butter is melted. Keep warm.

Drain the potatoes and return them to the pot. Stir over low heat until the potatoes are thoroughly dried, about 1 minute. Add the Parmesan, if using, salt and pepper. Set a ricer or food mill over a large bowl and press the potatoes into the bowl. Gently fold in the warm cream mixture with a silicone spatula until the cream is absorbed and the potatoes are thick and creamy. Serve immediately.

Zov's kitchen note: If you can't find Yukon Golds, try russet potatoes. Potatoes with high starch content, like russets, yield the fluffiest, lightest texture.

Mashed potatoes are best eaten the day you make them, but if you have leftovers, dilute them with some milk when reheating. For best results, however, try to make them no earlier than a few hours before serving.

SIDE DISHES: cheese enchiladas

My talented restaurant staff taught me this recipe, and we've perfected it over the years. These meat-free enchiladas are the tastiest I've ever had, and so easy to prepare. It makes a delicious family meal when rounded out with Spanish Rice Pilaf (page 278).

SERVES 6

Make the ranchero sauce: Heat the oil in a heavy, large saucepan over medium-high heat. Add the onion, celery, bell pepper, garlic and jalapeño and sauté until the vegetables are soft and the onion is translucent, about 4 minutes. Add the flour and next 5 ingredients. Add the broth slowly to the flour mixture, stirring constantly until well blended. Add the tomatoes and simmer very gently, uncovered, over medium-low heat until the sauce thickens, stirring occasionally, about 45 minutes. Stir in the chopped cilantro.

Make the enchiladas: Preheat the oven to 450°F. Spray both sides of the tortillas with the cooking spray. Lay the tortillas in a single layer on 2 large baking sheets and bake until soft and pliable, about 5 minutes. Meanwhile, mix 5 cups of the Monterey Jack cheese with the cheddar cheese and green onions in a medium bowl until well blended.

Place a generous 1/2 cup of the cheese mixture down the center of each tortilla and roll up the tortilla tightly. Place the enchiladas side by side and seam side down in a 13x9x2-inch baking dish. Spoon the ranchero sauce over the enchiladas and top with the remaining 1 cup of Monterey Jack cheese.

Do-ahead tip: At this point, the enchiladas can be stored in an airtight container and frozen for up to 1 month or refrigerated for up to 2 days. Thaw the frozen enchiladas before baking.

Bake the enchiladas uncovered until the cheese melts and the sauce is bubbly, about 15 minutes, or longer for enchiladas that have been chilled.

Transfer the enchiladas to plates and spoon a dollop of sour cream on one side and the guacamole on the other. Garnish with the cilantro sprigs and serve.

Zov's kitchen note: For a heartier version, add shredded roast chicken or cooked bay shrimp to the filling along with chopped cilantro. You can also add a layer of refried beans in the center of the enchiladas before rolling.

If you have extra sauce, use it for Spanish omelets: Fill your omelets with grated cheddar and 1/4 cup of the sauce, then top with more sauce and cheese.

Ranchero sauce

- 1/4 cup canola oil
- 1 small onion, finely chopped (about 1 cup)
- 1 celery stalk, finely chopped (about 1/2 cup)
- 1/2 cup finely chopped green bell pepper
- 5 garlic cloves, minced
- 1 jalapeño chile, seeded and finely chopped
- 3 tablespoons all-purpose flour
- 3/4 teaspoon freshly ground black pepper
- 1/2 teaspoon dried marjoram
- 1/2 teaspoon dried oregano
- 1/2 teaspoon kosher salt
- 1/2 teaspoon seasoned salt (see *Pantry and Produce*)
- 2 cups chicken broth or water
- 1 28-ounce can whole tomatoes, crushed well (with juices)
- 1/2 cup chopped fresh cilantro

Enchiladas

- Nonstick vegetable-oil cooking spray
- 12 corn tortillas
- 6 cups grated Monterey Jack cheese, divided
- 3 cups grated sharp cheddar cheese
- 6 green onions, finely chopped (about 1 cup)
- 1 cup sour cream
- 1 cup Perfect Guacamole (page 64)
- Fresh cilantro sprigs, for garnish

SIDE DISHES | lentil patties with tomato and cucumber

These lentil patties are popular with everyone, and for good reason: This traditional Lenten dish is a delicious expression of Armenian cooking, with its subtle spices and versatility. My mother always made them around Easter time, but they're a great alternative to the usual vegetarian fare anytime of the year. Rich in protein and seasoned with cumin and Red Pepper Paste (page 305), these patties are a hearty appetizer when served with lemon wedges and Tomato-Cucumber Relish (page 309). When preparing the relish for this recipe, cut the tomatoes and cucumbers into big, chunky pieces. I also love these patties stuffed into pita bread with chopped tomatoes, green onions and parsley.

SERVES 6 TO 8

1 cup red lentils
3 cups water
1 cup fine-grade bulgur (#1) (see *Pantry and Produce*)
3 tablespoons unsalted butter
6 tablespoons olive oil
2 onions, finely chopped (about 3 cups)
2 tablespoons Red Pepper Paste (page 305)
1½ teaspoons kosher salt
1½ teaspoons ground cumin
1 teaspoon Aleppo pepper (see *Pantry and Produce*)
½ teaspoon freshly ground black pepper
¼ teaspoon cayenne pepper
½ cup chopped fresh flat-leaf parsley, divided
3 green onions, chopped (about ½ cup), divided
Tomato-Cucumber Relish (page 309)

Pick through the lentils to remove any stones or debris. Wash the lentils in a sieve under cold running water until the water drains clear.

Bring 3 cups of water to a boil in a heavy 2-quart pot over medium-high heat. Add the lentils and return the water to a boil. Reduce the heat and simmer until most of the water is absorbed and the lentils are soft and mushy, about 18 minutes.

Place the bulgur in a large bowl. Fold the hot lentil mixture into the bulgur. Cover until the bulgur softens, about 25 minutes.

In the meantime, melt the butter with the olive oil in a heavy, large skillet over medium-high heat. Add the onions and sauté until the onions are very soft and almost medium brown in color, about 10 minutes. Stir the onion mixture into the lentils and bulgur. Add the red pepper paste, salt, cumin, Aleppo pepper, black pepper and cayenne. Cover and let rest for 5 minutes.

Using your hands, knead the mixture until the ingredients are completely incorporated and the bulgur is soft and absorbs the liquid. Let the mixture cool completely. Mix in half of the parsley and half of the green onions. Using moistened hands dipped in warm water, shape the mixture into walnut-size patties. Dipping your hands into warm water as you work prevents the patties from sticking to your hands. Garnish with the remaining parsley and green onions. Serve the relish on the side.

Zov's kitchen note: Red lentils turn almost yellow when cooked, and the bulgur expands as it sits. This dish does not freeze well, but tastes delicious the next day.

SIDE DISHES garlic roasted cauliflower with parsley and thyme

Ever since I began roasting cauliflower I have been absolutely hooked on the taste. Roasting cauliflower caramelizes its natural sugars, resulting in a sweet, nutty flavor and a texture that is both crispy and tender. All that's really needed is a splash of high-quality olive oil, but I like a touch of curry powder to add a pretty color without imparting too much flavor.

SERVES 4 TO 6

Preheat the oven to 400°F. Cut the cauliflower florets so they are somewhat uniform in size.

Whisk the oil, garlic, parsley, thyme, salt, black pepper and curry powder, if using, in a large bowl to blend. Add the cauliflower and toss to coat.

Place the cauliflower on a large, rimmed baking sheet and roast until it begins to soften and brown on the bottom, about 20 minutes. Stir the cauliflower and continue roasting, stirring and turning occasionally, until the cauliflower is tender and golden brown and the garlic bits are pale golden, about 10 minutes.

Transfer the cauliflower to a serving bowl or platter and serve.

Zov's kitchen note: For extra flavor, sprinkle with grated Parmesan cheese just before serving. Leftover cauliflower can be tossed into your favorite pasta dish or salad. For a terrific snack, stuff the roasted florets into pita bread with sliced tomatoes, feta cheese, fresh mint and cucumbers.

- 1 head cauliflower (about 2½ pounds), cored, florets separated
- 5 tablespoons olive oil
- 2 tablespoons minced garlic
- 1 tablespoon chopped fresh flat-leaf parsley
- 1 tablespoon chopped fresh thyme
- ½ teaspoon kosher salt
- ¼ teaspoon freshly ground black pepper
- ⅛ teaspoon curry powder (optional)

SIDE DISHES: tuscan eggplant parmesan

I have always loved eggplant Parmesan. A few years back on a culinary trip to Italy, I had the pleasure of dining at a restaurant called Mamma Gina in Florence. One of the courses was eggplant Parmesan. I took one bite and I thought I had gone to heaven. Here is my re-creation of that dish. I hope you enjoy it as much as I do. I love the casualness of the dish; it's a great centerpiece for a family meal. All you need is a green crispy salad, crunchy garlic bread and a bottle of Chianti.

SERVES 8

Position 1 rack in the center of the oven and the second rack just below the first rack. Preheat the oven to 350°F. Toss the mozzarella, Parmesan, Pecorino Romano, basil, parsley, oregano and thyme in a large bowl. Set the cheese mixture aside.

Cut the eggplants lengthwise into ¼-inch-thick slices. You should get around 9 to 10 slices from each eggplant. Mix the breadcrumbs and flour in a wide, shallow bowl. Whisk the eggs in another wide shallow bowl to blend. Coat the eggplant slices in the breadcrumb mixture, patting to adhere and shaking off any excess, then dip the eggplant slices in the beaten egg to coat, and then coat them again in the breadcrumb mixture.

Fill a large, deep skillet halfway with the oil and heat the oil over medium heat to 350°F. Working in batches, slide the coated eggplant slices into the hot oil and fry until they are golden brown on both sides, turning once, about 3 minutes per side. Drain the fried eggplant slices on paper towels and pat with another paper towel to absorb any excess oil.

Spread 1 cup of the sauce over the bottom of a 13x9x2-inch baking dish. Top with a single layer of the fried eggplant slices. Spread 1 cup of the sauce over the eggplant slices, then sprinkle 1¾ cups of the cheese mixture over. Form 2 more layers of the eggplant slices, sauce and cheese mixture. Make sure the entire surface of the dish is covered with the cheese mixture.

Do-ahead tip: At this point, the eggplant Parmesan can be covered tightly and refrigerated overnight or frozen for up to 1 month. Bake as directed, allowing more time if frozen. »

- 16 ounces whole-milk mozzarella cheese, grated
- 6 ounces grated Parmesan cheese
- 3 ounces grated Pecorino Romano cheese
- ½ cup chopped fresh basil
- 2 tablespoons chopped fresh flat-leaf parsley
- 2 tablespoons chopped fresh oregano
- 2 tablespoons chopped fresh thyme
- 2 large eggplants (about 2¼ pounds total), peeled
- 2 cups unseasoned dried breadcrumbs
- 1 cup all-purpose flour
- 6 large eggs
- Canola oil for deep-frying
- Tomato-Basil Sauce (page 308)

Cover the baking dish with foil and set the dish on the rack in the center of the oven. Place a heavy baking sheet on the rack below (this will catch any drippings). Bake until the eggplant Parmesan is hot in the center and the cheese has melted, about 50 minutes. Remove the foil and continue to bake until slightly puffed and the top is golden brown around the edges, about 20 minutes. Allow the eggplant Parmesan to rest for at least 10 minutes before serving so that it will be easier to cut.

Cut the eggplant Parmesan into 8 to 10 pieces and serve.

Do-ahead tip: Freeze individual portions for up to 1 month. Rewarm in the microwave for a quick meal. To reheat in the oven, thaw in the refrigerator, then cover with foil and bake at 350°F for 20 minutes. Uncover and bake until heated through, about 15 minutes longer.

Zov's kitchen note: If you don't want to make your own tomato sauce, most Italian markets carry high-quality homemade sauce.

Choose eggplants with smooth, glossy skin and store them in a cool, dry place. >

SIDE DISHES: spanish rice pilaf

Here's the secret to making perfect fluffy rice every time: Sauté the rice in the oil until it turns golden brown. This will prevent the rice from getting mushy and lumpy. This recipe is on the spicy side. To tame the heat, decrease the amount of jalapeños. Partner the rice with Cheese Enchiladas (page 268) or any grilled chicken or meat dish.

SERVES 6

Preheat the oven to 350°F. Blend the onions and diced tomatoes with their juices in a food processor until smooth and thoroughly pureed. You should have about 2 cups of puree.

Place the rice in a large strainer and rinse under cold running water, mixing the rice with your hand, until the water runs clear, about 1 minute. Drain well to remove any excess moisture.

Heat the oil in a heavy, ovenproof 12-inch-diameter nonstick or stainless-steel frying pan with 2½-inch-high straight sides over medium-high heat until the oil is very hot. Add the drained rice and stir constantly until the rice is light golden brown and looks fried, about 6 minutes. Reduce the heat to medium-low. Add ¼ cup of the minced jalapeños and all the garlic and sauté until the rice is opaque, about 1 minute. Add the pureed tomatoes and onions and the tomato paste, stirring until the paste is dissolved. Add the chicken broth, water and salt. Bring to a boil over medium-high heat.

Cover the pan and transfer it to the oven. Bake about 25 minutes until the liquid is absorbed and rice is tender and fluffy, scraping the sides and fluffing the rice mixture after the first 15 minutes. Fluff the rice with a fork, mixing in the cilantro and the remaining ¼ cup of jalapeños. Serve with lime wedges.

Zov's kitchen note: Fresh tomatoes can be substituted for canned tomatoes. Brown rice, long-grain white rice or medium-grain white rice can stand in for jasmine. The rice can also be cooked on the stove over medium-low heat.

- 1 onion, coarsely chopped (about 1½ cups)
- 1 14.5-ounce can diced tomatoes (with juices)
- 2 cups jasmine rice
- ⅓ cup vegetable oil
- ½ cup minced fresh jalapeño chiles (from about 4 jalapeño chiles), divided
- 7 garlic cloves, minced (about 2 tablespoons)
- 3 tablespoons tomato paste
- 2 cups chicken broth
- ½ cup water
- 2 teaspoons kosher salt
- ½ cup chopped fresh cilantro
- 1 lime, cut into wedges

SIDE DISHES: ultimate risotto with fresh peas, mushrooms and corn

There isn't anything quite like risotto. This creamy, luxurious rice requires careful cooking to achieve exactly the right texture. You begin by toasting short-grain rice in melted butter and then slowly adding hot broth bit by bit until the rice is al dente. Risotto can vary from something resembling a thick soup to a creamy porridge. The ingredients can be as simple as rice, white wine, stock and a sprinkling of Parmesan or more elaborate with vegetables, seafood or meat. Once you've mastered the basic technique, the variations are endless. This recipe is one of my favorites. It's a great accompaniment to short ribs, steaks or any grilled food.

SERVES 4 TO 6

- 5 cups chicken broth
- 6 tablespoons unsalted butter (¾ stick), divided
- 2 tablespoons olive oil
- 1 onion, finely chopped (about 1½ cups)
- 1½ cups arborio rice
- 1 tablespoon minced garlic
- 4 ounces cremini mushrooms, coarsely chopped
- ½ cup dry white wine
- 1 pound fresh English peas, shucked (about 1¼ cups)
- 1 large ear fresh corn, shucked (about 1¼ cups)
- 1 cup freshly grated Parmesan cheese, divided
- ½ teaspoon kosher salt
- ½ teaspoon freshly ground black pepper

Bring the broth to a simmer in a heavy medium saucepan, then cover and keep over very low heat.

Heat 2 tablespoons of the butter with the oil in a heavy 4-quart saucepan over medium-high heat. Butter adds a rich sweetness to risotto, while olive oil prevents the butter from burning. Add the onions and sauté until translucent, about 2 minutes.

Using a wooden spoon, stir in the rice (a wooden spoon will help create friction while a smooth spoon will glide through the grains). Continue stirring often to make sure that each grain is coated and the rice is nicely toasted and very lightly browned, about 8 minutes. Stirring creates friction on the grains of rice and releases a little of its starch. Add the garlic and the mushrooms and stir until the mushrooms begin to soften, about 2 minutes. Add the wine and cook until the liquid is absorbed, stirring frequently.

Reduce the heat to medium. Add the hot broth to the rice mixture ¾ cup at a time, stirring constantly and simmering gently until the broth is absorbed before more broth is added, about 15 minutes total. Stir in the peas and corn. Continue cooking and adding more broth until the rice is al dente and the mixture is creamy, about 5 minutes longer. Don't allow the rice to dry up completely before adding more broth, but make sure that there is no excess liquid in the pan either. »

Stir in ¾ cup of the Parmesan cheese and the remaining 4 tablespoons of butter. Season the risotto with ½ teaspoon salt and ½ teaspoon pepper. Serve, passing the remaining cheese alongside.

Zov's kitchen note: Toasting the rice is one of the secrets to creamy risotto. This important step creates a shell around each grain, allowing the rice to slowly absorb moisture without getting soggy or bursting open like a kernel of popcorn. Each grain maintains its own shape and doesn't get mushy.

The other secret to risotto is using hot broth, and adding it bit by bit. What sets risotto apart from all other rice dishes is that it's not just rice mixed with other ingredients but a perfect marriage of all the elements. Hot broth serves as the melding agent, releasing the rice's starch and making it creamy. It also keeps the risotto at a constant heat level, ensuring even cooking.

Adding hot broth slowly gives you more control over the texture. Rice loves to soak up liquid, and the gradual addition of broth is the only way the rice will cook thoroughly.

Risotto needs high-starch rice and a heavy pot (not nonstick). A thick bottom and sides help distribute the heat evenly and prevent burning; I often use stainless steel. A stainless steel, anodized aluminum or enameled interior won't react with high-acid ingredients such as white wine or tomato, which can turn gray in aluminum or unlined cast-iron pans.

A wooden spoon works best for stirring risotto. It's gentler on the rice than a metal spoon, and it won't scratch the inside of your pan.

Remember, there are no shortcuts to risotto.

SIDE DISHES: bulgur pilaf with tomatoes

Bulgur, a nutritious whole grain with a delicious nutty flavor, lightens up pilaf. This dish is truly comforting in every sense of the word. It is easy to prepare and tastes even better the next day. Serve it alongside Grilled Skirt Steak with Zahtar (page 204) or roasted chicken.

SERVES 6 TO 8

Preheat the oven to 350°F. Heat the oil in a medium ovenproof pot over medium heat. Add the onion and bell pepper and sauté until soft and translucent, about 6 minutes. Add the tomatoes with their juices and red pepper paste, and stir for 2 minutes. Add the bulgur and stir for 2 minutes, or until the mixture tightens up. Add the broth, basil, cumin, salt and pepper. Increase the heat to medium-high and bring just to a simmer.

Cover and bake the bulgur mixture in the oven until the bulgur is tender and the broth is absorbed, about 28 minutes. Do not stir the bulgur while it cooks. Keep covered and let stand at room temperature for about 10 minutes before serving.

Do-ahead tip: Cover and refrigerate for up to 1 day. To rewarm, cover with aluminum foil and bake in a 350°F oven until hot.

Serve with the Greek yogurt and tomato-cucumber relish.

Zov's kitchen note: Turn this dish into a complete meal by adding pulled chicken pieces. For a heartier vegetarian meal, mix in 1 cup of sautéed mushrooms, peas or corn. If you don't have time to make your own red pepper paste, pre-made paste, sold in jars, can be found at Middle Eastern markets (see *Pantry and Produce* for more information).

¼ cup olive oil
1 large onion, finely chopped (about 1¾ cups)
1 medium green bell pepper, finely chopped
1 15-ounce can chopped tomatoes with juices
2 tablespoons Red Pepper Paste (page 305)
2 cups coarse bulgur (#4) (see *Pantry and Produce*)
3 cups chicken broth
1 tablespoon dried basil
1 teaspoon ground cumin
1½ teaspoons kosher salt
½ teaspoon freshly ground black pepper
Greek yogurt
Tomato-Cucumber Relish (page 309)

SIDE DISHES zov's silky macaroni and cheese

Mac 'n' cheese is at its best when velvety, rich and homemade. The smooth cheese sauce sends this easy-to-make recipe over the top. For a fun presentation, bake individual portions in ramekins or 8-ounce soufflé dishes, or serve it family style in a large baking dish.
Go ahead and indulge. We all deserve some feel-good comfort food once in awhile.

SERVES 8

Cook the macaroni: Combine 4 quarts of water and 1 tablespoon of the salt in a large pot and bring to a boil over high heat. Add the macaroni and cook until tender but still firm to the bite, stirring often, about 6 minutes. Drain the macaroni in a colander, then toss it in the colander with the oil to coat; set the macaroni aside while preparing the cheese sauce. Reserve the pot to make the sauce.

Make the cheese sauce: Warm the milk in a large saucepan until it is hot but not boiling; cover and set aside. Melt the butter in the reserved large pot over medium heat until foaming. Add the flour and whisk until the mixture becomes fragrant and deepens in color, about 4 minutes. Gradually whisk in the hot milk. Increase the heat to medium-high and continue whisking until the mixture comes to a boil, about 3 minutes. The mixture must reach a full boil to fully thicken. Reduce the heat to medium and simmer, whisking occasionally, until the sauce thickens to the consistency of heavy cream, about 5 minutes.

Remove the sauce from the heat and gradually add the cheeses, whisking until they melt completely. Mix in the Worcestershire sauce, Tabasco, black pepper, cayenne and remaining 1 tablespoon of salt.

Do–ahead tip: The cheese sauce can be refrigerated for up to 7 days. When ready to serve, heat the sauce in a large saucepan before proceeding.

Assemble the casserole and make the topping: Position the oven rack in the lower middle position and preheat the oven to 325°F. Butter a 13x9x2-inch baking dish. Sprinkle ¼ cup of the panko over the bottom of the baking dish. Stir the cooked macaroni into the warm cheese sauce. Spoon the macaroni and cheese mixture into the prepared baking dish. »

Macaroni and cheese sauce

- 2 tablespoons kosher salt, divided
- 1 pound large elbow macaroni
- 2 tablespoons olive oil
- 9 cups whole milk
- 4 ounces (1 stick) unsalted butter
- ½ cup all-purpose flour
- 6 ounces Fontina cheese, cut into small cubes
- 6 ounces sharp cheddar cheese, shredded
- 4 ounces finely shredded Asiago cheese
- 4 ounces freshly grated Parmesan cheese
- 2 tablespoons Worcestershire sauce
- 1 teaspoon Tabasco Sauce
- ½ teaspoon freshly ground black pepper
- ¼ teaspoon cayenne pepper

Topping

- 1¾ cups panko (Japanese breadcrumbs), divided
- ¼ cup freshly grated Parmesan cheese
- 3 tablespoons chopped fresh flat-leaf parsley
- 3 tablespoons unsalted butter, melted

Toss the remaining 1½ cups of panko, Parmesan and parsley in a medium bowl. Drizzle the melted butter over and toss to coat. Sprinkle the crumb mixture over the macaroni and cheese.

Bake until the macaroni and cheese is bubbly around the sides and heated through, about 30 minutes. Turn the broiler on and broil the macaroni and cheese until the crumb topping is deep golden brown, rotating the baking dish for even browning, about 2 minutes.

Zov's kitchen note: It may seem like there is a lot of cheese sauce, but the pasta will absorb all of it.

For a heartier version, add sautéed sliced mushrooms to the sauce along with shredded rotisserie chicken, available at many grocery stores. Top it off with good-quality crumbled bacon and chopped green onions.

The cheese sauce is a fantastic topping on nachos, baked potatoes or fresh veggies. Garnish nachos and baked potatoes with chopped green onions and dollops of sour cream.

Milk and cheese are the starting points for this familiar favorite. >

SAUCES, ETC.

balsamic vinaigrette **294**

blue cheese dressing **294**

creamy hollandaise sauce **295**

preserved lemons **296**

ginger–sesame vinaigrette **298**

horseradish-yogurt sauce **298**

curry sauce **299**

mustard aïoli **299**

bolognese sauce **300**

red wine sauce **302**

red wine-dijon vinaigrette **302**

chile-lime chipotle sauce **303**

tzatziki sauce **303**

tomato-basil pistou **304**

tahini sauce **304**

red pepper paste **305**

marinara sauce **306**

parmesan croutons **308**

tomato-basil sauce **308**

tomato-cucumber relish **309**

harissa **310**

roasted red pepper and eggplant sauce **311**

romesco sauce **312**

SAUCES, ETC.

Many years ago I was on a culinary tour of Italy and after a long day of cooking, shopping and walking through the streets of Bologna, my husband and I stumbled into a quaint little restaurant. We both ordered pappardelle with Bolognese sauce. The moment the pasta touched my lips I was in heaven. Every bite was better than the last. It wasn't just the tender handmade pasta that made the difference; the sauce was the best I've ever had. | After that meal I realized that a homemade sauce or dressing was the key to delicious weeknight cooking. In this chapter I share with you my go-to sauces, marinades and salad dressings, most of which can be made ahead so they're ready whenever you need them. These are classics that I've updated for today's health-conscious cook. They add incredible flavor and balance to a variety of dishes, from pastas and meats to salads and vegetables. The Marinara Sauce adds dramatic color and flavor to any pasta. Tahini Sauce drizzled over grilled meats makes every bite mouth-watering and savory. I also re-created that Bolognese I had so many years ago. You will be hard-pressed to find another sauce so balanced and delicious. Try it on pappardelle, penne or spaghetti for a meal that is sure to please your family. | Here's a secret: fresh citrus. It's the common thread weaving through these recipes. The juice from fresh lemons balances vinaigrettes and sauces, adding a subtle brightness that isn't overpowering. Just a few drops of citrus juice and some lemon or lime zest instead of salt is not only more flavorful, but also a healthier way to enliven any dish. |

SAUCES, ETC.

balsamic vinaigrette

This all-purpose dressing gives salads a little lift. Keep a jar in your refrigerator and you'll never have to buy pre-made dressing again.

MAKES ABOUT 1 ½ CUPS

Blend the balsamic vinegar, rice vinegar, garlic, mustard, shallots, maple syrup, pomegranate molasses, salt and pepper in a blender until smooth. With the machine running, gradually add the oil in a thin stream, blending until the mixture is completely emulsified.

Do-ahead tip: Refrigerate the vinaigrette in a tightly sealed glass jar for up to 3 days. Shake to emulsify before using.

- ¼ cup balsamic vinegar
- ¼ cup rice vinegar
- 4 garlic cloves
- 2 tablespoons Dijon mustard
- 2 tablespoons finely chopped shallots
- 2 tablespoons pure maple syrup
- 1 tablespoon pomegranate molasses (see *Pantry and Produce*)
- 1 ½ teaspoons kosher salt
- 1 teaspoon freshly ground black pepper
- ½ cup canola oil

blue cheese dressing

My blue cheese dressing is rich and creamy, even with low-fat dairy products and reduced-fat mayonnaise. For the most flavor, choose the tangiest aged blue cheese possible. You'll find there is no comparison between homemade and store-bought; homemade simply tastes better. Try this recipe and see for yourself!

MAKES 3 ½ CUPS

Mix the first 11 ingredients in a large bowl to blend. Add the blue cheese and mash with a fork until incorporated. Slowly add the buttermilk, stirring to blend.

Do-ahead tip: Refrigerate the dressing in a tightly sealed glass jar for up to 2 weeks. Stir the dressing to blend before using.

Zov's kitchen note: You can substitute Greek yogurt for the sour cream. Greek yogurt is available at most grocery stores. If the dressing gets too thick, thin it out with milk or additional buttermilk.

- ½ cup low-fat mayonnaise
- ½ cup low-fat sour cream
- 6 tablespoons white-wine vinegar
- 2 tablespoons granulated onion powder
- 1 tablespoon Dijon mustard
- 1 tablespoon granulated garlic
- 1 tablespoon Worcestershire sauce
- 2 ½ teaspoons kosher salt
- 1 teaspoon seasoned salt (see *Pantry and Produce*)
- ½ teaspoon freshly ground black pepper
- ¼ teaspoon hot chili sauce (such as Sriracha) (see *Pantry and Produce*)
- 1 cup crumbled blue cheese (about 5 ounces)
- 1 ½ cups low-fat buttermilk

creamy hollandaise sauce

The secret to making a great hollandaise is to use very hot butter. Adding a touch of cream makes the sauce ultra-rich and smooth, and serves a practical purpose, too: It helps prevent the sauce from separating. The typical hollandaise is very delicate and can't be reheated, but this one can be made well in advance and rewarmed in the microwave.

MAKES 1 ¼ CUPS

Blend the first 5 ingredients in a blender for about 5 seconds. Heat the melted butter in a small saucepan over medium-high heat until it starts to sputter, but not brown. With the blender on high, slowly drizzle the hot butter into the yolk mixture until all the butter is incorporated and the sauce is thick and creamy. If too thick, thin it by whisking in 1 tablespoon of hot water at a time.

Do-ahead tip: The sauce can be refrigerated for up to 2 days. Transfer to a bowl, let cool and then cover and store. To serve, microwave on medium heat at 5-second intervals until melted and warm, whisking between each interval.

Zov's kitchen note: It's important to drizzle the butter into the egg yolks very slowly. If you add the butter too quickly, the sauce will have a thick, custard-like consistency. You can add 2 teaspoons of mayonnaise to stabilize the sauce. For a spicier version, add 1 teaspoon of chipotle sauce.

4 large egg yolks
3 tablespoons heavy cream
2 ½ tablespoons fresh lemon juice
½ teaspoon kosher salt
¼ teaspoon cayenne pepper
6 ounces (1 ½ sticks) unsalted butter, melted

SAUCES, ETC. preserved lemons

Preserved lemons are a staple of Moroccan cuisine, adding bright, delicious flavor to a wide range of dishes, from sauces and stews to salad dressings and marinades. It is a great condiment to have in your arsenal, and so easy to make. Simply marinate fresh lemons in additive-free coarse kosher salt for three weeks. Preserved lemons keep in the refrigerator for up to one year. For more information, see *Pantry and Produce*.

MAKES 1 QUART

Holding the lemon with the stem end on the cutting board, cut three-fourths of the way through the lemons, forming an X and making sure the lemons are still attached at the stem end. Do not cut all the way through. Open each lemon slightly and pack the inside with about ½ cup of salt.

Sprinkle ½ cup of salt into a 1-quart glass jar. With the cut ends facing downward, pack half of the lemons tightly in the jar. Scatter most of the remaining salt over the lemons and arrange the thyme sprigs, bay leaf and peppercorns in the jar. Pack the remaining lemons in the jar, pushing them down firmly to release their juices. Sprinkle with any remaining salt. Add enough lemon juice to nearly cover the lemons. Close the jar tightly.

Set the jar aside at room temperature until the lemon rinds soften, at least 3 weeks. After the first 3 days, the lemons should be completely immersed in lemon juice. If not, add more juice to cover the lemons (they must be completely submerged at all times). After 1 week, turn the jar upside down to redistribute the juices. Keep the jar upside down for a day or so, and then turn it over again. Refrigerate the preserved lemons for up to 1 year.

To use: Remove a lemon from the jar, discard the seeds, and rinse thoroughly in water to remove the salt.

Zov's kitchen note: If you want to increase the amount of preserved lemons, just use a larger container, packing in as many lemons as the jar allows. Add enough salt to completely coat the slices. Lemons must be covered with lemon juice at all times or they will turn moldy. Just refrigerate and use whenever a recipe calls for preserved lemons. Try using it in your own recipes. This delicious condiment is so versatile; the possibilities are endless.

---

5 to 6 whole medium-small lemons, scrubbed clean

1½ cups (about) kosher salt, divided

2 bushy thyme sprigs

1 bay leaf

4 whole black peppercorns

½ cup (about) fresh lemon juice

One 1-quart glass jar

SAUCES, ETC. ## ginger-sesame vinaigrette

The vinaigrette is delicious on grilled fish or chicken, or tossed with your favorite cooked noodles.

MAKES 2 ¼ CUPS

Blend the first 11 ingredients in a blender. With the machine running, gradually add the sesame oil, then the canola oil, blending well. Season the vinaigrette to taste with more salt and pepper.

Do-ahead tip: Refrigerate in a tightly sealed glass jar for up to 2 weeks. Whisk to blend before using.

Zov's kitchen note: The fish sauce is a must in this recipe. Its tangy, salty flavor is an integral part of the dressing. You can find it in the Asian foods section of many supermarkets or at Asian markets.

- ½ cup rice vinegar
- ¼ cup fresh lime juice
- ¼ cup honey
- ¼ cup minced peeled fresh ginger
- 3 tablespoons fish sauce
- 2 tablespoons soy sauce
- 2 tablespoons hot chili sauce (such as Sriracha) (see *Pantry and Produce*)
- 1 tablespoon minced garlic
- 1 tablespoon minced shallots
- ½ teaspoon kosher salt
- ¼ teaspoon freshly ground black pepper
- ¼ cup toasted sesame oil
- ½ cup canola oil

horseradish-yogurt sauce

Serve with Beef Short Ribs (page 198), drizzle over Crispy Vegetable Croquettes (page 42) or use as a tangy dip for crudités.

MAKES 1 CUP

Stir all the ingredients in a small bowl to blend.

Do-ahead tip: Refrigerate in a tightly sealed glass jar for up to 2 days.

- 1 cup Greek yogurt
- 3 tablespoons prepared horseradish
- 2 tablespoons finely chopped fresh chives
- 1 tablespoon olive oil
- ½ teaspoon kosher salt
- ¼ teaspoons freshly ground black pepper

curry sauce

This Indian curry is a key ingredient in my Spicy Shrimp Curry Bowl (page 182). You can also use this versatile sauce with pasta (especially linguini and angel hair), stir fries and as a marinade for chicken.

MAKES 4 CUPS

Blend all the ingredients in a blender on high speed until the mixture is smooth and thick. Use immediately or refrigerate in a tightly sealed glass jar for up to 2 weeks.

Zov's kitchen note: You can substitute chili paste for the dried red pepper.

- 1 13.5-ounce can unsweetened coconut milk
- ¾ cup creamy peanut butter
- ¾ cup soy sauce
- ½ cup fresh cilantro
- ¼ cup fresh lime juice (from about 2 limes)
- 2 tablespoons curry powder
- 2 teaspoons ground coriander (see *Pantry and Produce*)
- 2 teaspoons ground ginger
- 1½ teaspoons paprika
- 1¼ teaspoons dried crushed hot red pepper

mustard aïoli

Aïoli gets dressed up with honey mustard and dill. Serve with Gravlax (page 46), spread on sandwiches (in place of mayonnaise) or stir into soups and stews.

MAKES ¾ CUP

Whisk the mustard, vinegar and salt in a medium bowl to blend. Add the oil in a thin, steady stream, whisking constantly to blend. Stir in the dill.

Do-ahead tip: Refrigerate in a tightly sealed glass jar for up to 1 week.

- ½ cup honey mustard
- 1 tablespoon Sherry wine vinegar
- ¼ teaspoon kosher salt
- 5 tablespoons olive oil
- 2 tablespoons chopped fresh dill

SAUCES, ETC. bolognese sauce

This famous ragù is named for the Italian city of Bologna, where it originated, and where several years ago I had the best version I've ever tasted. It was served at a charming trattoria called Al Pappagallo, and to this day I can still remember the taste, texture and even the smell of that sauce. I have recreated the recipe here in all its rich and delicious glory. Serve over pappardelle pasta.

MAKES 5 QUARTS

Cook the pancetta in a heavy 8-quart pot over medium heat until the fat is completely rendered, about 6 minutes. Add the onions, carrots, celery and garlic and cook, stirring often, until the liquid evaporates and the vegetables are almost brown, about 25 minutes. Add the pork, veal and beef and cook until the meat and vegetables are brown, stirring to break up the meat and scraping any browned bits off the bottom of the pot, about 20 minutes.

Add the tomato paste and sugar and cook, stirring constantly, until the paste is dark maroon, about 8 minutes. Add the wine and cook until the mixture loosens up, about 2 minutes. Stir in the pureed tomatoes, 2 cups of chicken broth and 3 cups of water. Add the kosher salt, seasoned salt, dried thyme, black pepper, lemon pepper, bay leaves and fresh thyme. Cook until the sauce comes to a simmer, stirring often. Reduce the heat to medium-low and simmer gently, stirring occasionally, for 1½ hours. Add the remaining 2 cups of chicken broth and 1 cup of water and simmer until the sauce thickens into a ragù, stirring often, about 1½ hours longer.

Stir in the cheese, milk and butter. Simmer until the sauce is thick, about 25 minutes. Remove the bay leaves and the thyme stems and serve.

Do-ahead tip: Refrigerate for up to 4 days or freeze for up to 2 months. Transfer to five 1-quart containers, set the containers in a roasting pan and surround with ice. Set aside to cool, stirring occasionally. Cover and store. Rewarm in a covered saucepan over medium-low heat, stirring occasionally until it simmers. Add chicken broth if the sauce is too thick.

Zov's kitchen note: Bolognese is time-consuming, but if you plan it right, you'll have it at the ready whenever you need it. I usually make a big batch, portion out what I need (it's even better the next day), and freeze the rest.

For a richer taste, use cream instead of milk. Pappardelle is flat, wide pasta that holds up well with heavy meat sauces. You can also use penne or medium-size spaghetti. I also like using this sauce for lasagna, eggplant Parmesan, or any layered pasta dish.

½ pound pancetta, chopped
2 onions, finely chopped (about 3 cups)
5 carrots, peeled and finely chopped (about 2½ cups)
7 celery stalks, finely chopped (about 3½ cups)
6 garlic cloves, minced
8 ounces ground pork
8 ounces ground veal
8 ounces lean ground beef
3 6-ounce cans tomato paste
1 teaspoon sugar
1½ cups dry red wine
3 28-ounce cans whole tomatoes, pureed in food processor
4 cups chicken broth, divided
4 cups water, divided
2 tablespoons kosher salt
1 tablespoon seasoned salt (see *Pantry and Produce*)
1 tablespoon dried thyme
1 tablespoon freshly ground black pepper
1 teaspoon lemon pepper
4 bay leaves
1 large sprig fresh thyme
1 cup freshly grated Parmigiano-Reggiano
1 cup whole milk or heavy cream
3 tablespoons unsalted butter

SAUCES, ETC. ## red wine sauce

This richly flavored sauce comes together in minutes. Serve with Beef Tenderloin with Spinach, Leeks and Goat Cheese (page 200).

MAKES 1 1/3 CUPS

Heat a medium skillet over medium-high heat. Add the oil and the shallots and sauté until the shallots are tender, about 1 minute. Add the wine and cook until the wine is reduced by half, about 4 minutes. Add the tomato paste and cook until it is incorporated with the wine. Add 1 cup of the beef broth and bring to a boil, then continue to cook another 3 minutes. Dissolve the cornstarch in the remaining 1/4 cup of the beef broth. Add the cornstarch mixture to the sauce and simmer until thickened, about 2 minutes. Add the thyme and butter to the sauce and stir until the sauce is nice and velvety. Add the salt and pepper. Adjust the seasonings if necessary.

Do-ahead tip: Cover and refrigerate for up to 2 days.

Zov's kitchen note: This versatile sauce adds extra dimension to grilled or baked chicken as well. Keep the red wine, and just substitute chicken broth for the beef broth.

- 1 tablespoon olive oil
- 1 1/2 tablespoons minced shallots
- 1/2 cup dry red wine (such as Merlot or Syrah)
- 1 tablespoon tomato paste
- 1 1/4 cups beef broth, divided
- 1 tablespoon cornstarch
- 1 teaspoon chopped fresh thyme
- 3 tablespoons unsalted butter, cold, cut into small pieces
- 1/2 teaspoon kosher salt
- 1/2 teaspoon freshly ground black pepper

red wine-dijon vinaigrette

Drizzle this vinaigrette over Cauliflower and Broccoli Salad (page 162) or any green salad.

MAKES 1 CUP

Whisk the vinegar, shallots, mustard, garlic, salt, pepper and sugar in a large bowl to blend. Add the oil in a thin steady stream, whisking constantly and vigorously to emulsify the dressing.

Do-ahead tip: Refrigerate in a tightly sealed glass jar for up to 1 week. Whisk to blend before using.

- 5 tablespoons red wine vinegar
- 2 tablespoons minced shallots
- 1 tablespoon Dijon mustard
- 1 garlic clove, minced
- 1 tablespoon kosher salt
- 1/2 teaspoon freshly ground black pepper
- 1/8 teaspoon sugar
- 1/2 cup olive oil

chile-lime chipotle sauce

I like to dip my Crispy Onion Rings (page 34) in this tangy sauce, but it's a foolproof way to amp up the flavor in all kinds of dishes, from Greek Burgers (page 208) to sandwiches (especially grilled chicken and roast beef). Try it as a spicy replacement for sour cream in nachos, or any time you want a condiment with a kick.

MAKES 1 ¾ CUPS

Whisk all the ingredients in a medium bowl to blend. Cover and refrigerate for 1 hour for the flavors to blend.

Do-ahead tip: Cover and refrigerate the sauce for up to 5 days.

½ cup low-fat mayonnaise
½ cup sour cream
¼ cup plain Greek yogurt
2 tablespoons creamed horseradish
2 tablespoons fresh lime juice
2 tablespoons Red Pepper Paste (page 305)
1 tablespoon minced chipotle chiles (packed in adobo sauce), plus 1 teaspoon adobo sauce
1 teaspoon dried oregano
¼ teaspoon cayenne pepper
¼ teaspoon kosher salt

tzatziki sauce

Serve this Greek yogurt dip with Beef Brochettes (page 196), Spicy Pomegranate-Glazed Chicken Wings (page 62) or Tamarind Pork Kebabs (page 218).

MAKES 1 ¾ CUPS

Stir the cucumber, yogurt, garlic, salt and pepper in a medium bowl. The tzatziki can be served immediately, or for the flavors to blend more thoroughly, cover and refrigerate for 30 minutes before serving.

Do-ahead tip: Cover and refrigerate for up to 2 days.

1 large cucumber, peeled, seeded and finely diced
1 cup plain whole milk yogurt
1 garlic clove, minced
½ teaspoon kosher salt
¼ teaspoon freshly ground black pepper

SAUCES, ETC.

tomato-basil pistou

Garlic lovers should add this simple sauce to their bag of tricks. It's the French version of pesto. Stir into Vegetable Soup (page 138) or use as a sandwich spread or rub for meats.

MAKES 1¼ CUPS

Mince the garlic cloves in the food processor. Add the tomato paste, basil, Parmesan, salt and pepper and blend until the basil is finely chopped. With the machine running, drizzle the oil through the feed tube to blend well.

Do-ahead tip: Store in an airtight container and refrigerate for up to 2 days.

4 garlic cloves
1 6-ounce can tomato paste
¾ cup (packed) fresh basil leaves
½ cup grated Parmesan cheese
1 teaspoon kosher salt
½ teaspoon freshly ground black pepper
½ cup olive oil

tahini sauce

Most people know this classic Middle Eastern sauce as a condiment for falafels (Crispy Vegetable Croquettes, page 42), but I use it for so much more. It's the finishing touch on my elegant Stuffed Trout entrée (page 188). It's also delicious drizzled on sandwiches or as a quick dip for pita bread and crudités.

MAKES ABOUT 2½ CUPS

Finely chop the garlic in a food processor. Blend in the tahini, cilantro, parsley, salt and pepper. With the machine running, add the lemon juice. Using a rubber spatula, scrape down the sides and bottom of the work bowl. Slowly blend in enough water to form a sauce with a consistency of buttermilk.

Do-ahead tip: Refrigerate in a tightly sealed glass jar for up to 2 days.

Zov's kitchen note: Tahini is a paste made from sesame seeds that's sold at Middle Eastern markets and some supermarkets.

2 garlic cloves
1 cup tahini (see note)
¼ cup coarsely chopped fresh cilantro
¼ cup coarsely chopped fresh flat-leaf parsley
2 teaspoons kosher salt
¾ teaspoon freshly ground black pepper
½ cup fresh lemon juice
1 cup (about) cold water

red pepper paste

Every summer when I was a teen, my mother and I made a pilgrimage to Fresno to pick bushels of red peppers from her cousin's orchard. As soon as we got home, she would make pepper paste to last the entire year. I remember the beautiful aroma of the sweet peppers filling up the house, and all the creative ways my mom used the paste in her cooking. I have carried this tradition into adulthood, and now, when the mood strikes and I want to bring back childhood memories, I just make this paste. Though the recipe calls for eight pounds of peppers and a day of stewing, two modern conveniences — a food processor and a slow cooker — make it relatively easy. If you don't have the time, you can find both hot and mild red pepper paste at Middle Eastern markets (see *Pantry and Produce* for more information). It's fantastic in so many dishes, but I especially love it in spicy flatbread, swirled into stews and soups, and as a flavor enhancer for sauces like aïoli.

MAKES ABOUT 2½ CUPS

Place the bell peppers in a heavy 8-quart pot. Add enough water to cover the bell peppers by 1 inch. Bring the water to a boil over high heat. Simmer until the bell peppers are soft, stirring often, about 20 minutes. Drain the bell peppers in a colander.

Working in batches, puree the bell peppers in a food processor to form the consistency of lumpy mashed potatoes. Transfer the mixture into a slow cooker and mix in the salt, granulated garlic, cumin and cayenne pepper.

Cover and cook on the low-heat setting for 22 hours, stirring occasionally. Uncover and cook the paste on the high-heat setting until the liquid evaporates and the mixture resembles tomato paste, stirring occasionally, about 2 hours.

Transfer the paste to the sterilized jars and pour the olive oil on top to cover the surface of the paste. Close the jars to seal tightly and refrigerate.

Do-ahead tip: Refrigerate for up to 1 year and freeze for up to 2 years. To freeze, divide the paste into portions that are suitable to your uses and store in separate resealable freezer bags.

Zov's kitchen note: If the pepper paste has been in the refrigerator more than a few months, you might see a film around the edge of the jar. Don't worry. It is not spoiled. Just remove the film with a clean paper towel. Always use a clean spoon when taking paste out of the jar to make sure no bacteria get into the paste, which will speed up spoilage.

8 pounds red bell peppers, seeded and cut into about 1-inch pieces
1 tablespoon kosher salt
2 teaspoons granulated garlic
1 teaspoon ground cumin
½ teaspoon cayenne pepper or Aleppo pepper (see *Pantry and Produce*)
1½ tablespoons olive oil

Special equipment:

three 6-ounce glass jars and canning tongs, both sterlized (for Sterilization Instructions, see page 86)

SAUCES, ETC. marinara sauce

This robust marinara is a perfect partner for Spaghetti with Turkey Meatballs (page 242. It can also be used for lasagna, cannelloni (page 256) or as the base for the fish stew, cioppino.

MAKES 4 QUARTS

Puree the tomatoes with their juices in the bowl of a food processor. Set aside.

Heat the oil in an 8-quart Dutch oven over medium-high heat. Add the onion, garlic and crushed red pepper, if using, and sauté until the onion softens, about 7 minutes. Stir in the pureed tomatoes, water and tomato paste. Stir in the kosher salt, black pepper, seasoned salt and sugar and bring the sauce to a boil. Reduce the heat to medium-low and simmer gently until the flavors blend and the sauce thickens slightly, stirring occasionally, about 1 hour.

Add the basil and parsley to the sauce and simmer for 30 minutes to allow the flavors to blend. Stir the butter into the sauce. The butter gives the sauce a velvety, rich texture and flavor.

Do-ahead tip: The sauce can be refrigerated for up to 4 days or frozen for up to 2 months. Transfer to four 1-quart containers, set the containers in a roasting pan and surround with ice. Set aside to cool, stirring occasionally. Cover the containers and store. Rewarm the sauce in a covered saucepan over medium-low heat, stirring occasionally, until it simmers.

- 4 28-ounce cans whole plum tomatoes with juices
- ⅓ cup extra-virgin olive oil
- 1 large onion, minced
- 3 tablespoons minced garlic
- 1 teaspoon dried crushed hot red pepper (optional)
- 3 cups water
- 2 6-ounce cans tomato paste
- 1 tablespoon kosher salt
- 1 teaspoon freshly ground black pepper
- 1 teaspoon seasoned salt (see *Pantry and Produce*)
- ½ teaspoon granulated sugar
- ½ cup chopped fresh basil
- ½ cup chopped fresh flat-leaf parsley
- 2 tablespoons unsalted butter

No matter what's on the menu, it's a good idea to stock up on this adaptable sauce >

SAUCES, ETC.

parmesan croutons

Practically any type of bread, from a baguette to a sandwich loaf, makes a good crouton. But for a perfect crouton, there are a few basic rules to follow. First, cut the bread into uniform pieces to ensure even baking. Then, add flavor by tossing the cubes in an olive oil-spice mixture. Finally, bake them until almost golden brown. It's that easy. Sprinkle over soups and salads.

Preheat the oven to 375°F. Whisk the Parmesan cheese, parsley, olive oil, garlic and salt together in a large bowl. Add the bread cubes and toss until thoroughly coated. Spread the croutons onto a heavy, large baking sheet. Bake, stirring occasionally, until the croutons are pale golden brown and crisp on the outside and semi-soft in the center, about 20 minutes. Let cool to room temperature before serving. These are best served the day they are made.

- 1 cup grated Parmesan cheese
- ½ cup chopped fresh flat-leaf parsley
- ½ cup extra-virgin olive oil
- 3 garlic cloves, minced
- ¼ teaspoon kosher salt
- 5 cups bread cubes, cut or torn into ½-inch cubes

tomato-basil sauce

This super simple sauce livens up weeknight pasta. Use it for Tuscan Eggplant Parmesan (page 274) or as a snappy dip for Tomato-Basil Risotto Fritters (page 76).

MAKES ABOUT 5 CUPS

Heat the oil in a heavy, large saucepan over medium heat. Add the garlic and crushed red pepper, and stir until the garlic is fragrant and almost soft, about 30 seconds. Squeeze the tomatoes with your hands over the saucepan, then add the tomatoes. Stir in the remaining tomato juice from the cans and bring the sauce to a boil over high heat. Reduce the heat to low and simmer gently until the tomatoes break down and the flavors develop, stirring occasionally, about 30 minutes. Stir in the basil, salt and black pepper. Simmer very gently for 10 minutes longer to allow the flavors to blend.

- ⅓ cup olive oil
- 2 tablespoons minced garlic
- 1 teaspoon dried crushed hot red pepper
- 2 28-ounce cans whole tomatoes with juices
- ¼ cup fresh basil leaves, torn
- 1 teaspoon kosher salt
- 1 teaspoon freshly ground black pepper

tomato-cucumber relish

This relish is a must with Che Kofta (page 32), but it also enhances Bulgur Pilaf (page 284), Greek-Style Chicken Kebabs (page 232) and Breakfast Bake with Soujouk and Potatoes (page 88). If you're using this relish with Lentil Patties (page 270), cut the vegetables a little larger.

MAKES 3 ¾ CUPS

In a clear glass bowl, layer the tomatoes, then the cucumbers, jalapeño, and lastly, the feta cheese. Top with the oregano and mint.

Do-ahead tip: The relish can be made up to 1 hour ahead. Cover and keep at room temperature.

Whisk the olive oil, lemon juice, salt, Aleppo pepper and black pepper in a medium bowl to blend. When ready to serve, pour the dressing over the layered ingredients but do not stir the relish.

For che kofta: Spoon on top of the che kofta, scooping up the juices from the bottom of the bowl to pour over it. Serve any remaining relish alongside.

- 3 large plum tomatoes, seeded and cut into medium dice
- 1 large hothouse cucumber, peeled and cut into medium dice
- 1 jalapeño chile, very thinly sliced into rounds
- ¼ cup coarsely crumbled French feta cheese
- ½ cup (not packed) fresh oregano or savory leaves, torn
- 2 tablespoons torn fresh mint
- ½ cup extra-virgin olive oil
- ¼ cup fresh lemon juice
- 1 ½ teaspoons kosher salt
- 1 teaspoon Aleppo pepper (see *Pantry and Produce*)
- ½ teaspoon freshly ground black pepper

SAUCES, ETC. harissa

Harissa is a staple in Moroccan cooking and often appears on the dinner table as a condiment. Made with hot red chiles, tomatoes and salt, its spiciness enlivens many dishes. I first learned how to make harissa a few years ago on a culinary tour in Morocco, and I've been experimenting with it ever since. It's traditionally served alongside couscous and tagines, but I use this secret ingredient to lift the flavor of stews, soups and salad dressings, to name just a few. What's fun about harissa is that it's so easy to make. For a change of pace, try putting your own twist on this recipe. You'll be proud of yourself.

MAKES 2½ CUPS

Place the dried chiles and sun-dried tomatoes in a large saucepan of simmering water. Remove the pan from the heat and weigh the chiles and tomatoes down with a plate to ensure they're submerged. Set aside until the chiles soften, about 45 minutes. Drain well and tear the chiles in half.

Stir the caraway seeds, coriander seeds and cumin seeds in a heavy, dry skillet over medium heat until fragrant and a shade or two darker, about 5 minutes. Remove from the heat and set aside until cool. Coarsely crush the seeds in a mortar or clean coffee grinder.

Puree the drained chiles, sun-dried tomatoes, crushed toasted spices, granulated garlic, paprika, preserved lemons, salt and crushed red pepper in a food processor until smooth. With the machine running, add the olive oil in thin stream through the feed tube until well blended. Spoon the paste into sterilized glass jars and refrigerate.

Do-ahead tip: Refrigerate for up to 3 months, or freeze in small sealed bags for up to 1 year and use as needed.

Zov's kitchen note: You can substitute 6 cloves of fresh garlic for the granulated garlic. I typically use granulated garlic in condiments because it helps preserve freshness and slows down spoilage. Be sure to use the harissa in small amounts, as the flavor is quite strong and it can be spicy.

15 dried New Mexico or Anaheim chiles (about 3¾ ounces), stemmed and seeded
⅓ cup sun-dried tomatoes (not packed in oil)
1 tablespoon caraway seeds
1 tablespoon coriander seeds (see *Pantry and Produce*)
1 tablespoon cumin seeds
2 tablespoons granulated garlic
2 tablespoons paprika
1 tablespoon chopped Preserved Lemons (page xxx)
2½ teaspoons fine sea salt
1 teaspoon dried crushed hot red pepper
1 cup extra-virgin olive oil

Special equipment:
three 6-ounce glass jars and canning tongs, both sterilized (for Sterilization Instructions, see page 86)

roasted red pepper and eggplant sauce

Serve with Spicy Ground Meat Kebabs (page 212), or try it with grilled halibut or chicken. I love using this sauce for cooked pastas as well.

MAKES 2¼ CUPS

Preheat the broiler. Line a baking sheet with foil. Pierce the eggplant all over with a fork. Place the eggplant and red bell peppers on the prepared baking sheet. Broil until the bell peppers and eggplant are completely charred on all sides and the inside of the eggplant is very tender, turning as needed, about 15 minutes for the bell peppers, and 25 minutes for the eggplant. Place the roasted peppers in a plastic bag and let steam for 15 minutes. Set the eggplant aside until cool enough to handle.

Remove and discard the skins and seeds from the roasted peppers and place them in a food processor. Do not wash the roasted peppers while peeling, as doing so removes a lot of the smoky flavor. Puree the roasted peppers until smooth. Transfer the puree to a medium bowl.

Scoop the flesh from the roasted eggplant into the food processor and discard the skin. Add the olive oil and garlic to the eggplant flesh and pulse to form a coarse puree. Stir the eggplant mixture into the pepper puree. Stir in the vinegar, paprika, salt, pepper and sugar.

Do-ahead tip: Cover and refrigerate for up to 2 days.

- 1 eggplant
- 3 red bell peppers
- ¼ cup extra-virgin olive oil
- 1 garlic clove, minced
- 2 tablespoons red wine vinegar
- 1 teaspoon Hungarian paprika
- 1 teaspoon kosher salt
- ½ teaspoons freshly ground black pepper
- ½ teaspoon granulated sugar

SAUCES, ETC. romesco sauce

A good repertoire of sauces will bring complexity to your cooking, color to your dishes and smiles to your guests' faces. Here is one to keep in your back pocket. Romesco is a legendary Spanish sauce that is infinitely versatile. Its bold flavor takes any dish to the next level. I pair it with meats, pastas and vegetables, and it goes well with just about anything grilled. I use it to enhance basic soups and sauces, and also as a marinade. Try it as a topping for potatoes and seafood, or as a delicious dip for veggies and pita chips. It even works as a tangy spread for crostini. I'm not kidding when I say it goes with everything. And it tastes even better the next day.

MAKES ABOUT 5 CUPS

3 red bell peppers
½ cup blanched sliced almonds
2 plum tomatoes, cut in half
1 cup fresh basil leaves
½ cup unsalted roasted pistachios
2 ½-inch-thick slices day-old French bread (about 1½ ounces total), torn (about 1 cup)
6 tablespoons fresh lemon juice
3 tablespoons tomato paste
1 tablespoon Hungarian paprika
1 tablespoon minced shallots
4 garlic cloves, peeled
2½ teaspoons kosher salt
1 teaspoon cayenne pepper
1 teaspoon freshly ground black pepper
½ cup water
1 cup extra-virgin olive oil

Char the bell peppers over a gas flame or in a broiler until blackened on all sides. Enclose the bell peppers in a plastic bag and let stand at least 10 minutes. Peel and seed.

Meanwhile, preheat the oven to 350°F. Arrange the almonds on a rimmed baking sheet and bake until lightly toasted, about 8 minutes. Cool.

Combine the bell peppers, almonds, tomatoes, basil, pistachios, bread, lemon juice, tomato paste, paprika, shallots, garlic, salt, cayenne pepper and black pepper in a food processor. With the machine running, pour ½ cup of water through the feed tube. Slowly add the olive oil through the feed tube, blending until the sauce is well combined and relatively smooth. As you add the water and oil, stop the machine occasionally and scrape the bowl to ensure all the ingredients are evenly blended.

Do–ahead tip: Cover and refrigerate for up to 5 days. The sauce can also be frozen for up to 1 year. To freeze, divide the sauce into portions that are suitable to your uses and store each portion in separate resealable freezer bags.

Zov's kitchen note: If you don't have time to roast the peppers, use ½ cup of Red Pepper Paste (page 305) instead. Make sure to taste the sauce after blending and adjust the seasonings to balance the flavors. It is best to wait at least 10 minutes before adjusting the seasonings so the flavors have time to blend. Pre-made paste is sold at Middle Eastern markets and many supermarkets (see *Pantry and Produce* for more information).

SWEETS

almond crescent cookies **318**

cherry crisps **320**

apricot shortbread bars **322**

black and white pound cake **324**

blueberry muffins with almond streusel **326**

apple-cinnamon phyllo crumble **328**

choreg **330**

decadent chocolate cake **334**

jewel jam cookies **338**

jumble cookies **340**

mom's S cookies **342**

gata **344**

lemon sour cream pound cake **348**

quince coffee cake **350**

red velvet cupcakes **352**

simple moist carrot cake **354**

pineapple upside-down cake **356**

super easy holiday fruit and nut loaf **360**

simple poached pears **362**

SWEETS

No matter how much you like appetizers, salads, soups or entrées, there is one section of a cookbook that no one can pass up: desserts. Who can resist homemade cookies, decadent deep red velvet cupcakes smothered in cream cheese frosting, tart and moist lemon pound cake, and fruity apricot shortbread bars? It's impressive sweets like these that make the entire meal memorable. | For me, nothing brings back childhood memories like Gata, a moist Armenian sweet bread. I loved watching my mother roll out the dough, place the buttery streusel filling on one side, and then flip it over. After folding the dough over again and crimping the edges, she brushed the top with egg wash to give it a beautiful sheen. When she pulled it out of the oven, the entire house smelled amazing. It was excellent coffee bread, and we would eat it alongside tea. | Choreg (pictured here) is another slightly sweet bread traditionally made around Easter. Nigella seeds add a delicious smokiness, which contrasts nicely with the bread's light flavor and tender texture. No Armenian holiday breakfast is complete without it. | In this chapter, I share these treasured family recipes with you, along with old favorites like Pineapple Upside-Down Cake and new and delicious sweets that will make everyone's mouth water. |

SWEETS almond crescent cookies

These cookies have been a staple in our home for years. They make a tempting treat for the holidays or a terrific hostess gift. I guarantee they will disappear fast. To achieve a slightly chewy, soft texture, I use a double cookie sheet, which ensures even baking on both sides.

MAKES 24 COOKIES

12 ounces almond paste
¾ cup granulated sugar
1 large egg white
4 ounces (about) sliced blanched or toasted almonds
6 ounces (about) semisweet chocolate, chopped

Line 2 heavy, large baking sheets with parchment paper. Using a stand mixer fitted with the paddle attachment (or a handheld mixer), beat the almond paste and sugar in the mixer bowl until it is well blended and resembles cornmeal, about 5 minutes. Gradually blend in the egg white and continue to beat on medium speed until well blended (the dough will be soft).

Put the sliced almonds in a shallow plate and drop rounded tablespoonfuls of the dough into the almonds. Roll the spoonful of dough in the almonds with your fingers, coating generously, and shape the dough into 3-inch lengths. Arrange the cookies on the prepared baking sheets, shaping them into crescents when placing them down. Set the cookies aside uncovered at room temperature for 1 hour. Meanwhile, preheat the oven to 350°F.

Stack each baking sheet of cookies onto a second baking sheet. Bake for 15 minutes. Remove the second baking sheets and continue to bake the cookies until they are golden brown, about 8 minutes. Transfer the baking sheets to a rack to cool the cookies slightly, about 5 minutes. Using a metal spatula, transfer the cookies directly to the rack and cool completely.

Line the baking sheets with clean parchment paper. Set a small heatproof bowl over a saucepan of simmering water. Put the chocolate in the bowl and stir until melted. Dip the ends of each cookie into the melted chocolate. Set the cookies on the parchment-lined baking sheets and refrigerate until the chocolate is set, about 15 minutes. Serve at room temperature.

Do-ahead tip: Store in an airtight container at room temperature for up to 2 days or freeze for up to 1 month.

SWEETS cherry crisps

Fresh local cherries are the jewels of summer. Here's a perfect way to showcase them during their fleeting season, which lasts just a week or two in June. This recipe is a simple, old-fashioned way of preparing a crisp, but it's divided into individual portions, each with their own flavorful crumbly topping. Don't worry if you miss out on cherry season; blueberries, peaches and plums also work wonderfully. Serve the crisps warm with scoops of vanilla ice cream.

SERVES 8

Prepare the filling: Preheat the oven to 375°F. Generously butter eight 6-ounce oval gratin dishes that are about 6x4x1-inch. Line a heavy, large, rimmed baking sheet with foil, then spray the foil with nonstick spray. Set the gratin dishes on the prepared baking sheet (this will catch the juices that bubble over).

Toss the cherries, sugar and lemon juice in a 4-quart pot. Cook the mixture over medium-high heat until the juices form and come to a boil, about 6 minutes. Reduce the heat to medium-low and cook, stirring often, until the cherries are semi-tender, about 4 minutes longer.

Mix the cornstarch and the orange juice in a small bowl to blend well. Remove the pot from the heat and stir the cornstarch mixture into the cherries. Spoon the cherry mixture into the prepared baking dishes, dividing equally.

Prepare the topping: Mix the flour, sugar and salt in a large bowl. Add the butter cubes and rub them in with your fingertips until the mixture resembles a coarse meal and clumps together when squeezed in your hand. Crumble the topping generously over the cherry mixture.

Bake until the crust is golden brown and the filling bubbles thickly, about 40 minutes. Cool for 5 minutes.

Top each warm crisp with a scoop of vanilla ice cream and serve immediately.

Zov's kitchen note: Choose fresh ripe cherries. Pitting cherries can be a fun family activity. It's a great way to get the kids involved and excited about cooking. If fresh cherries are not available, you can use frozen or jarred (about 6 cups drained). I prefer jarred, pitted Michigan cherries over the canned variety.

Cherry filling
Unsalted butter for coating dishes
Nonstick vegetable-oil cooking spray
3 pounds fresh cherries, stemmed, split in half and pitted
2/3 cup granulated sugar
2 tablespoons fresh lemon juice
2 tablespoons cornstarch
2 tablespoons orange juice or cold water

Topping
2 cups all-purpose flour
1 cup granulated sugar
1/2 teaspoon fine-grained salt
8 ounces (2 sticks) cold unsalted butter, cut into small cubes

Accompaniments
Vanilla ice cream

SWEETS: apricot shortbread bars

I have been making these lovely shortbread bars for almost a decade. I adapted the recipe from my mentor and dear friend Julia Child. It's a real gem. You will never ever find a better shortbread than this. It is so flaky and tender that, without fail, people ask me for the recipe every time I serve it. Now I'm sharing it with all of you.

MAKES 36 BARS

- 4 cups all-purpose flour
- 2 teaspoons baking powder
- ¼ teaspoon fine-grained salt
- 1 pound (4 sticks) unsalted butter, at room temperature
- 2 cups granulated sugar
- 4 large egg yolks, at room temperature
- 2 cups Apricot Jam (page 84) or purchased apricot preserves
- ½ cup powdered sugar, divided

Whisk the flour, baking powder and salt in a large bowl to blend. Set aside.

Using a stand mixer fitted with the paddle attachment (or handheld mixer), beat the butter in the mixer bowl on high speed until it is pale and fluffy, about 3 minutes. Add the sugar and egg yolks and beat until the sugar is dissolved and the mixture is light, scraping the bowl occasionally, about 5 minutes. Lower the mixer speed to low. Add the flour mixture and mix just until blended (do not overmix the dough).

Divide the dough into 4 equal pieces. Transfer each piece to a separate sheet of plastic wrap, then flatten the dough pieces into discs. Wrap the 4 discs separately and freeze until firm, at least 45 minutes.

Preheat the oven 350°F. Using the largest holes of a box grater, grate 2 dough discs into a 13x9x2-inch baking dish. Keep the dough discs in the freezer until you are ready to grate them so they do not soften. Gently pat the dough just to distribute it evenly over the dish and into the corners. Do not press the dough down and/or compact it; it should be light and airy in the dish. Spread the apricot jam over the dough. Grate the remaining 2 dough discs evenly over the jam.

Bake the shortbread until the top is golden brown, about 45 minutes. Immediately dust the top of the hot shortbread with ¼ cup of the powdered sugar. Transfer the baking dish to a rack and cool the shortbread to room temperature. Cut the shortbread into thirty-six 2x1½-inch bars. Dust the bars with the remaining ¼ cup of powdered sugar just before serving.

Do-ahead tip: Store the bars at room temperature in an airtight container for up to 3 days. You can also store unbaked dough discs in freezer bags and freeze them for up to 1 month.

Zov's kitchen note: If you're using purchased apricot preserves and you find that they are chunky, give them a whiz in the food processor.

SWEETS: black and white pound cake

This classic pound cake is anything but boring. I have been making this cake for most of my married life, and it has always been a favorite with family and friends. Moist and tender, it's also fabulous with morning coffee or whenever you feel the need for a little afternoon pick-me-up.

MAKES ONE 10-INCH TUBE CAKE; SERVES 12 TO 16

Preheat the oven to 350°F. Generously butter a 10-inch plain tube pan, then dust the pan with flour; tap out any excess flour (be sure to butter and flour the center tube of the pan). Sift the flour, baking powder and salt into a medium bowl.

Using an electric mixer, beat the sugar, butter and cream cheese in a large bowl until light and fluffy. Add the eggs one at a time, beating well after each addition. Beat in the vanilla. Add the flour mixture to the butter mixture alternately with the sour cream, beating until smooth after each addition. Pour two-thirds of the batter (about 4½ cups) into the prepared pan. Stir the chocolate syrup and baking soda in another medium bowl to blend, then add the remaining batter (about 2½ cups) and stir lightly to blend. Pour the chocolate mixture over the batter in the pan, but do not swirl the batters.

Bake until a toothpick inserted near the center of the pan comes out with some crumbs attached, about 1 hour and 20 minutes, covering the cake with foil if it begins to brown too quickly. Transfer the pan to a rack and cool the cake for 30 minutes. Turn the cake out onto a plate, then turn it onto a cooling rack so that the chocolate portion of the cake is on top. Cool as desired. Transfer the cake, chocolate side up, to a cake plate and serve the cake warm or at room temperature.

Do-ahead tip: Cool the cake completely. Store the cake in an airtight container and refrigerate for up to 1 week or freeze for up to 2 months.

Sift powdered sugar over the cake. Cut the cake into wedges and serve with whipped cream and fresh berries and garnish with mint.

Zov's kitchen note: The chocolate syrup is the kind that you make chocolate milk from, and can be found at any grocery store.

You really only need one pound cake recipe in your file. Once you have it, you can do many variations of the same cake. If you don't like chocolate, just omit the syrup; the cake is still delicious. Or add lemon juice or lemon zest in its place. If you love orange flavor, add ½ cup orange juice with orange zest.

2½ cups all-purpose flour
2 teaspoons baking powder
½ teaspoon salt
2 cups granulated sugar
8 ounces (2 sticks) unsalted butter, at room temperature
3 ounces cream cheese, at room temperature
4 large eggs, at room temperature
2 teaspoons vanilla extract
1 cup sour cream, at room temperature
¾ cup chocolate syrup (such as Hershey's) (see note)
¼ teaspoon baking soda
Powdered sugar
Whipped cream
Assorted fresh berries
Fresh mint sprigs, for garnish

SWEETS: blueberry muffins with almond streusel

The moist and tender texture is more like a cake than a muffin. Enjoy this recipe as is or dress it up for a party by transforming it into a pound cake (just bake the batter in a loaf pan). Fresh citrus is best at bringing out the natural flavor of blueberries, but you can play around with the ingredients by adding chocolate chips, cranberries or bananas. These muffins are so simple and versatile, it's no wonder they have been a favorite in our bakery since the day we opened. Just don't forget the paper liners!

MAKES 12 JUMBO MUFFINS

Prepare the streusel topping: Mix the all-purpose flour, almond flour and sugar in a large bowl. Add the butter and mix it in with your fingertips until it's crumbly and just clumps together when squeezed in your hand. Set aside.

Prepare the muffins: Preheat the oven to 375°F. Line 12 jumbo muffin cups with paper muffin liners.

Using a stand mixer fitted with the paddle attachment, beat the sugar and butter in the mixer bowl until light and fluffy, about 5 minutes.

Whisk the flour, baking powder and salt in a medium bowl to blend. Whisk the eggs, buttermilk, and citrus zest in a large bowl to blend. Set aside.

Slowly beat the oil into the butter mixture. On low speed, beat in the flour mixture alternately with the buttermilk mixture until just blended. Do not overmix the batter. Using a large silicone spatula, gently fold the blueberries into the batter, being careful not to pierce the blueberries.

Spray a trigger ice cream scoop with nonstick cooking spray (this makes it easier to release the batter from the scoop). Using the scoop, divide the batter evenly among the prepared muffin cups. Sprinkle the streusel topping generously over the muffins.

Bake until the tops begin to brown and a toothpick inserted into the center of each muffin comes out clean, about 35 minutes. Cool for 10 minutes in the pan on a cooling rack, then remove the muffins from the pan and cool directly on the rack. Sift powdered sugar over the muffins just before serving.

Do-ahead tip: Store cooled muffins in an airtight container at room temperature for up to 2 days.

Zov's kitchen note: Frozen blueberries also work nicely in this recipe. Baking at a high oven temperature produces higher peaks on the muffins.

Streusel topping
¾ cup all-purpose flour
½ cup almond flour
½ cup granulated sugar
4 tablespoons (½ stick) cold unsalted butter, cut into small cubes

Batter
2 cups granulated sugar
8 ounces (2 sticks) unsalted butter, at room temperature
3 cups all-purpose flour
1 tablespoon baking powder
¼ teaspoon fine-grained salt
6 large eggs
¾ cup buttermilk
1 tablespoon lemon zest
1 tablespoon orange zest
¼ cup canola oil
1½ cups fresh blueberries
Nonstick vegetable-oil cooking spray
Powdered sugar

SWEETS | apple-cinnamon phyllo crumble

This delectable apple crumble with a topping made of light and crispy phyllo warms the heart as well as the tummy. There's nothing like the contrast of flaky pastry and creamy ice cream.

SERVES 12

Make the apple filling: Spray a 13x9x2-inch baking dish with nonstick spray. Toss the apples, sugar and cinnamon in a large bowl until the apples are completely coated.

Melt the butter in a large, deep skillet over medium-high heat. Once the butter begins to sizzle, add the apples. Cook the apples, stirring frequently, until they are crisp-tender, about 8 minutes. Transfer the apple mixture to a colander that is set over a bowl to catch the accumulated juices. Set aside for a couple of minutes to allow the juices to drain. Reserve the skillet.

Shake the colander a couple of times over the bowl to help drain the juices from the apples. Pour the accumulated juices into the same skillet and simmer over medium heat until the juices thicken into a sauce, stirring constantly, about 8 minutes. Add the drained apples to the sauce and toss gently to combine. Transfer the apple mixture to the prepared baking dish, forming an even layer. Cool completely.

Do-ahead tip: The apple filling can be made 1 day ahead. Cover the filling and refrigerate; bring to room temperature before continuing.

Make the phyllo topping: Position the rack in the center of the oven and preheat the oven to 375°F. Mix the sugar and cinnamon in a bowl to blend. Lay 1 phyllo rectangle on work surface. Brush the phyllo with some of the melted butter then sprinkle with some of the cinnamon-sugar. Gather the phyllo and form it into a loose rose-like formation that is about 3-inches wide, and place it on top of the apple filling. Repeat with the remaining phyllo rectangles, melted butter, and cinnamon-sugar, forming a single layer of phyllo roses that covers the apple filling.

Bake until the phyllo is brown and crisp and the filling is hot, about 35 minutes. Serve warm with vanilla ice cream.

Zov's kitchen note: Always thaw the phyllo in the refrigerator before using. Make sure the apples are cooled before topping them with phyllo; otherwise the phyllo will become soggy. You can prepare this dessert up to 1 day ahead.

Apple filling

Nonstick vegetable-oil cooking spray
10 large Granny Smith apples, peeled, cored and cut into ¼-inch-thick wedges
¾ cup granulated sugar
1 teaspoon ground cinnamon
6 tablespoons (¾ stick) unsalted butter, cut in small cubes

Phyllo topping

2 tablespoons granulated sugar
1 teaspoon ground cinnamon
6 fresh phyllo pastry sheets or frozen, thawed (each about 17x13 inches), stacked and halved crosswise, forming twelve 8½ x13-inch rectangles
3 tablespoons unsalted butter, melted

Accompaniments

Vanilla ice cream

SWEETS: choreg

It is the comforting aromas and tastes that make holiday celebrations so delicious—and so beautiful. This Armenian delicacy (pronounced "cho-reg") traditionally shows up on Easter, but my mother always made these soft little breads year round and brought large freezer bags full of them whenever she came to visit. Nigella seeds and mahlab, a Mediterranean spice, add a fragrant taste to these light, semi-sweet loaves. They're terrific with string cheese and olives, and make a wonderful snack all on their own.

MAKES 28

Mix ¼ cup warm water, yeast and 1 teaspoon of sugar in a medium bowl and set aside in a warm place until the yeast doubles in size, about 15 minutes. Whisk the milk, butter, shortening and eggs in a large bowl to blend. Mix in the yeast mixture.

Using a heavy-duty stand mixer fitted with the paddle attachment, mix 9 cups of flour, the remaining 1½ cups of sugar, nigella seeds, fennel seeds, mahlab and salt in the mixer bowl until well blended. With the mixer on low speed, slowly pour the milk mixture into the dry ingredients, mixing until the dough comes together. Replace the paddle attachment with the dough hook and knead the dough on medium-low speed until the dough is smooth and elastic, about 5 minutes. While mixing, add more flour as needed, 1 tablespoon at a time, to form a dough that is very tacky when touched but does not leave dough on your hand. Coat another large bowl with the canola oil then transfer the dough to the bowl. Cover with plastic wrap and set aside in a warm draft-free area until the dough has risen and doubled in size, about 1½ hours.

Line 4 heavy large baking sheets with parchment paper. Using three 1-ounce pieces of dough, roll out each piece between the work surface and the palms of your hand to form three 6-inch-long ropes. Braid the 3 ropes together. Pinch the ends together and tuck the ends under. Repeat with the remaining dough to form 28 braided loaves total. Arrange 6 to 8 braided loaves on each baking sheet, spacing evenly apart. Cover the loaves loosely with plastic wrap and let rise in a warm draft-free area for 45 minutes. Meanwhile, preheat the oven to 375°F.

Brush the loaves with the egg wash and sprinkle with sesame seeds. Bake until the loaves are golden brown, 15 to 20 minutes. Cool slightly on racks and serve warm. »

- ¼ cup warm water (105°F to 115°F)
- 2 ¼-ounce packages active dry yeast
- 1 teaspoon plus 1½ cups granulated sugar
- 2 cups warm whole milk (105°F to 115°F) or 1 15-ounce can evaporated milk, at room temperature
- 4 ounces (1 stick) unsalted butter, melted and cooled
- ½ cup solid vegetable shortening, melted and cooled
- 4 large eggs, at room temperature
- 9 ¼ cups (about) all-purpose flour, plus more for dusting
- 1 tablespoon nigella seeds (see *Pantry and Produce*)
- 1 teaspoon ground fennel seeds
- 1 teaspoon mahlab (see *Pantry and Produce*)
- 1 teaspoon salt
- 1 tablespoon canola oil
- 1 large egg yolk mixed with 1 tablespoon whole milk (for egg wash)
- 2 tablespoons sesame seeds

choreg
STEP BY STEP

1. Using 1-ounce pieces of dough, roll out each piece to form a 5- to 6-inch long rope.

2. Braid 3 ropes together for each loaf.

3. Pinch and tuck the ends, then transfer to a parchment-lined baking sheet.

4. Be sure to space the loaves evenly apart on the baking sheet.

(continued from page 330)

Do-ahead tip: The choregs can be frozen for up to 4 months. Cool completely, then store in freezer bags. To serve, wrap the choregs in foil and bake at 350°F or microwave for 20 seconds until warm.

Zov's kitchen note: You can make choregs in a variety of shapes.

To make a twisted choreg: Divide the dough into forty 2½-ounce pieces. Roll out each piece to form a 6- to 8-inch-long rope. Lay the rope horizontally in front of you. With one hand holding one end of the rope on the work surface, use your other hand to roll the opposite end of the rope, creating a twisted rope that resembles a straight peppermint stick. Fold the twisted rope lengthwise in half, then twist the folded rope 2 times.

To make a coil: Divide the dough into forty 2½-ounce pieces. Roll out each piece to form an 8-inch-long rope, then coil each rope and tuck the ends under the coiled buns.

To make 4 large braids: Divide the dough into 4 equal pieces, then divide each piece into 3 equal portions. Roll out each portion into 24-inch-long ropes, and braid 3 ropes for each loaf (follow the instructions on page 330 for making smaller braids).

SWEETS | decadent chocolate cake

Michelle Bracken, our executive pastry chef, is one of the most talented pastry chefs that I know, and she has been making this cake for as long as I can remember. It's an irresistible way to savor the deep intensity of dark chocolate. If you don't want to make a layer cake, you can always bake the cake in a 9x13-inch baking pan. Just make half of the chocolate ganache and use it only for the topping. For best results, use the highest-quality chocolate you can find.

SERVES 10 TO 12

Prepare the cakes: Position a rack in the center of the oven and preheat the oven to 350°F. Lightly coat the bottom and sides of two 9-inch round cake pans with butter. Line the bottom of the pans with parchment paper, then butter the parchment and coat the paper and sides of the pans lightly with flour; tap out any excess flour.

Using a stand mixer fitted with the paddle attachment (or a handheld mixer), mix the sugar, flour, cocoa powder, baking soda, baking powder and salt in the mixer bowl on low speed until blended. Mix in the eggs and oil. Add the buttermilk, hot coffee and vanilla and mix on medium speed just until the batter is well blended, stopping the machine and scraping the sides and bottom of the bowl as needed.

Divide the batter equally between the 2 prepared pans. Bake until the cake springs back to your touch, 30 to 35 minutes. Transfer the pans to a cooling rack and cool the cakes for 15 minutes. Run the tip of a small knife around the cakes to loosen them from the pans. Place a cooling rack upside down on top of each cake, then invert the cakes onto the racks. Carefully remove the pans and peel off the parchment paper. Cool the cakes completely.

Do-ahead tip: The cake layers can be made 1 day ahead. Wrap well with plastic wrap and store at room temperature.

Make the ganache: Place the chopped chocolate in a medium stainless-steel bowl. Combine the cream and corn syrup in a heavy saucepan over medium heat and bring to a boil, whisking until blended. Immediately pour the boiling cream over the chopped chocolate and let stand for 5 minutes. Using a whisk, stir the mixture just until the chocolate is completely melted and the mixture is smooth. Add the butter and mix just until blended. Let the ganache cool at room temperature, without stirring, about 3 hours. At this point, the ganache will be spreadable and thick. You will have about 4 cups of ganache. »

Cake

Unsalted butter for coating pans
2 cups granulated sugar
1½ cups all-purpose flour, plus more for coating pans
1 cup Dutch-processed cocoa powder (see *Pantry and Produce*)
2 teaspoons baking soda
1 teaspoon baking powder
¼ teaspoon fine-grained salt
4 large eggs
½ cup canola oil
1 cup buttermilk
1 cup hot coffee
1 teaspoon vanilla extract

Ganache

16 ounces bittersweet chocolate (do not exceed 60% cacao), finely chopped
2 cups heavy cream
2 tablespoons light corn syrup
3 tablespoons unsalted butter, cut into pieces, at room temperature

Assemble and frost the cake: Place 1 cake layer, top side up, on a flat plate or a cake stand. Using a mixer on medium-low speed, beat 1½ cups of the ganache in another medium bowl just until lighter in color, 1 to 1½ minutes. Do not overmix, as doing so will cause the ganache to look grainy.

Using an icing spatula, spread the whipped ganache evenly and smoothly over the top of the cake. Top with the second cake layer, placing it top side down. Refrigerate the cake until the filling is cold and the cake no longer wobbles, about 1 hour. Chilling the cake makes the cake more stable and easier to frost.

Spread one-fourth of the unwhipped ganache over the top and sides of the cake, filling in the gap around sides between the cake layers and covering completely. Refrigerate the cake just until the frosting is firm. Spread the remaining unwhipped ganache decoratively all over the cake.

Do-ahead tip: The finished cake can be made 1 day ahead. Cover with a cake dome and store at room temperature.

Zov's kitchen note: This cake is best eaten at room temperature. We like to decorate it with chocolate shavings, fresh raspberries and a dusting of powdered sugar.

Using a small amount of light corn syrup gives the chocolate frosting and filling a beautiful sheen. I prefer using Callebaut chocolate or another comparable high-quality chocolate, which you can find at specialty cookware stores and some supermarkets.

If you have extra frosting, make chocolate truffles by adding orange liqueur (such as Grand Marnier) or raspberry liquor. Shape into balls and then roll in cocoa powder or powdered sugar.

Extra dark bittersweet chocolate has a deeper, stronger flavor than semisweet. >

SWEETS jewel jam cookies

What would the holidays be without homemade cookies? It seems no one has time to cook anymore, so making goodies from scratch is really an act of love. Even the gift of a few cookies evokes the true spirit of the season, and this festive treat is the perfect choice. Fill them with your favorite jewel-toned jam.

MAKES ABOUT 2 DOZEN

Grind the almonds in a food processor until they form very fine crumbles that resemble sand; set aside.

Using a stand mixer with the paddle attachment (or a handheld mixer), beat the butter and granulated sugar in the mixing bowl on medium-high speed until light and fluffy, about 4 minutes. Add the vanilla and cinnamon and beat until blended. Add the flour and ground almonds and beat just until blended. Divide the dough into 3 portions and flatten into discs. Wrap each disc separately in plastic wrap and refrigerate for at least 1 hour.

Preheat the oven to 350°F. Line 4 large baking sheets with parchment paper. Roll out each disc between 2 sheets of plastic wrap to ⅛ inch thickness. Return the dough to the refrigerator until cold and firm.

Using a 2-inch round cookie cutter, cut out the cookies from 1 sheet of dough. Using a ¾-inch cookie cutter, cut out the center from half of the cookies. Transfer the cookies to one of the prepared baking sheets, spacing 1 inch apart. Gather the dough scraps and centers and set aside. Bake the cookies until they feel firm to the touch and are pale golden around the edges, about 12 minutes. Transfer the cookies to a rack to cool completely. Repeat with the remaining sheets of dough. Gather all the dough scraps, and repeat rolling and cutting to form more cookies.

Do-ahead tip: Store in an airtight container at room temperature for up to 2 days or freeze for up to 2 months. Fill and assemble the cookies just before serving so they retain their crisp texture.

Just before serving, arrange the cookie bottoms on a work surface and spoon about ½ teaspoon of jam in the center of each, then top each with a cookie ring, forming a sandwich-style cookie. Sift powdered sugar over the sandwich cookies and serve.

Zov's kitchen note: It's important to keep the dough chilled when cutting out the cookies. For a more decadent version, dip half of each cookie in melted chocolate. Cool the cookies on wax paper for the chocolate to set.

---

2 cups ground blanched slivered almonds
12 ounces (3 sticks) unsalted butter, at room temperature
⅔ cup granulated sugar
1 teaspoon vanilla extract
½ teaspoon ground cinnamon
2 cups all-purpose flour, plus more for dusting
1 cup (about) jam, such as apricot, strawberry or raspberry
Powdered sugar

SWEETS jumble cookies

This is the most popular cookie in our bakery; our executive pastry chef Michelle Bracken bakes three or four batches a day. We can't keep them on the shelves. They're moist and full of nutty flavor, and dads and kids especially love them.

MAKES 20 COOKIES

Position the rack in the center of the oven and preheat the oven to 350°F. Place the almonds and pecans on a heavy, large baking sheet and bake until golden brown and fragrant, about 11 minutes, stirring halfway through the baking time to ensure the almonds brown evenly. Transfer the nuts to a cutting board to cool completely. Coarsely chop the almonds and pecans, then set the nuts aside. Maintain the oven temperature.

Stir the flour, baking soda and salt in a medium bowl to blend. Set the flour mixture aside. Using a stand mixer with the paddle attachment (or a hand-held mixer), beat the butter, sugar and brown sugar in the mixing bowl until well blended, about 3 minutes. Add the eggs one at a time, beating well after each addition. Beat in the vanilla. With the machine on low speed, gradually add the flour mixture, beating just until incorporated (do not overmix or the cookies will be tough). Mix in the chocolate chips, raisins, and then lastly, the chopped nuts.

Line 4 heavy, large baking sheets with parchment paper or spray the baking sheets with nonstick cooking spray. Using ½ cup of dough for each cookie, mound the dough atop the prepared baking sheets, spacing evenly and forming 5 mounds on each baking sheet. With the palm of your hand lightly press down on the cookie dough to flatten. Working in batches, bake the cookies until they are golden brown all over and the very center is still pale golden, about 15 minutes. Cool the cookies on the baking sheet for 5 minutes. Transfer the cookies to a rack and cool completely.

Do-ahead tip: The dough freezes well unbaked, so you can prepare it up to 7 days before baking. The cookies are fantastic for shipping. Tightly sealed cookies keep for up to 3 days.

Zov's kitchen note: For this recipe, measure nuts whole before you toast them. But it's easier to chop the nuts after they are toasted. Dried cherries or dried cranberries can stand in for the raisins. A 4-ounce ice cream scoop makes mounding the dough onto the baking sheet quick and easy.

1 ¾ cups whole almonds
1 ½ cups pecan halves
2 ¼ cups all-purpose flour
2 teaspoons baking soda
½ teaspoon salt
10 ounces (2 ½ sticks) unsalted butter, room temperature
1 cup granulated sugar
⅔ cup (packed) golden brown sugar
2 large eggs, room temperature
1 ½ teaspoons pure vanilla extract
1 12-ounce package Hershey's dark chocolate chips
2 cups raisins
Parchment paper or nonstick vegetable-oil cooking spray

SWEETS mom's S cookies

I loved watching my mother make these cookies when I was a child, and I loved eating them, too. So light and flaky, they crumble in your mouth on the first bite. A longtime favorite at our bakery, they're lovely for a shower or afternoon tea, and would make a delicious hostess gift. Who wouldn't be delighted to get them?

MAKES ABOUT 6 DOZEN

12 ounces (3 sticks) unsalted butter, at room temperature
1 cup granulated sugar
1 tablespoon water
1 teaspoon vanilla extract
3 cups all-purpose flour
½ cup almond flour (see note)
1 cup powdered sugar, for dusting

Using a stand mixer with the paddle attachment (or a handheld mixer), beat the butter in the mixer bowl on medium-high speed until light and fluffy, about 5 minutes. Gradually add the sugar, beating until the sugar is no longer granulated or sandy, about 5 minutes. Beat in the water and vanilla. Add the all-purpose flour and almond flour and beat just until blended. Divide the dough into 6 equal pieces, then form each piece into a log. Wrap each dough log separately with plastic wrap and refrigerate until the dough becomes firm but still pliable, about 30 minutes. Meanwhile, preheat the oven to 350°F.

Roll each dough log it into a ½-inch-diameter rope. Cut the dough crosswise and on a diagonal into 3-inch-long strips. Shape the strips into S or crescent shapes on the prepared baking sheets. Bake until the cookies are a light golden pale color, about 18 minutes. Cool completely on a cooling rack, then dust the cookies with powdered sugar.

Do-ahead tip: Store the cookies between sheets of wax paper in an airtight container at room temperature for up to 4 days or in the freezer for up to 5 months. Do not dust with powdered sugar until you are ready to serve.

Zov's kitchen note: Almond flour is available at natural foods stores and specialty foods stores. As a substitute, pulse blanched slivered almonds in a food processor until a coarse powder forms.

SWEETS gata

This delicious Armenian sweet roll is similar to coffee cake. Begin preparing the dough a day ahead so it has time to rise.

MAKES 6

Make the dough: Using a heavy-duty stand mixer fitted with the paddle attachment, mix 6 cups of flour, sugar, yeast and salt in the mixer bowl until well blended. Whisk the sour cream, butter, 2 eggs and the egg yolks in a large bowl to blend. With the mixer on low speed, slowly pour the egg mixture into the dry ingredients, mixing until the dough comes together. Replace the paddle attachment with the dough hook and knead the dough on medium speed until soft and slightly tacky, about 3 minutes. Transfer the dough to a floured work surface and knead until smooth and elastic.

Line a large baking sheet with plastic wrap. Divide the dough evenly into 6 balls, each weighing about 10 ounces, or about 4 inches round. Wrap each ball separately in plastic wrap and place them on the prepared baking sheet. Cover the entire baking sheet with plastic wrap again and refrigerate overnight. Wrapping the dough balls separately prevents them from rising too much while in the refrigerator. The extra cover of plastic wrap ensures they do not dry out.

Unwrap each dough ball and return them to the baking sheet lined with plastic wrap. Cover and keep in a draft-free area and at room temperature until risen and nearly doubled in size, about 3 hours.

Meanwhile, make the streusel filling: Melt the butter in a large, nonstick skillet with 2-inch-high sides over medium heat. Add the flour and stir almost constantly until the flour becomes light brown and resembles golden brown sugar and small sand pebbles, about 20 minutes. Set aside to cool completely. Mix in the sugar. »

Dough
6 cups all-purpose flour plus
2 tablespoons granulated sugar
2 (¼-ounce) packages rapid-rise yeast
1 teaspoon salt
16 ounces sour cream, at room temperature
8 ounces (2 sticks) unsalted butter, softened
2 large eggs, at room temperature
2 large egg yolks, at room temperature

Streusel filling
8 ounces (2 sticks) unsalted butter
3½ cups all-purpose flour
2 cups sugar

Assembly
1 large egg mixed with 1 tablespoon water or whole milk (for egg wash)
3 tablespoons sesame seeds

Assemble the gata: Line 2 large baking sheets with parchment paper. Using a rolling pin, roll out 1 ball of dough at a time on a very lightly floured work surface to a thin 10-inch round. Do not flour the dough too much as you roll it out or it will become dry. Sprinkle about ¾ cup of the streusel filling over the entire surface of the dough; press the filling with your hands to flatten it. Starting with the edge closest to you, roll the dough tightly, as though you were making a cinnamon roll, to enclose the filling. Wrap the rolled cylinder of dough into a round coil, which will be about 5-inches in diameter. Place the gata on the prepared baking sheet and tuck the end under. Repeat with the remaining dough balls and filling, arranging 3 gatas on each baking sheet, spaced evenly apart. Flatten the gatas to 1½-inches thick and 6-inches in diameter. Pierce the dough all over with a fork. Cover lightly with plastic wrap and set aside in a warm draft-free area until the dough rises slightly, about 1 hour.

Meanwhile, preheat the oven to 350°F. Brush the gata with the egg wash and sprinkle with sesame seeds. Bake until golden brown all over, about 35 minutes. Cool for 30 minutes. Cut into wedges and serve warm.

Do-ahead tip Gata can be frozen for up to 6 months. Cool completely and store in freezer bags. To rewarm, wrap in foil and bake at 350°F.

The egg wash gives gata a shiny golden sheen. >

SWEETS: lemon sour cream pound cake

Not your typical pound cake, the secret to this extra moist and delicate version is instant lemon pudding. I love it with my morning coffee or whenever I'm in the mood for a treat. For dessert, serve warm with vanilla ice cream, blueberry compote and dollops of whipped cream.

SERVES 10 TO 12

Make the cake: Preheat the oven to 350°F. Generously butter a 10-inch tube pan, then dust the pan with flour and tap out any excess flour.

Sift the flour, instant pudding, baking powder, salt and baking soda into a medium bowl. Using an electric mixer, beat the sugar, butter, cream cheese and lemon zest in a large bowl until light and fluffy. Add the eggs one at a time, beating well after each addition. Beat in the lemon extract. Add the flour mixture alternately with the sour cream, beating until smooth after each addition. Pour the batter into the prepared pan.

Bake until a wooden skewer inserted near the center comes out clean, about 1 hour and 20 minutes. Transfer the cake to a rack and cool in the pan for 15 minutes. Invert the cake onto the cooling rack and remove the pan. Turn the cake so that the domed risen side is facing upward. Using a wooden skewer, poke holes all over the cake. Set the cooling rack on top of a baking sheet.

Glaze the cake: Mix the powdered sugar, lemon juice and zest in a heavy small saucepan over medium heat just until the sugar dissolves and the mixture comes to a simmer, about 3 minutes. While the cake is still warm, brush the syrup over the cake with a pastry brush, covering the entire cake and allowing the syrup to completely penetrate the cake.

Do-ahead tip: Refrigerate, tightly wrapped, for up to 1 week, or freeze for up to 2 months.

Cut the cake into wedges and serve with fresh berries and dollops of whipped cream.

Zov's kitchen note: If you serve the cake with vanilla ice cream and blueberry compote, a sprig of mint makes a lovely and delicious garnish. If you love orange flavor, just add ½ cup of orange juice and 1 tablespoon of orange zest.

Cake
- 2½ cups all-purpose flour
- 1 3.4-ounce package instant lemon pudding
- 2 teaspoons baking powder
- ½ teaspoon fine salt
- ¼ teaspoon baking soda
- 2 cups granulated sugar
- 8 ounces (2 sticks) unsalted butter, at room temperature
- 3 ounces cream cheese, at room temperature
- 2 tablespoons finely grated lemon zest (from about 2 lemons)
- 4 large eggs, at room temperature
- 2 teaspoons lemon extract
- 1 cup sour cream, at room temperature

Glaze
- ¾ cup powdered sugar
- ½ cup fresh lemon juice
- 1 tablespoon finely grated lemon zest (from 1 lemon)

Toppings
- Assorted fresh berries
- Whipped cream

SWEETS quince coffee cake

This is everything coffee cake should be: moist, tender and buttery. Quince jam adds brightness.

SERVES 6 TO 8

Preheat the oven to 350°F. Lightly oil a 9-inch square baking pan.

Using an electric mixer, beat the butter and sugar in a large bowl until fluffy, about 3 minutes. Add the yolks one at a time, beating well after each addition. Beat in the salt.

In a medium bowl, mix the yogurt and vanilla. In a small bowl, stir the vinegar and baking soda (the mixture will bubble and foam). Stir the vinegar mixture into the yogurt mixture (this mixture will bubble too).

Beat the flour into the butter mixture alternately with the yogurt mixture, beginning and ending with the flour and scraping down the sides of the bowl. The batter will be semi-soft.

Transfer the batter to the prepared baking pan. Spoon the jam atop the batter in five mounds, spacing evenly apart. Using a knife or skewer, swirl the jam decoratively through the batter. Bake for 35 to 40 minutes or until a toothpick inserted into the center of the cake comes out with some crumbs attached.

Transfer the pan to a rack and cool the cake to room temperature. Sift the powder sugar over the cake. Cut into squares and serve.

Zov's kitchen note: Sour cream can stand in for yogurt. If you don't have time to make your own quince jam, use store-bought apricot or strawberry preserves instead.

When adding the vinegar and baking soda to the yogurt, the mixture will bubble and rise. This is the leavening part of the recipe. Anytime you use vinegar in dough, it always softens the mixture.

- 2 teaspoons vegetable oil
- 8 ounces (2 sticks) unsalted butter
- 1 cup granulated sugar
- 4 large egg yolks
- ¼ teaspoon salt
- 1 cup plain yogurt
- 1 tablespoon vanilla extract
- 2 teaspoons distilled white vinegar
- 1 teaspoon baking soda
- 2½ cups all-purpose flour
- ⅔ cup Quince Jam, stirred to loosen (page 112)
- Powdered sugar, for dusting

SWEETS: red velvet cupcakes

So moist and tender with extra creamy icing, these cupcakes literally melt in your mouth. No wonder they are one of the most popular cupcakes at our bakery. It's a fun dessert that kids love. The icing is terrific with carrot cake and apple cake, too.

MAKES 24 STANDARD-SIZE CUPCAKES OR 12 JUMBO CUPCAKES

Make the cupcakes: Preheat the oven to 350°F. Line 24 standard (⅓-cup) muffin cups or 12 jumbo muffin cups with paper cupcake liners.

Sift the flour, cocoa powder and salt in a medium bowl to blend; set aside. Using a stand mixer fitted with the paddle attachment (or a handheld mixer), beat the oil and sugar in the mixer bowl on medium speed until well combined. Add eggs one at a time and beat well after each addition. Stop the machine and add the food coloring and vanilla. Using the lowest speed, mix until the food coloring is well combined. Add the flour mixture in 2 additions, alternating with the buttermilk in 2 additions, and beating on low speed just until well blended between additions. Whisk the vinegar and baking soda in a small bowl for 10 seconds (the mixture will bubble), then quickly mix it into the batter. Using ¼ cup of batter for standard-size cupcakes and ½ cup of batter for jumbo cupcakes, divide the batter among the prepared muffin cups. Bake until a tester inserted into the center comes out clean, about 18 minutes for standard cupcakes and 22 minutes for jumbo. Cool the cupcakes for 5 minutes, then transfer them to a rack to cool completely.

Make the cream cheese frosting: Using an electric mixer on medium speed, beat the cream cheese and butter in a large bowl until smooth and creamy, about 3 minutes. Beat in the vanilla. Gradually add the powdered sugar, beating constantly until smooth and creamy. At this point, the frosting will be very soft but can be spooned atop the cupcakes. For stiffer frosting, cover the frosting and refrigerate until it is thick enough to spread or pipe onto the cupcakes, about 1 hour. Do not refrigerate the frosting for more than 2 hours or it may become too firm to spread.

Frost the cupcakes: Spread the frosting on the cupcakes or spoon the frosting into a piping bag and pipe decoratively atop the cupcakes.

Do-ahead tip: The cupcakes can be made 1 day ahead. Store in an airtight container at room temperature.

Cupcakes

- 2½ cups cake flour
- ¼ cup unsweetened Dutch-process cocoa powder (see *Pantry and Produce*)
- 1 teaspoon salt
- 1½ cups canola oil
- 1½ cups granulated sugar
- 2 large eggs, at room temperature
- ¼ cup red food coloring
- 1 teaspoon vanilla extract
- 1 cup buttermilk
- 2 teaspoons distilled white vinegar
- 1½ teaspoons baking soda

Cream cheese frosting

- 2 8-ounce packages cream cheese, at room temperature
- 6 tablespoons (¾ stick) unsalted butter, at room temperature
- 1½ teaspoons vanilla extract
- 3½ cups powdered sugar, sifted

SWEETS: simple moist carrot cake

This feel-good dessert has cast its sweet spell on our customers; it's one of the biggest sellers in our bakery. Everyone loves this rich and comforting cake. Toasted walnuts and coconut give it a moist and chewy texture.

SERVES 12

Make the cake: Preheat the oven to 350°F. Place the walnuts on a baking sheet and bake until lightly browned and fragrant, stirring occasionally, about 8 minutes. Scatter the coconut over another baking sheet and bake until golden brown, stirring occasionally so that the coconut browns evenly, about 10 minutes. Set the toasted walnuts and coconut aside to cool. Maintain the oven temperature.

Butter a 13x9x2-inch metal baking pan. Line the bottom of the pan with parchment paper. Whisk the flour, baking powder, baking soda, cinnamon, nutmeg and salt in a medium bowl to blend; set aside. Whisk the granulated sugar, brown sugar and eggs in a large bowl to blend. Slowly add the oil while whisking to blend well. Using a wooden spoon, stir in the flour mixture alternately with the buttermilk. Using a rubber spatula, fold in the carrots, pineapple with juices, toasted walnuts and toasted coconut. Do not overmix. Pour the batter into the prepared pan.

Bake until a toothpick inserted in the center of the cake comes out clean, about 1 hour. Transfer the cake to a cooling rack and cool in the pan for 30 minutes. Invert the cake onto the cooling rack and remove the parchment paper. Cool completely.

Make the frosting: Using an electric mixer on medium speed, beat the cream cheese and butter in a large bowl until smooth, about 3 minutes. Add the vanilla and beat well. Gradually add the powdered sugar, beating constantly until smooth, fluffy and creamy.

Spread the frosting over the top of the cake (not the sides). Cut the cake into squares and serve.

Do-ahead tip: The frosted cake can be refrigerated in an airtight container for up to 2 days. Serve cold or at room temperature.

Zov's kitchen note: The cake can also be made in a greased 10-inch tube pan. And you can use the batter for carrot cupcakes. To make, spray 12 muffin tins with nonstick cooking spray and divide the batter evenly. Bake for 15-18 minutes, or until a tester comes out clean.

Cake
- 1 cup walnuts, coarsely chopped
- 1 cup sweetened flaked coconut
- 2½ cups all-purpose flour
- 1 tablespoon baking powder
- 2 teaspoons baking soda
- 1½ teaspoons ground cinnamon
- ½ teaspoon ground nutmeg
- ¼ teaspoon salt
- 2 cups granulated sugar
- ½ cup (packed) golden brown sugar
- 4 large eggs
- 1½ cups canola oil
- ¾ cup buttermilk
- 3 cups shredded peeled carrots (from about 1 pound)
- 1 8-ounce can crushed pineapple with juices

Frosting
- 2 8-ounce packages cream cheese, at room temperature
- 6 tablespoons (¾ stick) unsalted butter, at room temperature
- 1½ teaspoons vanilla extract
- 1¾ cups powdered sugar

SWEETS pineapple upside-down cake

For so many people, just the thought of pineapple upside-down cake brings back fond memories of mom making this simple dessert for a perfect end to a Sunday dinner. There was a reason why it was so popular: You can make it in about 20 minutes from ingredients you probably have on hand. But the appeal goes beyond convenience. The sweet-tart juice from the pineapple combines with the brown sugar to create a delicious sauce that slowly soaks into the light, fluffy cake. Top it off with whipped cream or ice cream and you've got a dessert that's close to perfection. Why don't you try it right now?

SERVES 8

Preheat the oven to 350°F. Lightly spray a 10-inch round cake pan that is 2-inches high with cooking spray.

Melt 4 ounces (1 stick) of the butter in a heavy, large skillet over medium heat. Add the brown sugar and stir until the sugar is dissolved, about 5 minutes. Pour the mixture into the prepared cake pan and set the pan over very low heat to allow the brown sugar mixture to spread evenly over the bottom of the cake pan.

While the cake pan is still on the stove, arrange 8 pineapple slices over the brown sugar mixture, making sure there is 1 pineapple slice in the center. Cut the remaining 4 pineapple slices in half and overlap the cut slices around inside edge of the pan. Fill the centers of the pineapple slices with pecan halves.

Whisk the flour, baking powder and salt into a medium bowl to blend. Using an electric mixer on high speed, beat the remaining 6 ounces (1½ sticks) of butter and the sugar in a large bowl until creamy. Add the eggs one at a time, beating until well blended. Beat in the vanilla. Scrape down the sides of the bowl. Add the flour mixture alternating with the milk in batches until the flour is completely incorporated into the batter. Gently pour the batter over the pineapple mixture, spreading evenly and being careful not to rearrange the pineapple or pecans.

Bake until the cake is golden on top and springs back when gently pressed with your fingertips, about 1 hour and 5 minutes. Transfer the pan to a cooling rack and let cool for 10 minutes. »

Nonstick vegetable-oil cooking spray
10 ounces (2½ sticks) unsalted butter, at room temperature, divided
1½ cups packed dark brown sugar
3 8-ounce cans sliced pineapple in syrup (about 12 slices), drained
16 pecan halves
2 cups all-purpose flour
2½ teaspoons baking powder
¾ teaspoon fine-grained salt
1 cup granulated sugar
2 large eggs
1 teaspoon vanilla extract
1 cup whole milk

Accompaniments
Whipped cream or vanilla ice cream

Using a small spatula, loosen the cake from the edge of the cake pan. Place a rimmed serving platter over the cake and invert the cake and platter together at once. Gently shake to help the cake release from the pan, if necessary, then lift off the pan. Rearrange any pieces of pineapple or pecans, if necessary. Cut the warm cake into wedges and serve with whipped cream or ice cream.

Do-ahead tip: This cake is best served warm the day it is made, but it can be made up to 1 day ahead. Wrap with plastic wrap and refrigerate. Bring to room temperature before serving or microwave the cake slices on high at 10-second intervals just until warm.

Zov's kitchen note: Pineapple upside-down cake was traditionally made on top of the stove in a cast-iron skillet (the handle made it easy to flip the cake upside down). These upside-down skillet cakes, also made with apples and cherries, can be traced back in United States as far as the early 1900s. But it wasn't until canned pineapple hit the market that the version we all know and love became popular. I still prefer to use canned pineapple, just as home cooks did in the '50s and '60s, because of its consistency, ease and availability.

SWEETS super easy holiday fruit and nut loaf

This flavorful sweet bread is packed with dried fruit and nuts. Wrap in cellophane or cheesecloth and tie with a pretty ribbon for a festive holiday treat or hostess gift.

MAKES 1 LOAF

Preheat the oven to 325°F. Spray a 9x5x3-inch loaf pan with cooking spray, then line the pan with parchment paper. Toss the walnuts, dates, apricots and flour in a large bowl to coat the fruit with the flour. Using an electric hand mixer, beat the brown sugar, eggs and vanilla in a large bowl to blend. Mix in the baking powder and baking soda. Pour the egg mixture into the flour mixture and stir until all the fruits are well coated. Transfer the mixture to the prepared loaf pan, pressing the mixture into the pan to make sure it covers the bottom and fills the corners. Bake until the cake is dark brown on top and a tester comes out clean when inserted into the center, about 1 hour. Transfer the pan to a rack and cool the cake (the cake will fall as it cools).

Do-ahead tip: Store in an airtight container at room temperature for up to 2 weeks, or freeze in a freezer bag for up to 3 months.

- Nonstick vegetable-oil cooking spray
- 2 cups walnut halves (about 7 ounces)
- 2 cups whole dates, pitted (about 11 ounces)
- 1 cup whole dried apricots (about 7 ounces)
- ½ cup all-purpose flour
- ¾ cup (packed) golden brown sugar
- 3 large eggs
- 1 teaspoon vanilla extract
- 1 teaspoon baking powder
- 1 teaspoon baking soda

SWEETS simple poached pears

For an elegant and simple dessert, drizzle with chocolate or caramel sauce or serve with ice cream. I also like to team these sweet pears with Parmesan-Crusted Chicken Salad (page 240). Adding a vitamin C tablet to the water prevents the pears from browning.

SERVES 4 TO 8

Toss the pears in a large bowl with lemon juice to coat.

Combine 5 cups of water and the sugar in a 4-quart saucepan and bring to a boil over high heat. Add the vitamin C tablet and the pears. Decrease the heat to medium-low and simmer until the pears are tender, about 10 minutes. Transfer the pears and liquid to a deep bowl; make sure the pears are completely submerged in the liquid. Refrigerate until ready to use.

Do-ahead tip: Refrigerate the pears and syrup together in an airtight container for up to 3 days.

4 ripe Anjou pears (about 2 pounds), peeled, halved and cored
2 tablespoons fresh lemon juice
5 cups water
2 cups granulated sugar
1 vitamin C tablet

Index

Note: Page numbers in **boldface** type indicate recipes themselves.

A

Aleppo pepper
about, 18
Couscous with Preserved Lemon, Aleppo Pepper and Pine Nuts, 175, 199, 200, **250–251**

Almond(s)
Crunchy Granola with Almonds, Oats and Dried Fruits, **100–101**
Jewel Jam Cookies, **338–339**
Jumble Cookies, **340–341**
Romesco Sauce, **312–313**
Stuffed Trout with Tahini Sauce, **188–189**, 304

Almond flour
Blueberry Muffins with Almond Streusel, **326–327**
Mom's S Cookies, **342–343**

Almond paste
Almond Crescent Cookies, **318–319**

Anchovies
Olive Tapenade, **60–61**
Tuscan Tomato Salad (Panzanella), **164–165**, 197

Appetizers, 24–79
Beef Pirozhki with Mushrooms, **28–31**, 56, 263
Che Kofta, **32–33**, 309
Cheese Boreg, **36–38**
Crispy Onion Rings, **34–35**, 220, 303
Crispy Vegetable Croquettes (Falafels), **42–44**, 304
Gravlax, **46–48**, 74
Grilled Eggplant, Olive and Tomato Bruschetta, **50–51**
Koufta, **52–56**
Old World Sliders, **58–59**
Olive Tapenade, **60–61**
Oven-Fried Parmesan Chicken Fingers, 224, **236–237**
Parmesan Bruschetta, **40–41**, 138
Perfect Guacamole, **64–65**, 205
Pureed Bean Dip with Yogurt and Dill, **72–73**
Spicy Pomegranate-Glazed Chicken Wings, **62–63**, 303
Spicy Sesame Seed Flatbreads with Pepper Paste, **66–70**
Tomato-Basil Risotto Fritters, **78–80**, 308
Tomato-Mint Salsa, **58–59**
Yogurt and Feta Cheese Spread, **58–59**
Zucchini Fritters with Gravlax, **74–75**

Apples
Apple-Cinnamon Phyllo Crumble, **328–329**

Apricot(s)
Apricot Jam, **84–86**, 323
Apricot Shortbread Bars, **322–323**
Super Easy Holiday Fruit and Nut Loaf, **360–361**

Aquavit
Gravlax, **46–48**, 74

Arugula
Greek Burgers with Baby Arugula and Feta, **208–209**, 303

Asiago cheese
Cheese Sauce, **286–288**
Zov's Silky Macaroni and Cheese, **286–288**

Asian Noodle Chicken Salad, 224, **226–227**

Avocados
about, 64
Black Bean and Avocado Salad, **150–151**, 197
Grilled Halibut with Mango Salsa, Cilantro and Mint, **170–171**
Perfect Guacamole, **64–65**, 205
Seared Ahi with Edamame, **184–185**
Summer Corn Salad with Avocados and Sherry, **160–161**, 208

B

Baby greens
in Parmesan-Crusted Chicken Salad with Poached Pears and Candied Walnuts, 240

Bacon
in Breakfast Bake with Soujouk and Potatoes, 89
Classic Manhattan Clam Chowder, **126–127**
Wedge Salad with Applewood-Smoked Bacon and Maytag Blue Cheese, **154–155**
in Zov's Silky Macaroni and Cheese, 288

Balsamic Vinaigrette, 294

Bananas
Bananas Foster French Toast, 82, **90–91**

Bar(s)
Apricot Shortbread Bars, **322–323**

Barley
about, 18
Barley Salad with Summer Vegetables and Feta Cheese, **152–153**

Barramundi
Barramundi with Preserved Lemons and Chickpeas, 160, **174–175**

Basil
Grilled Eggplant, Olive and Tomato Bruschetta, **50–51**
Marinara Sauce, 242, 292, **306–307**
Romesco Sauce, **312–313**
Seared Ahi with Edamame, **184–185**
Shrimp with Cannellini Beans, **172–173**
Spicy Shrimp Curry Bowl, **182–183**
Summer Corn Salad with Avocados and Sherry, **160–161**, 208
Tomato-Basil Pistou, **304**
Tomato-Basil Risotto Fritters, **78–80**, 308
Tomato-Basil Sauce, 76, 275, **308**
Tuscan Tomato Salad (Panzanella), **164–165**, 197

Beans. See Black beans; Butter beans; Cannellini beans; Edamame beans; Fava beans; Garbanzo beans; »

Index

Green beans; Kidney beans
Beef
  Beef and Eggplant Tagine, **194–195**
  Beef Brochettes with Garlic-Thyme Marinade, **196–197,** 303
  Beef Pirozhki with Mushrooms, **28–31,** 56, 263
  Beef Short Ribs with Horseradish-Yogurt Sauce, **198–199**
  Beef Stroganoff with Mushrooms and Green Onions, **202–203**
  Beef Tenderloin with Spinach, Leeks and Goat Cheese, **200–201,** 302
  Bolognese Sauce, 199, 292, **300–301**
  Braised Green Beans with Beef and Tomatoes, **206–207**
  in Cabbage Salad with Bulgur, 148
  Che Kofta, **32–33,** 309
  in Greek Burgers with Baby Arugula and Feta, 208
  Grilled Skirt Steak with Zahtar and Fresh Lime, **204–205,** 284
  Koufta, **52–56**
  Meat and Potato Casserole, **216–217**
  in Moroccan Harira Soup, 134
  Old World Sliders, **58–59**
  in Spaghetti with Turkey Meatballs and Marinara Sauce, 242
  Spicy Ground Meat Kebabs, 163, **212–213,** 311
  Zov's Favorite Meatloaf, **220–221**
Beets
  Beet Salad with Watercress, Spinach and Fennel, **158–159,** 228
Bell peppers
  Asian Noodle Chicken Salad, 224, **226–227**
  Barley Salad with Summer Vegetables and Feta Cheese, **152–153**
  Black Bean and Avocado Salad, **150–151,** 197
  Bulgur Pilaf with Tomatoes, 228, 246, **284–285,** 309
  Cauliflower and Broccoli Salad with Red Wine-Dijon Vinaigrette, **162–163,** 200, 228
  Chicken Tagine with Currants, **238–239**
  Classic Manhattan Clam Chowder, **126–127**
  Fusilli Pasta Salad with Rotisserie Chicken, **230–231**
  Grilled Halibut with Mango Salsa, Cilantro and Mint, **170–171**
  Ranchero Sauce, **268–269**
  Red Pepper Paste, 66, 303, **305**
  Roasted Red Pepper and Eggplant Sauce, 213, **311**
  Romesco Sauce, **312–313**
  Seared Ahi with Edamame, **184–185**
  Spanish Omelet with Manchego and Cheddar Cheese, **114–115**
  Spicy Shrimp Curry Bowl, **182–183**
  Summer Corn Salad with Avocados and Sherry, **160–161,** 208
  Tomato and Watermelon Salad with Feta Cheese, **156–157**
  Torte Milanese with Spinach, **106–108**
  Tuscan Tomato Salad (Panzanella), **164–165,** 197
Biscuits
  Simple Buttermilk Biscuits, **110–111,** 131
Bistro Potato Gratin, 181, 200, 208, **254–255**
Black and White Pound Cake, 324–325
Black beans
  about, 131, 150
  Black Bean and Avocado Salad, **150–151,** 197
  Black Bean Soup with Vegetables, **130–131**
Blue cheese
  about, 154
  Blue Cheese Dressing, 34, 154, **294**
  Creamy Angel Hair Pasta with Tomatoes and Gorgonzola Cheese, 176, **264–265**
  in Spicy Sesame Seed Flatbreads with Pepper Paste, 66–70
  Wedge Salad with Applewood-Smoked Bacon and Maytag Blue Cheese, **154–155**
Blueberries
  Blueberry Muffins with Almond Streusel, **326–327**
  Blueberry Syrup, **98–99**
Blueberries, dried
  Crunchy Granola with Almonds, Oats and Dried Fruits, **100–101**
Bolognese Sauce, 199, 292, **300–301**
Bouillabaisse
  Mediterranean Bouillabaisse with Pearled Couscous, **186–187**
Braised Green Beans with Beef and Tomatoes, 206–207
Bread. See also Quick breads; Yeast breads
  Bananas Foster French Toast, 82, **90–91**
  Butternut Squash Parmesan Bread Pudding, 214, **260–261**
  Eggs Benedict with Gravlax and Creamy Hollandaise Sauce, 95, **102–103**
  Greek Burgers with Baby Arugula and Feta, **208–209,** 303
  Grilled Eggplant, Olive and Tomato Bruschetta, **50–51**
  Meat and Potato Casserole, **216–217**
  Old World Sliders, **58–59**
  Parmesan Bruschetta, **40–41,** 138
  Parmesan Croutons, 131, 132, **308**
  Romesco Sauce, **312–313**
  Tuscan Tomato Salad (Panzanella), **164–165,** 197
  Zov's Favorite Meatloaf, **220–221**
Bread pudding
  Butternut Squash Parmesan Bread Pudding, 214, **260–261**
Breadcrumbs
  Japanese. See Panko
  Tuscan Eggplant Parmesan, **274–277,** 308

Breakfast, 80–121
  Apricot Jam, **84–86,** 323
  Bananas Foster French Toast, 82, **90–91**
  Blueberry Syrup, **98–99**
  Breakfast Bake with Soujouk and Potatoes, **88–89,** 309
  Breakfast Potato Cakes, **94–96,** 103
  Crunchy Granola with Almonds, Oats and Dried Fruits, **100–101**
  Eggs Benedict with Gravlax and Creamy Hollandaise Sauce, 95, **102–103**
  Harisah (Pelted Wheat Porridge with Chicken), **234–235**
  Oatmeal Brûlée, **92–93**
  Old-Fashioned Pancakes with Blueberry Syrup, 82, **98–99**
  Quince Jam, **112–113,** 350
  Simple Buttermilk Biscuits, **110–111,** 131
  Sour Cherry Jam, **104–105**
  Spanish Omelet with Manchego and Cheddar Cheese, **114–115**
  Super Easy Fig Jam, **116–117**
  Torte Milanese with Spinach, **106–108**
  Ultimate Cinnamon Buns, **118–121**
Broccoli
  Cauliflower and Broccoli Salad with Red Wine-Dijon Vinaigrette, **162–163,** 200, 228
  in Creamy Potato-Leek Soup, 132
Brochettes
  Beef Brochettes with Garlic-Thyme Marinade, **196–197,** 303
Bruschetta
  Grilled Eggplant, Olive and Tomato Bruschetta, **50–51**
  Parmesan Bruschetta, **40–41,** 138
Buffalo wings
  Spicy Pomegranate-Glazed Chicken Wings, **62–63,** 303
Bulgur
  about, 18
  Bulgur Pilaf with Tomatoes, 228, 246, **284–285,** 309
  Cabbage Salad with Bulgur, **148–149,** 197, 219
  Che Kofta, **32–33,** 309
  Koufta, **52–56**
Burgers
  Greek Burgers with Baby Arugula and Feta, **208–209,** 303
  Old World Sliders, **58–59**
Burrata cheese, about, 60
Butter beans
  about, 252
  Butter Beans with Pancetta and Leeks, 246, **252–253**
Buttermilk
  Blue Cheese Dressing, 34, 154, **294**
  Blueberry Muffins with Almond Streusel, **326–327**
  Crispy Onion Rings, **34–35,** 220, 303
  Decadent Chocolate Cake, **334–337**
  Old-Fashioned Pancakes with Blueberry Syrup, 82, **98–99**
  Red Velvet Cupcakes, **352–353**
  Simple Buttermilk Biscuits, **110–111,** 131
  Simple Moist Carrot Cake, **354–355**
Butternut squash
  Butternut Squash Parmesan Bread Pudding, 214, **260–261**

C

Cabbage. *See also* Napa cabbage
  Cabbage Salad with Bulgur, **148–149,** 197, 219
Cakes
  Black and White Pound Cake, **324–325**
  Decadent Chocolate Cake, **334–337**
  Lemon Sour Cream Pound Cake, **348–349**
  Pineapple Upside-Down Cake, 316, **356–358**
  Red Velvet Cupcakes, **352–353**
  Simple Moist Carrot Cake, **354–355**

Cannellini beans
  in Butter Beans with Pancetta and Leeks, 252
  Shrimp with Cannellini Beans, **172–173**
Cannelloni Stuffed with Cheese, 256–257
Canning instructions, 86
Carrots
  Beef Short Ribs with Horseradish-Yogurt Sauce, **198–199**
  Black Bean Soup with Vegetables, **130–131**
  Bolognese Sauce, 199, 292, **300–301**
  Chicken and Rice Soup with Lemon, **136–137**
  Chicken Tagine with Currants, **238–239**
  Coconut Chicken Chowder with Lemongrass, **128–129**
  Fusilli Pasta Salad with Rotisserie Chicken, **230–231**
  Simple Moist Carrot Cake, **354–355**
  Spicy Shrimp Curry Bowl, **182–183**
  Vegetable Soup with Tomato-Basil Pistou, **138–139,** 304
Casseroles
  Breakfast Bake with Soujouk and Potatoes, **88–89,** 309
  Meat and Potato Casserole, **216–217**
  Zov's Silky Macaroni and Cheese, **286–288**
Cauliflower
  Cauliflower and Broccoli Salad with Red Wine-Dijon Vinaigrette, **162–163,** 200, 228
  in Creamy Potato-Leek Soup, 132
  Garlic Roasted Cauliflower with Parsley and Thyme, **272–273**
  Velvety Cream of Spinach and Cauliflower Soup, 124, **140–141**
Celery
  Asian Noodle Chicken Salad, 224, **226–227**
  Beef Short Ribs with Horseradish-Yogurt Sauce, **198–199** »

Index

Black Bean and Avocado Salad, **150–151,** 197
Black Bean Soup with Vegetables, **130–131**
Bolognese Sauce, 199, 292, **300–301**
Chicken and Rice Soup with Lemon, **136–137**
Classic Manhattan Clam Chowder, **126–127**
Coconut Chicken Chowder with Lemongrass, **128–129**
Creamy Potato-Leek Soup, 124, **132–133**
Fusilli Pasta Salad with Rotisserie Chicken, **230–231**
Moroccan Harira Soup, **134–135**
Ranchero Sauce, **268–269**
Spanish Omelet with Manchego and Cheddar Cheese, **114–115**
Summer Corn Salad with Avocados and Sherry, **160–161,** 208
Vegetable Soup with Tomato-Basil Pistou, **138–139,** 304
Velvety Cream of Spinach and Cauliflower Soup, 124, **140–141**

Che Kofta, 32–33, 309

Cheddar cheese
Beef Pirozhki with Mushrooms, **28–31,** 56, 263
Breakfast Bake with Soujouk and Potatoes, **88–89,** 309
Butternut Squash Parmesan Bread Pudding, 214, **260–261**
Cheese Enchiladas, **268–269**
Cheese Sauce, **286–288**
Spanish Omelet with Manchego and Cheddar Cheese, **114–115**
Tomato-Basil Risotto Fritters, **78–80,** 308
Zov's Silky Macaroni and Cheese, **286–288**

Cheese. See Asiago cheese; Blue cheese; Burrata cheese; Cheddar cheese; Cream cheese; Feta cheese; Fontina cheese; Goat cheese; Gouda cheese; Gruyère cheese; Manchego cheese; Monterey Jack cheese; Mozzarella cheese; Parmesan cheese; Parmigiano-Reggiano cheese; Pecorino Romano cheese; Ricotta cheese

Cheese Boreg, 36–38
Cheese Enchiladas, 268–269
Cherries
Cherry Crisps, **320–321**
Sour Cherry Jam, **104–105**
Sour Cherry Sauce, **214–215**

Cherries, dried
in Jumble Cookies, 341

Chicken
Asian Noodle Chicken Salad, 224, **226–227**
in Beef and Eggplant Tagine, 194
in Bulgur Pilaf with Tomatoes, 284
in Cabbage Salad with Bulgur, 148
Chicken and Rice Soup with Lemon, **136–137**
Chicken Tagine with Currants, **238–239**
Coconut Chicken Chowder with Lemongrass, **128–129**
cutting up wings, 62
Fusilli Pasta Salad with Rotisserie Chicken, **230–231**
Greek-Style Chicken Kebabs with Lemon and Oregano, 160, 163, 224, **232–233,** 309
Grilled Ginger-Lime Chicken Thighs with Harissa, **228–229**
Harisah (Pelted Wheat Porridge with Chicken), **234–235**
in Moroccan Harira Soup, 134
Oven-Fried Parmesan Chicken Fingers, 224, **236–237**
Parmesan-Crusted Chicken Salad with Poached Pears and Candied Walnuts, **240–241,** 362
Pelted Wheat Porridge with Chicken, **234–235**
Spicy Pomegranate-Glazed Chicken Wings, **62–63,** 303
in Spicy Shrimp Curry Bowl, 182
in Zov's Silky Macaroni and Cheese, 288

Chickpeas. See Garbanzo beans

Chile peppers
Chile-Lime Chipotle Sauce, 34, 208, **303**
handling, 64
Harissa, 175, 228, 239, **310**
Pureed Bean Dip with Yogurt and Dill, **72–73**
Spanish Rice Pilaf, 268, **278–279**

Chile-Lime Chipotle Sauce, 34, 208, 303

Chocolate
Almond Crescent Cookies, **318–319**
Black and White Pound Cake, **324–325**
Decadent Chocolate Cake, **334–337**
Ganache, **334–337**
Jumble Cookies, **340–341**

Chopped ingredients, photo of, 15

Choreg, 316, **330–333**

Chowders
Classic Manhattan Clam Chowder, **126–127**
Coconut Chicken Chowder with Lemongrass, **128–129**

Cilantro
Asian Noodle Chicken Salad, 224, **226–227**
Black Bean and Avocado Salad, **150–151,** 197
Black Bean Soup with Vegetables, **130–131**
Braised Green Beans with Beef and Tomatoes, **206–207**
Crispy Vegetable Croquettes (Falafels), **42–44,** 304
Curry Sauce, 182, **299**
Grilled Halibut with Mango Salsa, Cilantro and Mint, **170–171**
Moroccan Harira Soup, **134–135**

Perfect Guacamole, **64–65,** 205
Seared Ahi with Edamame, **184–185**
Spanish Rice Pilaf, 268, **278–279**
Spicy Grilled Salmon with Fresh Herbs and Ginger, **180–181**
Stuffed Trout with Tahini Sauce, **188–189,** 304
Tahini Sauce, 42, 292, **304**
Tamarind Pork Kebabs with Ginger and Soy, **218–219,** 303
Tortilla Soup with Fresh Corn, Cilantro and Lime, **142–143**

Clam(s)
Classic Manhattan Clam Chowder, **126–127**
Mediterranean Bouillabaisse with Pearled Couscous, **186–187**
shopping for, 187

Clam juice
Classic Manhattan Clam Chowder, **126–127**
Mediterranean Bouillabaisse with Pearled Couscous, **186–187**

Classic Manhattan Clam Chowder, 126–127

Cocoa powder
about, 18
Decadent Chocolate Cake, **334–337**
Red Velvet Cupcakes, **352–353**

Coconut
in Crunchy Granola with Almonds, Oats and Dried Fruits, 100
Simple Moist Carrot Cake, **354–355**

Coconut milk
about, 128
Coconut Chicken Chowder with Lemongrass, **128–129**
Curry Sauce, 182, **299**

Cod
in Stuffed Trout with Tahini Sauce, 188

Coffee
Decadent Chocolate Cake, **334–337**

Coffee cake
Quince Coffee Cake, **350–351**

Coho salmon
in Stuffed Trout with Tahini Sauce, 188

Cold soup
Creamy Potato-Leek Soup, 124, **132–133**

Condiments
Harissa, 175, 228, 239, **310**
Preserved Lemons, 60, 139, 175, 229, 239, 251, **296–297,** 310
Tomato-Cucumber Relish, 33, 89, 233, 271, 284, **309**

Cookies
Almond Crescent Cookies, **318–319**
Jewel Jam Cookies, **338–339**
Jumble Cookies, **340–341**
Mom's S Cookies, **342–343**

Coriander, about, 20

Corn
in Bulgur Pilaf with Tomatoes, 284
Coconut Chicken Chowder with Lemongrass, **128–129**
Holiday Creamed Corn, **258–259**
Summer Corn Salad with Avocados and Sherry, **160–161,** 208
Tortilla Soup with Fresh Corn, Cilantro and Lime, **142–143**
Ultimate Risotto with Fresh Peas, Mushrooms and Corn, 214, **280–283**

Corn syrup
in Ganache, 336

Cornstarch, diluting, 258

Couscous
Couscous with Preserved Lemon, Aleppo Pepper and Pine Nuts, 175, 199, 200, **250–251**
Mediterranean Bouillabaisse with Pearled Couscous, **186–187**

Crabmeat
in Zucchini Fritters with Gravlax, 74–75

Cranberries, dried
Crunchy Granola with Almonds, Oats and Dried Fruits, **100–101**
in Jumble Cookies, 341

Cream
Bistro Potato Gratin, 181, 200, 208, **254–255**
Bolognese Sauce, 199, 292, **300–301**
Butternut Squash Parmesan Bread Pudding, 214, **260–261**
Creamy Angel Hair Pasta with Tomatoes and Gorgonzola Cheese, 176, **264–265**
Creamy Hollandaise Sauce, 103, **295**
Creamy Mashed Potatoes, 199, 200, 220, **266–267**
Creamy Potato-Leek Soup, 124, **132–133**
Decadent Chocolate Cake, **334–337**
Ganache, **334–337**
Holiday Creamed Corn, **258–259**
Meat and Potato Casserole, **216–217**
Pan-Seared Scallops with Tarragon Mushroom Sauce, **176–178**
Velvety Cream of Spinach and Cauliflower Soup, 124, **140–141**
Zov's Favorite Meatloaf, **220–221**

Cream cheese
Black and White Pound Cake, **324–325**
Cream Cheese Frosting, **352–353, 354–355**
Lemon Sour Cream Pound Cake, **348–349**
Ultimate Cinnamon Buns, **118–121**

Creamy Angel Hair Pasta with Tomatoes and Gorgonzola Cheese, 176, **264–265**
Creamy Hollandaise Sauce, 103, **295**
Creamy Mashed Potatoes, 199, 200, 220, **266–267**
Creamy Potato-Leek Soup, 124, **132–133**

Cremini mushrooms
Beef Stroganoff with Mushrooms and Green Onions, **202–203**
Black Bean and Avocado Salad, **150–151,** 197
Pan-Seared Scallops with Tarragon Mushroom Sauce, **176–178**
Seared Ahi with Edamame, **184–185** »

Index

Ultimate Risotto with Fresh Peas, Mushrooms and Corn, 214, **280–283**
Crespelle, 256–257
Crisps
Cherry Crisps, **320–321**
Crispy Onion Rings, 34–35, 220, 303
Crispy Vegetable Croquettes, 42–44, 304
Croquettes
Crispy Vegetable Croquettes (Falafels), **42–44,** 304
Croutons
Parmesan Croutons, 131, 132, **308**
Crumbles
Apple-Cinnamon Phyllo Crumble, **328–329**
Crunchy Granola with Almonds, Oats and Dried Fruits, 100–101
Cucumbers
Asian Noodle Chicken Salad, 224, **226–227**
Barley Salad with Summer Vegetables and Feta Cheese, **152–153**
Summer Corn Salad with Avocados and Sherry, **160–161,** 208
Tomato and Watermelon Salad with Feta Cheese, **156–157**
Tomato-Cucumber Relish, 33, 89, 233, 271, 284, **309**
Tomato-Mint Salsa, **58–59**
Tuscan Tomato Salad (Panzanella), **164–165,** 197
Tzatziki Sauce, 62, 197, 219, **303**
Cupcakes
Red Velvet Cupcakes, **352–353**
Simple Moist Carrot Cake, 354
Currants
Chicken Tagine with Currants, **238–239**
Curry
Curry Sauce, 182, **299**
Spicy Shrimp Curry Bowl, **182–183**

D

Daikon
in Wedge Salad with Applewood-Smoked Bacon and Maytag Blue Cheese, 154
Dates
Super Easy Holiday Fruit and Nut Loaf, **360–361**
Decadent Chocolate Cake, 334–337
Diced ingredients, photo of, 15
Dill
Gravlax, **46–48,** 74
Pureed Bean Dip with Yogurt and Dill, **72–73**
Zucchini Fritters with Gravlax, **74–75**
Dips
Perfect Guacamole, **64–65,** 205
Pureed Bean Dip with Yogurt and Dill, **72–73**
Dough
for Cheese Boreg, **36–38**
yeast. *See* Yeast breads
Dressings. *See also* Vinaigrettes
for Barley Salad with Summer Vegetables and Feta Cheese, **152–153**
Blue Cheese Dressing, 34, 154, **294**
Lemon-Lime Dressing, **150–151**

E

Edamame beans
Seared Ahi with Edamame, **184–185**
Egg(s)
about, 82
Bananas Foster French Toast, 82, **90–91**
Beef Pirozhki with Mushrooms, **28–31,** 56, 263
Black and White Pound Cake, **324–325**
Blueberry Muffins with Almond Streusel, **326–327**
Breakfast Bake with Soujouk and Potatoes, **88–89,** 309
Butternut Squash Parmesan Bread Pudding, 214, **260–261**
Cannelloni Stuffed with Cheese, **256–257**
Cheese Boreg, **36–38**
Choreg, 316, **330–333**
Crespelle, **256–257**
Decadent Chocolate Cake, **334–337**
Eggs Benedict with Gravlax and Creamy Hollandaise Sauce, 95, **102–103**
Gata, **344–347**
Jumble Cookies, **340–341**
Lemon Sour Cream Pound Cake, **348–349**
Meat and Potato Casserole, **216–217**
Old-Fashioned Pancakes with Blueberry Syrup, 82, **98–99**
Pineapple Upside-Down Cake, 316, **356–358**
Red Velvet Cupcakes, **352–353**
Simple Moist Carrot Cake, **354–355**
Spaghetti with Turkey Meatballs and Marinara Sauce, **242–243,** 306
Spanish Omelet with Manchego and Cheddar Cheese, **114–115**
Super Easy Holiday Fruit and Nut Loaf, **360–361**
Torte Milanese with Spinach, **106–108**
Tuscan Eggplant Parmesan, **274–277,** 308
Zov's Favorite Meatloaf, **220–221**
Zucchini Fritters with Gravlax, **74–75**
Egg yolks
Apricot Shortbread Bars, **322–323**
Creamy Hollandaise Sauce, 103, **295**
Quince Coffee Cake, **350–351**
Ultimate Cinnamon Buns, **118–121**
Eggplant
Beef and Eggplant Tagine, **194–195**
Grilled Eggplant, Olive and Tomato Bruschetta, **50–51**
Roasted Red Pepper and Eggplant Sauce, 213, **311**
in Summer Corn Salad with Avocados and Sherry, 160
Tuscan Eggplant Parmesan, **274–277,** 308

Enchiladas
  Cheese Enchiladas, **268–269**
English muffins
  Eggs Benedict with Gravlax and Creamy Hollandaise Sauce, 95, **102–103**
Extra-virgin olive oil, about, 20

F

Falafels
  Crispy Vegetable Croquettes (Falafels), **42–44,** 304
Fava beans
  Crispy Vegetable Croquettes (Falafels), **42–44,** 304
  dried, about, 44
  peeling, 44
Fennel bulbs
  Beef Short Ribs with Horseradish-Yogurt Sauce, **198–199**
  Beet Salad with Watercress, Spinach and Fennel, **158–159,** 228
Feta cheese
  about, 156
  Barley Salad with Summer Vegetables and Feta Cheese, **152–153**
  in Beet Salad with Watercress, Spinach and Fennel, 159
  Cheese Boreg, **36–38**
  Greek Burgers with Baby Arugula and Feta, **208–209,** 303
  Tomato and Watermelon Salad with Feta Cheese, **156–157**
  Tomato-Cucumber Relish, 33, 89, 233, 271, 284, **309**
  Yogurt and Feta Cheese Spread, **58–59**
Figs
  about, 116
  Super Easy Fig Jam, **116–117**
Figs, dried
  Beef Short Ribs with Horseradish-Yogurt Sauce, **198–199**
  Crunchy Granola with Almonds, Oats and Dried Fruits, **100–101**
Fish. See Seafood
Fish sauce
  about, 298
  Ginger-Sesame Vinaigrette, 226, **289**
Flatbreads
  Spicy Sesame Seed Flatbreads with Pepper Paste, **66–70**
Fontina cheese
  Cheese Boreg, **36–38**
  Cheese Sauce, **286–288**
  in Tomato-Basil Risotto Fritters, 78
  Zov's Silky Macaroni and Cheese, **286–288**
French toast
  Bananas Foster French Toast, 82, **90–91**
Fritters
  Tomato-Basil Risotto Fritters, **78–80,** 308
Frosting
  Cream Cheese Frosting, **352–353, 354–355**
  Ganache, **334–337**
Fruit. See specific fruits
Fusilli Pasta Salad with Rotisserie Chicken, 230–231

G

Ganache, 334–337
Garbanzo beans
  in Barley Salad with Summer Vegetables and Feta Cheese, 153
  Barramundi with Preserved Lemons and Chickpeas, 160, **174–175**
  Crispy Vegetable Croquettes (Falafels), **42–44,** 304
  Lamb Stew with Swiss Chard, **210–211**
  Moroccan Harira Soup, **134–135**
  Pureed Bean Dip with Yogurt and Dill, **72–73**
Garlic
  about, 310
  Beef Brochettes with Garlic-Thyme Marinade, **196–197,** 303
  Stuffed Trout with Tahini Sauce, **188–189,** 304
Garlic Roasted Cauliflower with Parsley and Thyme, 272–273
Gata, 344–347
Ginger
  Coconut Chicken Chowder with Lemongrass, **128–129**
  Crispy Vegetable Croquettes (Falafels), **42–44,** 304
  Ginger-Sesame Vinaigrette, 226, **289**
  Grilled Ginger-Lime Chicken Thighs with Harissa, **228–229**
  Spicy Grilled Salmon with Fresh Herbs and Ginger, **180–181**
  Tamarind Pork Kebabs with Ginger and Soy, **218–219,** 303
Goat cheese
  Beef Tenderloin with Spinach, Leeks and Goat Cheese, **200–201,** 302
  Beet Salad with Watercress, Spinach and Fennel, **158–159,** 228
  Parmesan-Crusted Chicken Salad with Poached Pears and Candied Walnuts, **240–241,** 362
Gorgonzola cheese
  Creamy Angel Hair Pasta with Tomatoes and Gorgonzola Cheese, 176, **264–265**
Gouda cheese
  Beef Pirozhki with Mushrooms, **28–31,** 56, 263
  Breakfast Bake with Soujouk and Potatoes, **88–89,** 309
  in Spicy Sesame Seed Flatbreads with Pepper Paste, 66–70
Granola
  Crunchy Granola with Almonds, Oats and Dried Fruits, **100–101**
Grape(s)
  Beef and Eggplant Tagine, **194–195**
Grape(s), sour
  about, 194 »

Index

Beef and Eggplant Tagine, **194–195**
Grapefruit
    Grilled Halibut with Mango Salsa, Cilantro and Mint, **170–171**
Gravlax, 46–48, 74
Greek Burgers with Baby Arugula and Feta, 208–209, 303
Greek-Style Chicken Kebabs with Lemon and Oregano, 160, 163, 224, **232–233,** 309
Green beans
    Braised Green Beans with Beef and Tomatoes, **206–207**
    Fusilli Pasta Salad with Rotisserie Chicken, **230–231**
    Seared Ahi with Edamame, **184–185**
    Vegetable Soup with Tomato-Basil Pistou, **138–139,** 304
Green onions
    Asian Noodle Chicken Salad, 224, **226–227**
    Barley Salad with Summer Vegetables and Feta Cheese, **152–153**
    Beef Stroganoff with Mushrooms and Green Onions, **202–203**
    Black Bean and Avocado Salad, **150–151,** 197
    Breakfast Bake with Soujouk and Potatoes, **88–89,** 309
    Cabbage Salad with Bulgur, **148–149,** 197, 219
    Fusilli Pasta Salad with Rotisserie Chicken, **230–231**
    Grilled Ginger-Lime Chicken Thighs with Harissa, **228–229**
    Seared Ahi with Edamame, **184–185**
    Summer Corn Salad with Avocados and Sherry, **160–161,** 208
    in Zov's Silky Macaroni and Cheese, 288
Grilled Eggplant, Olive and Tomato Bruschetta, 50–51
Grilled Ginger-Lime Chicken Thighs with Harissa, 228–229
Grilled Halibut with Mango Salsa, Cilantro and Mint, 170–171
Grilled Skirt Steak with Zahtar and Fresh Lime, 204–205, 284
Gruyère cheese
    Torte Milanese with Spinach, **106–108**

H

Halibut
    in Barramundi with Preserved Lemons and Chickpeas, 175
    Grilled Halibut with Mango Salsa, Cilantro and Mint, **170–171**
Ham. *See also* Pancetta
    in Breakfast Bake with Soujouk and Potatoes, 89
    Torte Milanese with Spinach, **106–108**
Harisah (Pelted Wheat Porridge with Chicken), 234–235
Harissa, 175, 228, 239, **310**
    Grilled Ginger-Lime Chicken Thighs with Harissa, **228–229**
Holiday Creamed Corn, 258–259
Honey
    Ginger-Sesame Vinaigrette, 226, **289**
Horseradish
    Chile-Lime Chipotle Sauce, 34, 208, **303**
    Horseradish-Yogurt Sauce, 199, **289**
Hot chile sauce
    Spicy Pomegranate-Glazed Chicken Wings, **62–63,** 303
Hummus
    Pureed Bean Dip with Yogurt and Dill, **72–73**
Hydroponic watercress. *See* Watercress

I

Icing. *See* Frosting

J

Jam
    Apricot Jam, **84–86,** 323
    Jewel Jam Cookies, **338–339**
    Quince Coffee Cake, **350–351**
    Quince Jam, **112–113,** 350
    Sour Cherry Jam, **104–105**
    Super Easy Fig Jam, **116–117**
Jasmine rice
    about, 263
    Jasmine Rice Pilaf with Vermicelli, 182, 188, 194, 202, 216, **262–263**
Jewel Jam Cookies, 338–339
John Dory
    in Stuffed Trout with Tahini Sauce, 188
Julienned ingredients, photo of, 15
Jumble Cookies, 340–341

K

Kalamata olives
    Grilled Eggplant, Olive and Tomato Bruschetta, **50–51**
    Olive Tapenade, **60–61**
    Tuscan Tomato Salad (Panzanella), **164–165,** 197
Kebabs and skewers
    Beef Brochettes with Garlic-Thyme Marinade, **196–197,** 303
    Greek-Style Chicken Kebabs with Lemon and Oregano, 160, 163, 224, **232–233,** 309
    Spicy Ground Meat Kebabs, 163, **212–213,** 311
    Tamarind Pork Kebabs with Ginger and Soy, **218–219,** 303
Kidney beans
    Vegetable Soup with Tomato-Basil Pistou, **138–139,** 304
Koufta, 52–56

L

Lamb
    in Beef and Eggplant Tagine, 194
    in Che Kofta, 33
    Greek Burgers with Baby Arugula and Feta, **208–209,** 303
    Lamb Stew with Swiss Chard, **210–211**
    Moroccan Harira Soup, **134–135**

Spicy Ground Meat Kebabs, 163, **212–213,** 311

Leeks
Beef Tenderloin with Spinach, Leeks and Goat Cheese, **200–201,** 302
Black Bean Soup with Vegetables, **130–131**
Butter Beans with Pancetta and Leeks, 246, **252–253**
Coconut Chicken Chowder with Lemongrass, **128–129**
Creamy Potato-Leek Soup, 124, **132–133**
Vegetable Soup with Tomato-Basil Pistou, **138–139,** 304
Velvety Cream of Spinach and Cauliflower Soup, 124, **140–141**
washing, 252

Lemon(s)
about, 21
Chicken and Rice Soup with Lemon, **136–137**
photo of, 19
Preserved Lemons, 60, 139, 175, 229, 239, 251, **296–297,** 310
Sautéed Swiss Chard with Lemon and Pine Nuts, 176, **248–249**

Lemon juice
Creamy Hollandaise Sauce, 103, **295**
Greek-Style Chicken Kebabs with Lemon and Oregano, 160, 163, 224, **232–233,** 309
Lemon Sour Cream Pound Cake, **348–349**
Lemon-Lime Dressing, **150–151**
Pureed Bean Dip with Yogurt and Dill, **72–73**
Romesco Sauce, **312–313**
Stuffed Trout with Tahini Sauce, **188–189,** 304
Tahini Sauce, 42, 138, 292, **304**
Tomato-Cucumber Relish, 33, 89, 233, 271, 284, **309**

Lemongrass
about, 20
Coconut Chicken Chowder with Lemongrass, **128–129**
photo of, 19

Lentils
Lentil Patties with Tomato and Cucumber, **270–271,** 309
Moroccan Harira Soup, **134–135**

Lettuce
Asian Noodle Chicken Salad, 224, **226–227**
in Parmesan-Crusted Chicken Salad with Poached Pears and Candied Walnuts, 240
Wedge Salad with Applewood-Smoked Bacon and Maytag Blue Cheese, **154–155**

Lime(s)
Grilled Skirt Steak with Zahtar and Fresh Lime, **204–205,** 284

Lime juice
Chile-Lime Chipotle Sauce, 34, 208, **303**
Curry Sauce, 182, **299**
Ginger-Sesame Vinaigrette, 226, **289**
Grilled Ginger-Lime Chicken Thighs with Harissa, **228–229**
Lemon-Lime Dressing, **150–151**
Spicy Grilled Salmon with Fresh Herbs and Ginger, **180–181**

M

Mâche
in Parmesan-Crusted Chicken Salad with Poached Pears and Candied Walnuts, 240

Mahi mahi
in Grilled Halibut with Mango Salsa, Cilantro and Mint, 170

Mahlab, about, 21

Manchego cheese
Spanish Omelet with Manchego and Cheddar Cheese, **114–115**

Mangoes
Grilled Halibut with Mango Salsa, Cilantro and Mint, **170–171**

Maple syrup
Balsamic Vinaigrette, **294**
Blueberry Syrup, **98–99**
Crunchy Granola with Almonds, Oats and Dried Fruits, **100–101**

Marinara Sauce, 242, 292, **306–307**

Marsala wine
Sour Cherry Sauce, **214–215**

Mayonnaise
Blue Cheese Dressing, 34, 154, **294**
Chile-Lime Chipotle Sauce, 34, 208, **303**
to stabilize Creamy Hollandaise Sauce, 295

Meat(s), 190–221. *See also* Bacon; Beef; Ham; Lamb; Pancetta; Pork; Sausage; Veal

Meat and Potato Casserole, 216–217

Meatballs
Spaghetti with Turkey Meatballs and Marinara Sauce, **242–243,** 306

Meatloaf
Zov's Favorite Meatloaf, **220–221**

Mediterranean Bouillabaisse with Pearled Couscous, 186–187

Mezze, 26. *See also* Appetizers

Milk
Bananas Foster French Toast, 82, **90–91**
Bolognese Sauce, 199, 292, **300–301**
Breakfast Bake with Soujouk and Potatoes, **88–89,** 309
Butternut Squash Parmesan Bread Pudding, 214, **260–261**
Cheese Sauce, **286–288**
Choreg, 316, **330–333**
Creamy Potato-Leek Soup, 124, **132–133**
Holiday Creamed Corn, **258–259**
Oatmeal Brûlée, **92–93**
Pineapple Upside-Down Cake, 316, **356–358** »

Index

Ultimate Cinnamon Buns, **118–121**
Zov's Silky Macaroni and Cheese, **286–288**
Minced ingredients, photo of, 15
Mint
  Barley Salad with Summer Vegetables and Feta Cheese, **152–153**
  Cabbage Salad with Bulgur, **148–149,** 197, 219
  Fusilli Pasta Salad with Rotisserie Chicken, **230–231**
  Grilled Halibut with Mango Salsa, Cilantro and Mint, **170–171**
  Moroccan Harira Soup, **134–135**
  Old World Sliders, **58–59**
  Spicy Grilled Salmon with Fresh Herbs and Ginger, **180–181**
  Summer Corn Salad with Avocados and Sherry, **160–161,** 208
  Tomato and Watermelon Salad with Feta Cheese, **156–157**
  Tomato-Mint Salsa, **58–59**
  Zucchini Fritters with Gravlax, **74–75**
Mom's S Cookies, 342–343
Monterey Jack cheese
  Beef Pirozhki with Mushrooms, **28–31,** 56, 263
  Cheese Boreg, **36–38**
  Cheese Enchiladas, **268–269**
Moroccan Harira Soup, 134–135
Moroccan Spice Mix, 214–215
Mozzarella cheese
  Canneloni Stuffed with Cheese, **256–257**
  Tomato-Basil Risotto Fritters, **78–80,** 308
  Tuscan Eggplant Parmesan, **274–277,** 308
  Tuscan Tomato Salad (Panzanella), **164–165,** 197
Muffins
  Blueberry Muffins with Almond Streusel, **326–327**

Mushrooms. *See also* Cremini mushrooms; Shiitake mushrooms
  about, 220
  Beef Pirozhki with Mushrooms, **28–31,** 56, 263
  Beef Tenderloin with Spinach, Leeks and Goat Cheese, **200–201,** 302
  Braised Green Beans with Beef and Tomatoes, **206–207**
  in Breakfast Bake with Soujouk and Potatoes, 89
  in Bulgur Pilaf with Tomatoes, 284
  Mushroom Sauce, **220–221**
  Spanish Omelet with Manchego and Cheddar Cheese, **114–115**
  in Summer Corn Salad with Avocados and Sherry, 160
  in Zov's Silky Macaroni and Cheese, 288
Mussels
  Mediterranean Bouillabaisse with Pearled Couscous, **186–187**
  shopping for, 187
Mustard
  Mustard Aïoli, 46, **299**
  Red Wine-Dijon Vinaigrette, **302**

N

Napa cabbage
  Asian Noodle Chicken Salad, 224, **226–227**
Nigella seeds, about, 21
Nuts. *See specific kinds of nuts*

O

Oats
  Crunchy Granola with Almonds, Oats and Dried Fruits, **100–101**
  Oatmeal Brûlée, **92–93**
Old World Sliders, 58–59
Old-Fashioned Pancakes with Blueberry Syrup, 82, **98–99**
Olive(s). *See* Kalamata olives

Olive oil
  extra-virgin, about, 20
  photo of, 23
Olive Tapenade, 60–61
Omelets
  Spanish Omelet with Manchego and Cheddar Cheese, **114–115**
Onions. *See also* Green onions; Red onions
  Beef and Eggplant Tagine, **194–195**
  Beef Short Ribs with Horseradish-Yogurt Sauce, **198–199**
  Beef Stroganoff with Mushrooms and Green Onions, **202–203**
  Black Bean Soup with Vegetables, **130–131**
  Bolognese Sauce, 199, 292, **300–301**
  Braised Green Beans with Beef and Tomatoes, **206–207**
  Bulgur Pilaf with Tomatoes, 228, 246, **284–285,** 309
  Chicken and Rice Soup with Lemon, **136–137**
  Chicken Tagine with Currants, **238–239**
  Classic Manhattan Clam Chowder, **126–127**
  Coconut Chicken Chowder with Lemongrass, **128–129**
  Crispy Onion Rings, **34–35,** 220, 303
  Crispy Vegetable Croquettes (Falafels), **42–44,** 304
  Greek Burgers with Baby Arugula and Feta, **208–209,** 303
  Harisah (Pelted Wheat Porridge with Chicken), **234–235**
  Koufta, **52–56**
  Lamb Stew with Swiss Chard, **210–211**
  Lentil Patties with Tomato and Cucumber, **270–271,** 309
  Marinara Sauce, 242, 292, **306–307**
  Meat and Potato Casserole, **216–217**
  Moroccan Harira Soup, **134–135**

Pelted Wheat Porridge with Chicken, 234–235
Ranchero Sauce, 268–269
Spicy Ground Meat Kebabs, 163, **212–213**, 311
Tortilla Soup with Fresh Corn, Cilantro and Lime, **142–143**
Ultimate Risotto with Fresh Peas, Mushrooms and Corn, 214, **280–283**
Vegetable Soup with Tomato-Basil Pistou, **138–139**, 304
Velvety Cream of Spinach and Cauliflower Soup, 124, **140–141**

Orange juice
Blueberry Syrup, **98–99**
in Lemon Sour Cream Pound Cake, 349
Sherry-Orange Vinaigrette, 158–159

Oregano
Greek-Style Chicken Kebabs with Lemon and Oregano, 160, 163, 224, **232–233**, 309
Tomato-Cucumber Relish, 33, 89, 233, 271, 284, **309**

Oven-Fried Parmesan Chicken Fingers, 224, **236–237**

P

Pancetta
Bolognese Sauce, 199, 292, **300–301**
Butter Beans with Pancetta and Leeks, 246, **252–253**
in Creamy Angel Hair Pasta with Tomatoes and Gorgonzola Cheese, 176, 264–265

Panko
Breakfast Potato Cakes, **94–96**, 103
Crispy Vegetable Croquettes (Falafels), **42–44**, 304
Old World Sliders, **58–59**
Oven-Fried Parmesan Chicken Fingers, 224, **236–237**
Parmesan-Crusted Chicken Salad with Poached Pears and Candied Walnuts, **240–241**, 362
Spaghetti with Turkey Meatballs and Marinara Sauce, **242–243**, 306
Tomato-Basil Risotto Fritters, **78–80**, 308
Zov's Silky Macaroni and Cheese, **286–288**
Zucchini Fritters with Gravlax, **74–75**

Pan-Seared Scallops with Tarragon Mushroom Sauce, 176–178

Panzanella, 164–165, 197

Parmesan cheese
Beef Pirozhki with Mushrooms, **28–31**, 56, 263
Bistro Potato Gratin, 181, 200, 208, **254–255**
Breakfast Potato Cakes, **94–96**, 103
Butternut Squash Parmesan Bread Pudding, 214, **260–261**
Canneloni Stuffed with Cheese, **256–257**
Cheese Sauce, **286–288**
Creamy Mashed Potatoes, 199, 200, 220, **266–267**
in Garlic Roasted Cauliflower with Parsley and Thyme, 272
Oven-Fried Parmesan Chicken Fingers, 224, **236–237**
Parmesan Bruschetta, **40–41**, 138
Parmesan Croutons, 131, 132, **308**
Parmesan-Crusted Chicken Salad with Poached Pears and Candied Walnuts, **240–241**, 362
Spaghetti with Turkey Meatballs and Marinara Sauce, **242–243**, 306
Tomato-Basil Pistou, **304**
Tomato-Basil Risotto Fritters, **78–80**, 308
Tuscan Eggplant Parmesan, **274–277**, 308
Ultimate Risotto with Fresh Peas, Mushrooms and Corn, 214, **280–283**
Zov's Favorite Meatloaf, **220–221**
Zov's Silky Macaroni and Cheese, **286–288**

Parmigiano–Reggiano cheese
Bolognese Sauce, 199, 292, **300–301**

Parsley
Beef Pirozhki with Mushrooms, **28–31**, 56, 263
Bistro Potato Gratin, 181, 200, 208, **254–255**
Chicken and Rice Soup with Lemon, **136–137**
Chicken Tagine with Currants, **238–239**
Classic Manhattan Clam Chowder, **126–127**
Crispy Vegetable Croquettes (Falafels), **42–44**, 304
Garlic Roasted Cauliflower with Parsley and Thyme, **272–273**
Koufta, **52–56**
Marinara Sauce, 242, 292, **306–307**
Meat and Potato Casserole, **216–217**
Moroccan Harira Soup, **134–135**
Old World Sliders, **58–59**
photo of, 19
Tahini Sauce, 42, 188, 292, **304**
Tuscan Tomato Salad (Panzanella), **164–165**, 197
Zucchini Fritters with Gravlax, **74–75**

Pasta
Asian Noodle Chicken Salad, 224, **226–227**
Canneloni Stuffed with Cheese, **256–257**
Creamy Angel Hair Pasta with Tomatoes and Gorgonzola Cheese, 176, **264–265**
Crespelle, **256–257**
Fusilli Pasta Salad with Rotisserie Chicken, **230–231**
Jasmine Rice Pilaf with Vermicelli, 182, 188, 194, 202, 216, **262–263**
Spaghetti with Turkey Meatballs and ▸▸

Index

Marinara Sauce, **242–243**, 306
Zov's Silky Macaroni and Cheese, **286–288**
Pastry. *See* Phyllo pastry; Puff pastry
Pea(s)
 in Bulgur Pilaf with Tomatoes, 284
 Ultimate Risotto with Fresh Peas, Mushrooms and Corn, 214, **280–283**
Peanut(s)
 Asian Noodle Chicken Salad, 224, **226–227**
Peanut butter
 Curry Sauce, 182, **299**
Pears
 Simple Poached Pears, **362–363**
Pecans
 Crunchy Granola with Almonds, Oats and Dried Fruits, **100–101**
 Jumble Cookies, **340–341**
 Pineapple Upside-Down Cake, 316, **356–358**
Pecans, candied
 in Parmesan-Crusted Chicken Salad with Poached Pears and Candied Walnuts, 240
Pecorino Romano cheese
 Tuscan Eggplant Parmesan, **274–277**, 308
Pelted wheat
 about, 21
 Harisah (Pelted Wheat Porridge with Chicken), **234–235**
Perfect Guacamole, 64–65, 205
Phyllo pastry
 Apple-Cinnamon Phyllo Crumble, **328–329**
Pilaf
 Bulgur Pilaf with Tomatoes, 228, 246, **284–285**, 309
 Jasmine Rice Pilaf with Vermicelli, 182, 188, 194, 202, 216, **262–263**
 Spanish Rice Pilaf, 268, **278–279**
Pine nuts
 Beef Tenderloin with Spinach, Leeks and Goat Cheese, **200–201**, 302
 Beet Salad with Watercress, Spinach and Fennel, **158–159**, 228
 Couscous with Preserved Lemon, Aleppo Pepper and Pine Nuts, 175, 199, 200, **250–251**
 Koufta, **52–56**
 Sautéed Swiss Chard with Lemon and Pine Nuts, 176, **248–249**
 Stuffed Trout with Tahini Sauce, **188–189**, 304
Pineapple
 Pineapple Upside-Down Cake, 316, **356–358**
 Simple Moist Carrot Cake, **354–355**
Pirozhki
 Beef Pirozhki with Mushrooms, **28–31**, 56, 263
Pistachios
 Grilled Halibut with Mango Salsa, Cilantro and Mint, **170–171**
 Romesco Sauce, **312–313**
 Stuffed Trout with Tahini Sauce, **188–189**, 304
Pomegranate molasses
 about, 21
 photo of, 23
 Spicy Pomegranate-Glazed Chicken Wings, **62–63**, 303
Pork. *See also* Bacon; Ham; Pancetta
 Bolognese Sauce, 199, 292, **300–301**
 Greek Burgers with Baby Arugula and Feta, **208–209**, 303
 Pork Tenderloin with Sour Cherry Sauce, **214–215**, 260
 Spicy Ground Meat Kebabs, 163, **212–213**, 311
 in Spicy Shrimp Curry Bowl, 182
 Tamarind Pork Kebabs with Ginger and Soy, **218–219**, 303
Porridge
 Harisah (Pelted Wheat Porridge with Chicken), **234–235**

Potato(es)
 about, 266
 Beef Pirozhki with Mushrooms, **28–31**, 56, 263
 Bistro Potato Gratin, 181, 200, 208, **254–255**
 Braised Green Beans with Beef and Tomatoes, **206–207**
 Breakfast Bake with Soujouk and Potatoes, **88–89**, 309
 Breakfast Potato Cakes, **94–96**, 103
 Classic Manhattan Clam Chowder, **126–127**
 Creamy Mashed Potatoes, 199, 200, 220, **266–267**
 Creamy Potato-Leek Soup, 124, **132–133**
 Meat and Potato Casserole, **216–217**
 Vegetable Soup with Tomato-Basil Pistou, **138–139**, 304
 Velvety Cream of Spinach and Cauliflower Soup, 124, **140–141**
Potato flakes
 Crispy Vegetable Croquettes (Falafels), **42–44**, 304
Poultry. *See* Chicken; Turkey
Pound cake
 Black and White Pound Cake, **324–325**
 Lemon Sour Cream Pound Cake, **348–349**
Preserved Lemons, 60, 139, 175, 229, 239, 251, **296–297**, 310
Preserved lemons
 about, 22, 60
 photo of, 23
Puff pastry
 Cheese Boreg Dough, **36–37**
 Torte Milanese with Spinach, **106–108**
Pureed Bean Dip with Yogurt and Dill, 72–73

Q

Quick breads
 Simple Buttermilk Biscuits, **110–111**, 131

Super Easy Holiday Fruit and Nut Loaf, **360–361**

Quinces
Quince Coffee Cake, **350–351**
Quince Jam, **112–113**, 350

R

Radishes
Wedge Salad with Applewood-Smoked Bacon and Maytag Blue Cheese, **154–155**

Ragù
Bolognese Sauce, 99, 292, **300–301**

Raisins
in Crunchy Granola with Almonds, Oats and Dried Fruits, 100
Jumble Cookies, **340–341**
Oatmeal Brûlée, **92–93**

Ranchero Sauce, 268–269

Red onions
Asian Noodle Chicken Salad, 224, **226–227**
Barley Salad with Summer Vegetables and Feta Cheese, **152–153**
Black Bean and Avocado Salad, **150–151**, 197
Cabbage Salad with Bulgur, **148–149**, 197, 219
Cauliflower and Broccoli Salad with Red Wine-Dijon Vinaigrette, **162–163**, 200, 228
Che Kofta, **32–33**, 309
Fusilli Pasta Salad with Rotisserie Chicken, **230–231**
Seared Ahi with Edamame, **184–185**
Spanish Omelet with Manchego and Cheddar Cheese, **114–115**
Spicy Shrimp Curry Bowl, **182–183**
Summer Corn Salad with Avocados and Sherry, **160–161**, 208
Tomato and Watermelon Salad with Feta Cheese, **156–157**
Tuscan Tomato Salad (Panzanella), **164–165**, 197

Wedge Salad with Applewood-Smoked Bacon and Maytag Blue Cheese, **154–155**

Red Pepper Paste, 66, 303, **305**

Red pepper paste
about, 22, 70, 312
photo of, 23
in Romesco Sauce, 312

Red Velvet Cupcakes, 352–353

Red wine
Beef Short Ribs with Horseradish-Yogurt Sauce, **198–199**
Bolognese Sauce, 199, 292, **300–301**
Red Wine Sauce, 200, **302**

Red wine vinegar
Red Wine Vinaigrette, **184–185**
Red Wine-Dijon Vinaigrette, **302**
Vinaigrette, **156–157**

Relishes
Tomato-Cucumber Relish, 33, 89, 233, 271, 284, **309**

Rice
about, 263
Black Bean Soup with Vegetables, **130–131**
Chicken and Rice Soup with Lemon, **136–137**
Coconut Chicken Chowder with Lemongrass, **128–129**
Jasmine Rice Pilaf with Vermicelli, 182, 188, 194, 202, 216, **262–263**
Moroccan Harira Soup, **134–135**
Spanish Rice Pilaf, 268, **278–279**
toasting, 282
Tomato-Basil Risotto Fritters, **78–80**, 308
Ultimate Risotto with Fresh Peas, Mushrooms and Corn, 214, **280–283**

Rice flour
Crispy Onion Rings, **34–35**, 220, 303
for fried foods, 34

Ricotta cheese
Cannelloni Stuffed with Cheese, **256–257**

Spicy Sesame Seed Flatbreads with Pepper Paste, **66–70**

Risotto
about, 281, 282
Tomato-Basil Risotto Fritters, **78–80**, 308
Ultimate Risotto with Fresh Peas, Mushrooms and Corn, 214, **280–283**

Roasted Red Pepper and Eggplant Sauce, 213, **311**

Rock cod
in Stuffed Trout with Tahini Sauce, 188

Rolls
Gata, **344–347**
Ultimate Cinnamon Buns, **118–121**

Romesco Sauce, 312–313

S

Sage leaves, frying, 252

Salads, 144–165
Asian Noodle Chicken Salad, 224, **226–227**
Barley Salad with Summer Vegetables and Feta Cheese, **152–153**
Beet Salad with Watercress, Spinach and Fennel, **158–159**, 228
Black Bean and Avocado Salad, **150–151**, 197
Cabbage Salad with Bulgur, **148–149**, 197, 219
Cauliflower and Broccoli Salad with Red Wine-Dijon Vinaigrette, **162–163**, 200, 228
dressings for. *See* Dressings; Vinaigrettes
Fusilli Pasta Salad with Rotisserie Chicken, **230–231**
Jasmine Rice Pilaf with Vermicelli in, 182, 188, 194, 202, 216, **262–263**
Panzanella, **164–165**
Parmesan-Crusted Chicken Salad with Poached Pears and Candied Walnuts, **240–241**, 362 »

Index

Seared Ahi with Edamame, **184–185**
Summer Corn Salad with Avocados and Sherry, **160–161,** 208
Tomato and Watermelon Salad with Feta Cheese, **156–157**
Tuscan Tomato Salad (Panzanella), **164–165,** 197
Wedge Salad with Applewood-Smoked Bacon and Maytag Blue Cheese, **154–155**
Salmon
  in Barramundi with Preserved Lemons and Chickpeas, 175
  in Cabbage Salad with Bulgur, 148
  Gravlax, **46–48,** 74
  Spicy Grilled Salmon with Fresh Herbs and Ginger, **180–181**
  in Stuffed Trout with Tahini Sauce, 188
Salmon, smoked
  Eggs Benedict with Gravlax and Creamy Hollandaise Sauce, 95, **102–103**
Sauces, 290–313
  Bolognese Sauce, 199, 292, **300–301**
  Cheese Sauce, **286–288**
  Chile-Lime Chipotle Sauce, 34, 208, **303**
  Creamy Hollandaise Sauce, 103, **295**
  Curry Sauce, 182, **299**
  Horseradish-Yogurt Sauce, 199, **289**
  Marinara Sauce, 242, 292, **306–307**
  Mushroom Sauce, **220–221**
  Mustard Aïoli, 46, **299**
  Ranchero Sauce, **268–269**
  Red Wine Sauce, 200, **302**
  Roasted Red Pepper and Eggplant Sauce, 213, **311**
  Romesco Sauce, **312–313**
  Sour Cherry Sauce, **214–215**
  Tomato-Basil Pistou, **304**
  Tomato-Basil Sauce, 76, 275, **308**
  Tomato-Mint Salsa, **58–59**
  Tzatziki Sauce, 62, 197, 219, **303**

Sausage
  Breakfast Bake with Soujouk and Potatoes, **88–89,** 309
Sautéed Swiss Chard with Lemon and Pine Nuts, 176, **248–249**
Savory
  Tomato-Cucumber Relish, 33, 89, 233, 271, 284, **309**
Scallions. *See* Green onions
Scallops
  Pan-Seared Scallops with Tarragon Mushroom Sauce, **176–178**
  shopping for, 178
Sea bass
  in Barramundi with Preserved Lemons and Chickpeas, 175
  in Grilled Halibut with Mango Salsa, Cilantro and Mint, 170
  Mediterranean Bouillabaisse with Pearled Couscous, **186–187**
  in Stuffed Trout with Tahini Sauce, 188
Seafood, 166–189
  Barramundi with Preserved Lemons and Chickpeas, 160, **174–175**
  Classic Manhattan Clam Chowder, **126–127**
  Gravlax, **46–48,** 74
  Grilled Halibut with Mango Salsa, Cilantro and Mint, **170–171**
  Mediterranean Bouillabaisse with Pearled Couscous, **186–187**
  Olive Tapenade, **60–61**
  Pan-Seared Scallops with Tarragon Mushroom Sauce, **176–178**
  Seared Ahi with Edamame, **184–185**
  Shrimp with Cannellini Beans, **172–173**
  Spicy Grilled Salmon with Fresh Herbs and Ginger, **180–181**
  Spicy Shrimp Curry Bowl, **182–183**
  Stuffed Trout with Tahini Sauce, **188–189,** 304
  Tomato-Basil Risotto Fritters, **78–80,** 308

Tuscan Tomato Salad (Panzanella), **164–165,** 197
Seared Ahi with Edamame, **184–185**
Seasoned salt, about, 22
Sesame oil
  Ginger-Sesame Vinaigrette, 226, **289**
Sesame seeds
  Seared Ahi with Edamame, **184–185**
  Spicy Sesame Seed Flatbreads with Pepper Paste, **66–70**
Shallots
  Beef Stroganoff with Mushrooms and Green Onions, **202–203**
  Bistro Potato Gratin, 181, 200, 208, **254–255**
  Butternut Squash Parmesan Bread Pudding, 214, **260–261**
  Mediterranean Bouillabaisse with Pearled Couscous, **186–187**
  Old World Sliders, **58–59**
  Perfect Guacamole, **64–65,** 205
  Vinaigrette, **230–231**
Shellfish. *See* Seafood
Sherry wine vinegar
  Sherry-Orange Vinaigrette, **158–159**
Shiitake mushrooms
  Coconut Chicken Chowder with Lemongrass, **128–129**
  Pan-Seared Scallops with Tarragon Mushroom Sauce, **176–178**
Shortbread
  Apricot Shortbread Bars, **322–323**
Shrimp
  Mediterranean Bouillabaisse with Pearled Couscous, **186–187**
  Shrimp with Cannellini Beans, **172–173**
  Spicy Shrimp Curry Bowl, **182–183**
  Tomato-Basil Risotto Fritters, **78–80,** 308
  in Zucchini Fritters with Gravlax, 74–75
Side dishes, 244–289
  Bistro Potato Gratin, 181, 200, 208, **254–255**

Bulgur Pilaf with Tomatoes, 228, 246, **284–285**, 309
Butter Beans with Pancetta and Leeks, 246, **252–253**
Butternut Squash Parmesan Bread Pudding, 214, **260–261**
Cannelloni Stuffed with Cheese, **256–257**
Cheese Enchiladas, **268–269**
Couscous with Preserved Lemon, Aleppo Pepper and Pine Nuts, 175, 199, 200, **250–251**
Creamy Angel Hair Pasta with Tomatoes and Gorgonzola Cheese, 176, **264–265**
Creamy Mashed Potatoes, 199, 200, 220, **266–267**
Garlic Roasted Cauliflower with Parsley and Thyme, **272–273**
Holiday Creamed Corn, **258–259**
Jasmine Rice Pilaf with Vermicelli, 182, 188, 194, 202, 216, **262–263**
Lentil Patties with Tomato and Cucumber, **270–271**, 309
Sautéed Swiss Chard with Lemon and Pine Nuts, 176, **248–249**
Spanish Rice Pilaf, 268, **278–279**
Tuscan Eggplant Parmesan, **274–277**, 308
Ultimate Risotto with Fresh Peas, Mushrooms and Corn, 214, **280–283**
Zov's Silky Macaroni and Cheese, **286–288**
Simple Buttermilk Biscuits, 110–111, 131
Simple Moist Carrot Cake, 354–355
Simple Poached Pears, 362–363
Skewers. See Kebabs and skewers
Smoked salmon
Eggs Benedict with Gravlax and Creamy Hollandaise Sauce, 95, **102–103**
Soujouk
Breakfast Bake with Soujouk and Potatoes, **88–89**, 309
Soups, 122–143. See also Chowders; Stews; Tagines
Black Bean Soup with Vegetables, **130–131**
Chicken and Rice Soup with Lemon, **136–137**
Creamy Potato-Leek Soup, 124, **132–133**
Moroccan Harira Soup, **134–135**
Tortilla Soup with Fresh Corn, Cilantro and Lime, **142–143**
Vegetable Soup with Tomato-Basil Pistou, **138–139**, 304
Velvety Cream of Spinach and Cauliflower Soup, 124, **140–141**
Sour Cherry Jam, 104–105
Sour Cherry Sauce, 214–215
Sour cream
Beef Stroganoff with Mushrooms and Green Onions, **202–203**
Black and White Pound Cake, **324–325**
Blue Cheese Dressing, 34, 154, **294**
Cheese Enchiladas, **268–269**
Chile-Lime Chipotle Sauce, 34, 208, **303**
Gata, **344–347**
Lemon Sour Cream Pound Cake, **348–349**
preventing curdling of, 202
in Quince Coffee Cake, 350
Spicy Ground Meat Kebabs, 163, **212–213**, 311
in Zucchini Fritters with Gravlax, 74–75
Soy sauce
Curry Sauce, 182, **299**
Tamarind Pork Kebabs with Ginger and Soy, **218–219**, 303
Spaghetti with Turkey Meatballs and Marinara Sauce, 242–243, 306
Spanish Omelet with Manchego and Cheddar Cheese, 114–115
Spanish Rice Pilaf, 268, **278–279**
Spices, 16–23
Spicy Grilled Salmon with Fresh Herbs and Ginger, 180–181
Spicy Ground Meat Kebabs, 163, **212–213**, 311
Spicy Pomegranate-Glazed Chicken Wings, 62–63, 303
Spicy Sesame Seed Flatbreads with Pepper Paste, 66–70
Spicy Shrimp Curry Bowl, 182–183
Spinach
Beef Tenderloin with Spinach, Leeks and Goat Cheese, **200–201**, 302
Beet Salad with Watercress, Spinach and Fennel, **158–159**, 228
in Creamy Potato-Leek Soup, 132
in Sautéed Swiss Chard with Lemon and Pine Nuts, 176, 248–249
Torte Milanese with Spinach, **106–108**
Velvety Cream of Spinach and Cauliflower Soup, 124, **140–141**
Spreads
Olive Tapenade, **60–61**
Yogurt and Feta Cheese Spread, **58–59**
Sriracha, about, 22
Sterilizing jars, 86
Stews. See also Tagines
Lamb Stew with Swiss Chard, **210–211**
Mediterranean Bouillabaisse with Pearled Couscous, **186–187**
Striped sea bass
in Barramundi with Preserved Lemons and Chickpeas, 175
Stuffed Trout with Tahini Sauce, 188–189, 304
Summer Corn Salad with Avocados and Sherry, 160–161, 208
Super Easy Fig Jam, 116–117
Super Easy Holiday Fruit and Nut Loaf, 360–361
Sweets, 314–363. See also Cakes; Cookies; Cupcakes; Frosting ≫

Index

Apple-Cinnamon Phyllo Crumble, **328–329**
Apricot Shortbread Bars, **322–323**
Blueberry Muffins with Almond Streusel, **326–327**
Cherry Crisps, **320–321**
Choreg, 316, **330–333**
Ganache, **334–337**
Gata, **344–347**
Quince Coffee Cake, **350–351**
Simple Poached Pears, **362–363**
Super Easy Holiday Fruit and Nut Loaf, **360–361**

Swiss chard
about, 210, 248
Creamy Angel Hair Pasta with Tomatoes and Gorgonzola Cheese, 176, **264–265**
Lamb Stew with Swiss Chard, **210–211**
Sautéed Swiss Chard with Lemon and Pine Nuts, 176, **248–249**

Syrup
Blueberry Syrup, **98–99**

T

Tagines
Beef and Eggplant Tagine, **194–195**
Chicken Tagine with Currants, **238–239**

Tahini
Tahini Sauce, 42, 188, 292, **304**

Tamarind paste
about, 219
Tamarind Pork Kebabs with Ginger and Soy, **218–219,** 303

Thyme
Beef Brochettes with Garlic-Thyme Marinade, **196–197,** 303
Garlic Roasted Cauliflower with Parsley and Thyme, **272–273**

Toasted nuts
in Parmesan-Crusted Chicken Salad with Poached Pears and Candied Walnuts, 240

Tomatoes
about, 160
Barley Salad with Summer Vegetables and Feta Cheese, **152–153**
Barramundi with Preserved Lemons and Chickpeas, 160, **174–175**
Beef and Eggplant Tagine, **194–195**
Beet Salad with Watercress, Spinach and Fennel, **158–159,** 228
Black Bean and Avocado Salad, **150–151,** 197
Black Bean Soup with Vegetables, **130–131**
Bolognese Sauce, 199, 292, **300–301**
Braised Green Beans with Beef and Tomatoes, **206–207**
Bulgur Pilaf with Tomatoes, 228, 246, **284–285,** 309
Butter Beans with Pancetta and Leeks, 246, **252–253**
Cabbage Salad with Bulgur, **148–149,** 197, 219
Canneloni Stuffed with Cheese, **256–257**
Chicken Tagine with Currants, **238–239**
Classic Manhattan Clam Chowder, **126–127**
Creamy Angel Hair Pasta with Tomatoes and Gorgonzola Cheese, 176, **264–265**
Eggs Benedict with Gravlax and Creamy Hollandaise Sauce, 95, **102–103**
Greek Burgers with Baby Arugula and Feta, **208–209,** 303
Grilled Eggplant, Olive and Tomato Bruschetta, **50–51**
Harissa, 175, 228, 239, **310**
Marinara Sauce, 242, 292, **306–307**
Moroccan Harira Soup, **134–135**
Olive Tapenade, **60–61**
peeling, 126
Perfect Guacamole, **64–65,** 205
Ranchero Sauce, **268–269**
Romesco Sauce, **312–313**
Seared Ahi with Edamame, **184–185**
Shrimp with Cannellini Beans, **172–173**
Spaghetti with Turkey Meatballs and Marinara Sauce, **242–243,** 306
Spanish Omelet with Manchego and Cheddar Cheese, **114–115**
Spanish Rice Pilaf, 268, **278–279**
Spicy Sesame Seed Flatbreads with Pepper Paste, **66–70**
Stuffed Trout with Tahini Sauce, **188–189,** 304
Summer Corn Salad with Avocados and Sherry, **160–161,** 208
Tomato and Watermelon Salad with Feta Cheese, **156–157**
Tomato-Basil Pistou, **304**
Tomato-Basil Risotto Fritters, **78–80,** 308
Tomato-Basil Sauce, 76, 275, **308**
Tomato-Cucumber Relish, 33, 89, 233, 271, 284, **309**
Tomato-Mint Salsa, **58–59**
Tortilla Soup with Fresh Corn, Cilantro and Lime, **142–143**
Tuscan Tomato Salad (Panzanella), **164–165,** 197
Vinaigrette, **230–231**
Wedge Salad with Applewood-Smoked Bacon and Maytag Blue Cheese, **154–155**

Torte Milanese with Spinach, 106–108

Tortillas
Cheese Enchiladas, **268–269**
Tortilla Soup with Fresh Corn, Cilantro and Lime, **142–143**

Trout
Stuffed Trout with Tahini Sauce, **188–189,** 304
Truffles, making, 336

Tuna
Seared Ahi with Edamame, **184–185**

Turkey
 in Greek Burgers with Baby Arugula and Feta, 208
 Spaghetti with Turkey Meatballs and Marinara Sauce, **242–243**, 306

Turmeric, about, 22

Tuscan Eggplant Parmesan, 274–277, 308

Tuscan Tomato Salad (Panzanella), **164–165,** 197

Tzatziki Sauce, 62, 197, 219, **303**

U

Ultimate Cinnamon Buns, 118–121

Ultimate Risotto with Fresh Peas, Mushrooms and Corn, 214, **280–283**

V

Veal
 Bolognese Sauce, 199, 292, **300–301**

Vegetable Soup with Tomato-Basil Pistou, 138–139, 304

Velvety Cream of Spinach and Cauliflower Soup, 124, **140–141**

Vinaigrettes
 Balsamic Vinaigrette, **294**
 for Fusilli Pasta Salad with Rotisserie Chicken, **230–231**
 Ginger-Sesame Vinaigrette, 226, **289**
 Red Wine Vinaigrette, **184–185**
 Red Wine-Dijon Vinaigrette, **302**
 Sherry-Orange Vinaigrette, **158–159**
 Vinaigrette, **156–157**

Vodka
 Gravlax, **46–48,** 74

W

Walnuts
 Barley Salad with Summer Vegetables and Feta Cheese, **152–153**
 Crunchy Granola with Almonds, Oats and Dried Fruits, **100–101**
 Simple Moist Carrot Cake, **354–355**
 Stuffed Trout with Tahini Sauce, **188–189,** 304
 Super Easy Holiday Fruit and Nut Loaf, **360–361**

Walnuts, candied
 Parmesan-Crusted Chicken Salad with Poached Pears and Candied Walnuts, **240–241,** 362

Watercress
 about, 20
 Beet Salad with Watercress, Spinach and Fennel, **158–159,** 228
 Pan-Seared Scallops with Tarragon Mushroom Sauce, **176–178**
 photo of, 19

Watermelon
 Tomato and Watermelon Salad with Feta Cheese, **156–157**

Wedge Salad with Applewood-Smoked Bacon and Maytag Blue Cheese, 154–155

White wine
 Mediterranean Bouillabaisse with Pearled Couscous, **186–187**
 Pan-Seared Scallops with Tarragon Mushroom Sauce, **176–178**
 Ultimate Risotto with Fresh Peas, Mushrooms and Corn, 214, **280–283**

Wine. *See* Red wine; White wine

Y

Yeast breads
 for Beef Pirozhki with Mushrooms, **28–31,** 56, 263
 Choreg, 316, **330–333**
 Gata, **344–347**
 Spicy Sesame Seed Flatbreads with Pepper Paste, **66–70**
 Ultimate Cinnamon Buns, **118–121**

Yogurt
 in Blue Cheese Dressing, 34, 154, 294
 Horseradish-Yogurt Sauce, 199, **289**
 Lamb Stew with Swiss Chard, **210–211**
 Pureed Bean Dip with Yogurt and Dill, **72–73**
 Quince Coffee Cake, **350–351**
 Spicy Ground Meat Kebabs, 163, **212–213,** 311
 Tzatziki Sauce, 62, 197, 219, **303**
 Yogurt and Feta Cheese Spread, **58–59**
 Zucchini Fritters with Gravlax, **74–75**

Z

Zahtar
 about, 22
 Grilled Skirt Steak with Zahtar and Fresh Lime, **204–205,** 284
 Spicy Sesame Seed Flatbreads with Pepper Paste, **66–70**

Zov's Favorite Meatloaf, 220–221

Zov's Silky Macaroni and Cheese, 286–288

Zucchini
 Barley Salad with Summer Vegetables and Feta Cheese, **152–153**
 Black Bean Soup with Vegetables, **130–131**
 Cauliflower and Broccoli Salad with Red Wine-Dijon Vinaigrette, **162–163,** 200, 228
 Fusilli Pasta Salad with Rotisserie Chicken, **230–231**
 Spicy Shrimp Curry Bowl, **182–183**
 in Summer Corn Salad with Avocados and Sherry, 160
 Zucchini Fritters with Gravlax, **74–75**

If you would like to order hard cover editions of this book, please call 1 800 980-ZOVS (9687) or visit www.zovs.com.

Zov's Publishing, LLC
17440 E. 17th Street,
Tustin, CA 92780 U.S.A.
Phone: 800 980-ZOVS (9687)
www.zovs.com

Set in Helvetica Neue and Prelo Slab